IN THE FOOTSTEPS OF THE SNOW LEOPARD

TIM EASTON

First published in 2021 by Tim Easton
Brisbane, Australia
Contact: tjeaston3@gmail.com

Copyright © 2021 Tim Easton

All rights reserved. Except as permitted under the Australian Copyright Act 1968, no part of this publication may be reproduced, stored in a retrieval system, or transmitted in any form or by any means, electronic, mechanical, photocopying, recording or otherwise, without prior written permission. All enquiries should be made to the author.

Author: Tim Easton
In the Footsteps of the Snow Leopard
ISBN: 978 0 646 82557 1

ISBN 978-0-646-82557-1

Subjects: Travel | Memoir
Book design: Jennifer Hall – jellyfishcreative.com.au

Cover photo: *Dwarfed by the 6,000 metre mountain Norbung Kang; Poona, my porter, at our campsite at Danighar.* © Tim Easton 2020

DISCLAIMER

Every effort has been made to ensure this book is free from error and omission and has been kept up to date. The information in this publication is of a general nature only and does not take into account personal needs, objectives or current situation. It should not be considered advice. The intent is to offer a variety of information to the reader. However, the author, publisher, editor or their agents or representatives shall not accept responsibility for any loss or inconvenience caused to a person or organisation relying on this information. Except as required by law, the author and publisher, their licensee, their entities, directors and employees do not accept any liability for any person acting, or refraining from acting, as a result of material in this book. The names of the people referred to in the case studies are not real and have been changed to maintain their privacy. We strongly recommend that professional advice is taken before making any decisions regarding personal needs.

This is a limited edition of only 100 copies,
which includes quotes from
Peter Matthiessen's **The Snow Leopard**
written more than forty years ago on the
same journey as Tim Easton in 2019.

ACKNOWLEDGEMENTS

With so many people to thank, I hope I manage to remember everybody.

Firstly, the team in Kathmandu who enabled me to do this journey; without their knowledge, expertise and love for their country and the Himalayas this trip wouldn't have been possible.

Giri Kewal, the business brains behind Nepal Mountain Adventure; Akash, the company accountant and guide for 21 Days in the Himalayas; Dilip, my guide for the twenty-four day trek and Poona, our porter who appears on the front cover. These men possess the greatest integrity coupled with their gentle ways and a very deep conviction for the work they do.

I want to thank the many readers who read the first draft. Their feedback was invaluable in shaping this book. To them my heartfelt thanks - Anne Kemp, Libby Anderson, Annette Millar, Sandra Winzar, Shannon Bratton, Vanessa Or, Robert A'hoon, David King, Dr Sam Korman, Mike Mee, Tony Groom, Dr Michael Meadows, Anthony Logan, Brendan Easton, Georgia Easton, Imogen Easton, Rita Tisdall, Susan Bainbridge, Ian Stevenson, Steve Bellamy and Lee Jediah.

To my editor Rob Holden, I think it is fair to say I do far better on the creativity of writing than the details of correct spelling, punctuation and grammar. Thank you Rob for your patience and perseverance on all 80,000 words or thereabouts.

To my publishing advisor, Bev Ryan for her professional overview.

To Jennifer Hall from Jellyfish Creative for the book cover design, website design and alterations and final preparation of layout for printing.

I am very grateful to Tim Fisk, George Gummow, Peter Mrzyglocki and Victor Odman for their financial support.

And it is to my parents John and Diana Easton that I owe this very last thankyou and my grateful appreciation for their love and support over a lifetime.

Nepal Mountain Adventure

FOREWORD

By Steve Bellamy

The sheer magnitude of the mountain vistas and the warmth of the local people of the Himalayas touch me in a way that is hard to describe. I have been travelling to the mountains of Nepal and India for over twenty years and am delighted that my good friend Tim has been similarly captivated.

These days my time is spent more in the foothills helping needy children with educational programmes and basic supplies, through the Australian charity *The Pencil Tree*, which was set up to assist the underprivileged children who live in this majestic part of the world.

From providing pencils, exercise books, and scholarships to private schools, to feeding whole communities and actually building an entire school in 2019, *The Pencil Tree* is determined to give these amazing children a chance of a better life that their illiterate parents could only dream of.

Tim's book will transport you to a land of ancient culture and smiling hospitable people and maybe, one day, you too can visit and be touched by this special place. But for now, sit back and enjoy a good read and imagine yourself on this journey with Tim in a land that nourishes the soul and challenges you in every way.

You are in safe hands.

Namaste,
Steve Bellamy
Founder of *The Pencil Tree*

CHAPTER I

The moment you accept what troubles you have been given; the door will open.
RUMI

It was almost nightfall when we arrived in Beni, a twelve-hour bus ride north-west from Kathmandu along busy roads with many potholes and dangers that were best not observed too closely, for fear of becoming accident-paranoid. Our driver seemed to have the job well in hand, but it paid to turn the other way when passing the mangled buses on the side of the road covered in dirt and dust, vines growing over and through them, a reminder of our impermanence on this Earth.

I found myself looking out the window at the long lines of buses and trucks that at times waited patiently for the next obstacle to pass, where the road was narrow due to a washout or on-going road works. Black diesel fumes pumped from the trucks loaded with produce for Kathmandu. We were in the foothills of the Himalayas; open flat stretches of road were almost non-existent. The generally courteous nature of the Nepalese people and their ability to decorate their vehicles with predominantly Hindu or Buddhist blessings somehow made the journey seem safer.

In places the people on this main road reminded me of ants – scurrying along their own highways of food production, where they wait for their own to pass or to help another with a heavy load. I find ants remarkable in so many ways; but this story is of a human nature – our frailties, our beauty and perhaps above all, our willingness to exist, to live through this tumbling, precarious life of Samsara.

I was back in Nepal for the first time since writing and publishing my experiences in the Annapurna region of the Himalayas in December 2017. In that book I mentioned a visit to Kopan Monastery, which was established in the early 1960s just north-east of Kathmandu on a high ridge. I had vowed I would return to learn more of Buddhist philosophy, an ancient art of some 2,500 years. This journey included a ten-day stay in Kopan, where I learned to meditate more correctly in the main temple – a teaching temple with over one hundred eager participants from around the world, mostly under 30 years of age, but all believing in the value of this ancient practice.

Kopan is part of the global teaching, Foundation for the Preservation of the Mahayana Tradition (or FPMT), which was founded by Lama Thubten Yeshe and Lama Thubten Zopa Rinpoche in 1975. It is now spread out to 160 Dharma centres in 37 countries across the globe that have the blessing of His Holiness the 14th Dalai Lama. (1)

It was a ten-day journey into my Western mind, which keeps me at times miserable and competitive, but above all exhausted. I was enthralled with the changes I needed to make. As this course came to an end, I knew I would be signing up again at some time for a 30-day course. I was hooked on this inward journey and the wholesome ways that I could direct my life by understanding my thoughts and what drives me as a Western human being.

Now, more than ever, we are responsible for the well-being and survival of this planet that sits in a small solar system, placed in a vast universe we know little about. It's as though we stand willing to learn more of this planet when we reach this place of need and willingness to change. I believe these times are upon us.

As a descendant of the 1900's, the Great Depression and two major world wars, there is much for me to heal inwardly –

a trauma passed down through the generations. I felt I had much to understand of what my family went through in World War One and World War Two, and the monuments created to remember our destructive past as a species ravaged by cruelty, killing and destruction. Yet we all breathe the same air, we all need healthy food, clean water, shelter, clothing, sanitation – but most of all love and connection. Everything after that I question.

I had come to these mountains, these Nepalese mountains, the Himalayas, to unpack more of my British past; yet I was born in Australia where, as a very young man of nineteen, I sought out the culture of the Indigenous Aboriginal people, to hear their stories firsthand at Lockhart River Mission on Cape York where I spent several weeks in the wilderness, observing the moon and stars from the Kennedy River and the beach near Lockhart River Mission. By day I would hunt with the elders for pig, bat, fish and goanna. Most of all I sought their knowledge, their wisdom, with a lineage of 60,000 to 100,000 years. They belong to the 'silent heartbeat' of the Earth. Yet these people were survivors of a brutal campaign to destroy them – it was genocide - and Lockhart River Mission offered a salvation from a now 'White Australia' – but things are shifting, Indigenous culture is returning.

The main component of this journey to Nepal was a twenty-four-day trek, *In the Footsteps of the Snow Leopard*. In 1973, Peter Matthiessen ventured to the remote Dolpo region in the northwest Himalayas to assist George Schaller, a German zoologist in search of bharal, a goat that is genetically close to the domesticated sheep and whose numbers have been rising steadily in the Himalayas. *(1a)*

They were excessively hunted in the 1800s by Europeans intent on showing the world their ability to shoot and kill bharal for their decorative horns. It was, however, the elusive snow leopard that had also been hunted almost to extinction – mostly by Europeans in the 1800s – that Peter and George sought to find. They were a party of twenty, with fourteen porters and four Sherpas for the duration of sixty-four days.

Peter's journey, however, was not just about assisting in the search for the bharal and the snow leopard in one of the coldest and most remote parts of the Himalayas, the Inner Dolpo region, where Shey Monastery has existed for countless generations and where just to the west sits Crystal Mountain (5,416m), so named from this Buddhist legend:

"The holiness of Crystal Mountain is based on legend. A thousand years ago Buddhist ascetic ,Gyamgon Rimpoche, the main Lama of the Thiwong Gyamgon Gompa, the main gompa of the Kakyupa sect, one of the four major sects of Buddhism, once dreamt about the Shey area where he'd never been before, and he sent one of his most brilliant disciples to explore the Shey pilgrimage. Drutop Shinge Yeshe, as per his guru's order, left Tibet and visited Dolpo. He first saw Shey from Saikpa Kang, of present Bhijer. When he found the people, whose supreme god was a wild mountain spirit, he tried to overcome the fierce mountain spirit, using the flying snow lion, a legendary companion of the snow leopard, but the spirit resisted by unleashing a horde of snake-beings. However, the snow lion reproduced itself 108 times, once for each book of Buddhist scriptures, and with this reinforcement, Drutop vanquished the spirit and transformed into 'a thundering Mountain of purest

*Crystal'."(*www.himalayancompanion.com*)* (1b)

Peter's story is also an inner journey about the loss of his wife, Deborah, to cancer a year earlier and how he, "by his own spiritual standards was grieving too much". Peter's knowledge of Zen Buddhism was modest, in his own words. It was Deborah who introduced him to this inner journey, and what better place to continue that journey than the natural wonderland where Tibetan Buddhism can be found carved into so many ancient stone texts – known as *Mani stones* – so as to preserve and repeat the Buddhist scripts for eternity. I marvelled at many hundreds of these ancient stone texts and for Peter, it was an ideal place to "renounce craving and neediness...detachment". He had to let go of his grieving for his wife. (2)

Peter's journey was an opportunity for me to walk in his footsteps, starting at Beni and following the ancient trails northwest that eventually lead to Tibet and Mongolia through many valleys and over seven passes ranging in height from 3,390m to 5,290m. The terrain is desolate but wildly exciting due to its remoteness where marijuana grows to four metres and in April/May caterpillar fungus flourish for the Chinese market that will pay upward of US$20,000/kg.

I have hired a guide and porter for this 24-day trek; we become good friends and without their professional help I could not have done this trip. Dilip is a man in his forties and speaks good English. He is the son of a British Army Gurkha which in many ways connects us; my own father being British Army had enormous respect for the Gurkha regiments that have fought against and alongside the British since the early 1800s.

Poona is our porter, as strong as an ox; he never complains and at times is carrying over 30kg. He is similar in age to Dilip but alas my limited Nepalese and his limited English prevent much verbal communication; however, I have the greatest respect for him. He does the lion's share of the cooking and carries most of the food and equipment. Between them, they bring sweet, hot milky coffee to my tent at dawn when at times the temperature was -15 degrees Celsius. Our bond for the 24 days is important – we must understand each other – and I am pleased to say we pass with flying colours; our respect for each other is solid.

I make special efforts on arriving in Kathmandu to meet with Akash, my guide in my first book, *21 Days in the Himalayas*. We both so wanted this meeting to happen – we both respected each other – despite the 'careless' events for which I take full responsibility. I was not the 'perfect' foreign trekker, doing as I was told all of the time. Akash was just doing his job on the Annapurna circuit and I wrongly wanted my freedom in his backyard – the Himalayas.

Akash now works as the accountant for the trekking company I use, which is based in Thamel, Kathmandu. He was unfamiliar with the remote Dolpo region, but he picks me up from my guesthouse and drives me to Kopan Monastery for the start of the ten-day course in Buddhism. This event in itself gave credibility to me as a Westerner wanting to understand the Nepalese people more deeply. For Akash and me, our friendship and love for the Himalayas was now an unbreakable bond. At the airport before leaving Australia I found some green and gold Australian shirts for him and his daughter – gifts I wanted him to have as an offering of peace and friendship. Next time I will take Indigenous designs, where a similar depth of culture and heritage can be found; both cultures are ancient and connect us to the Earth and her natural cycles.

Dilip, Poona and I would coincidently meet a British Army contingent camped by Phoksundo Lake who were drying their climbing equipment after a challenging snow-filled expedition to one of the many 5,000m peaks near Shey Monastery. One of their team was rescued by helicopter due to altitude sickness, and of the sixteen army personnel, eight were English and eight were Nepalese Gurkhas. Their captain, who was from Kent, was the only woman on this expedition, and they all smoked like Dolpo tent-teahouses.

My plan was to complete Peter Matthiessen's trek in September/October 2020 – however COVID-19 has altered things – someday I would like to fly into Juphal and trekking up to Phoksundo Lake and then onto Shey Monastery and Crystal Mountain, where there might be a chance of spotting a snow leopard. But it is unlikely – they hunt by stealth and are most unlikely to allow a human to catch them out. The bharal is certainly in number – however, the adventure of getting to this remote part of the Himalayas and spending time in this very special part of the planet will be exciting enough with the precious opportunity to hear the silent heartbeat of the Earth, still alive amongst the human noise of 2020.

CHAPTER II

Yesterday I was clever so I wanted to change the world.
Today I am wise so I am changing myself.
RUMI

The bus had been comfortable, a recent model Toyota, very new compared with what Peter Matthiessen had journeyed on from Kathmandu to Pokhara. Their enormous party of twenty assembled in Pokhara – George Schaller was to catch up with them soon after Beni.

Sitting for twelve hours on an often bumpy and very slow road has the effect of making me want to 'jump to the heavens' when I step off this metal container of still and cramped discomfort. In an attempt to loosen the grip of sitting in one position for so long I relish the tea breaks and an opportunity to uncoil my legs and stretch my body. When meditating, I am the same – sixty minutes at a time is about my best effort; however, I will happily do this three times per day. The lotus position is not my perfected art at age fifty-eight; instead I use a wooden chair that was made by my great-grandfather's workmen when he was forced to retire at just forty-five. With the wisdom of hindsight, I suggest it was most likely bipolar disorder that caused his early retirement, but he was a very clever man who could win the confidence of his workers in the West Country of England, the place my father grew up and loved dearly.

The chair is made of English oak with a maroon padded cushion which forms my 'lotus position'. It is a chair I treasure and I've been tasked with its safe delivery to my children. I feel comfortable that the Buddhist gods find this chair most favourable for a man growing up in the West and who, to date, is perhaps five to seven percent Buddhist; I still have thirty or more years to improve, and this twenty-four day trek will continue to create a thirst for spiritual knowledge and Earth connection.

When we arrive in Beni after the last 50 kilometres from Pokhara on a very, very, very slow rough road, I wasn't in the mood to find the cheapest guesthouse – "What does she want Dilip? 1000NPR per room (AU$16) – that will do. No, we're not sharing – that's 2000NPR. Good, pay the lady."

This family-run guesthouse was only ten minutes walk from the bus station. The daughter, in her early twenties, showed us the two rooms: "That's great, thank you – and there's hot water (she shows me the taps) thank you – come down for dinner when you're ready – thank you." Her broken English was somewhat better than my Nepalese, which embarrassingly extends to 'Namaste'; however, I did come to fully appreciate this greeting during my studies at Kopan Monastery.

The spiritual description, written in Sanskrit, comes from Hindu, Buddhist and other Southeast Asian religions, and translates something like this:

"I honour the place in you in which the entire universe dwells. I honour the place in you which is of love, of truth, of light and of peace. When you are in that place in you and I am in that place in me – WE ARE ONE!"

I find this deeply moving and respectful – to acknowledge such beauty in another human being – and that's just the start really. The connection only deepens as one progresses through life. I love the respect, which I could have done a lot more with in terms of my own growth and respect for the wider community. We are combative in the West, so willing to put the next person down or at least these have been my experiences.

In Australia we love to simplify things, and language is certainly one area where we take away complications and get straight to the point – perhaps it stems from our colonial rule of 130 years and our willingness to 'up yours mate' any form of a pretentious nature – the British being a case in question. Our version, therefore, of this very beautiful Sanskrit expression dating back many generations could, in fact, translate to: "bonza bottler – g'day."

I do think, however, it is best we stay with the aforementioned and more deeply spiritual version that connects us with each other, the Earth we inhabit, and the universe beyond. It gives further light to us all being connected on a deeper spiritual plane – "bonza bottler" – really? That's just embarrassing.

The room wasn't quite decorated to Kopan Monastery standards; there was a single window to the corridor with a dusty drape that most likely hadn't been washed since the day it was installed. Dilip and Poona got the window views to the darkened street below. The hot water was more a refreshingly cool room temperature. Beni was a transport hub in the foothills of the Himalayas with a very modest altitude of 899m, so we were still in positive temperatures.

Our 12-hour bus ride up and down so many smaller mountain ranges from Kathmandu had me wanting for some form of shower – even a refreshing bird bath would do as the water dribbled to the concrete floor – the shower was not working today. However, it was good to wash off the bus journey and begin to think about our trek ahead, knowing the comforts and luxuries were leaving us for twenty-four days, not forgetting the internet's disappearance – now that was something to rejoice.

I met Dilip and Poona downstairs for a dinner of dal bhat, the traditional Nepalese meal consisting of rice, lentil soup, vegetables, chutney and sometimes chicken, goat or cow. It's nutritious and goes well with a glass of Nepalese beer. It soon becomes clear through Dilip's interpretation that the young daughter of the house is looking for an Australian husband – I had just turned fifty-eight while staying at Kopan Monastery and I have three adult children of my own, so perhaps I was not her best choice – especially as we had only just met.

This discussion brings great laughter to the table but, alas, I'm not far from needing to sleep. I can only manage so much culture shock after a twelve-hour bus ride – notwithstanding the possibility of marriage to such a lovely young lady. No doubt her father could see the funny side of this absurdity. It was time for me to quietly leave for my room and with a thorough bolting of the door, I was finally alone.

My yellow down sleeping bag is stretched out on the hard mattress with a still very clean orange liner lying on top. I am asleep within minutes, dreaming of snow leopards expertly hunting bharal sheep; their large paws adapted for the snow, with a long heavy tail for balance – they are master stealth hunters. Their grey/green eyes – unlike the deep yellow colour of their African cousins – only add to making them seem quite supernatural. (3)

Poona is gone early in the morning to find a bamboo basket, which he'll fill with food and equipment. He rigs up a five-millimetre cord that he draws from the base of the basket up and over his forehead where he has a small white cloth to keep his sweat from falling into his eyes and to offer relief from the pressure of the rope. He will carry up to 30 kilograms on this trip; however, porters and Sherpas have been known to carry up to 50 kilograms, mostly on climbing expeditions. These weights are far more than any calculation we would make in the West in terms of backpacks, where roughly one quarter of our bodyweight is the best guide.

For me this is less than 20 kilograms – and I plan to make it 17 kilograms including three litres of water. I'm personally not happy to see a man carrying that kind of load, no matter how many US dollars are being offered. Poona with 30 kilograms I can accept; he has the build of a porter – solid, with calf muscles the size of small footballs.

We find alternate digs for breakfast, another guesthouse just down from the Australian 'marriage suite'. The family is very friendly and the man of the house just happens to be an ex-Gurkha so he is very interested in our expedition. Dilip discloses his father's connections with the British Gurkhas and their conversation turns into an explosion of Nepalese brotherhood. It's a coded conversation – military talk – of a proud position held by Nepalese men and their families alike. His wife and young daughter prepare our breakfast and serve us while the men talk...and talk...and talk.

I explain to Dilip I'm going to stretch my legs and explore the small town as we wait for Poona to find all he needs to make our journey and for the ex-Gurkha's conversation to run its course. I'm guessing I have a generous fifty minutes to see where two major rivers – the Kali Gandaki and the Myagdi – converge, crashing down from the Himalayas, the strategic town of Jomsom and the Annapurna Conservation Area, where I had trekked just two years before: a breathtakingly beautiful landscape, rich in Tibetan culture.

My walk takes me past an elderly lady sitting in the sun as she sews; behind her is a shop that sells colourful cloth and a young man operating a peddle-driven sewing machine. The elderly lady smiles at me, and I feel welcomed back in the Himalayas where countless travellers, over thousands of years, have come. It's my turn in this brief dance on the planet.

I pass a large four-wheel-drive truck that is being loaded, I'm guessing for the wild ride north to Jomsom. It's built like a tough off-road machine; its clearance is over 500mm, the tyres are chunky, and the whole exterior of the truck is decorated in the protective streamers and coloured designs of the Hindu religion. For the men and women making these trips, it is protection they request from their gods. Having journeyed on part of that 'road' on my last trip I wished these people safe passage; there was nothing simple about the road ahead, and even though it's just seventy kilometres to Jomsom it will take them most of the day depending on how well the road has been maintained and the natural forces of the Himalayas. The gods laugh at us with landslides, torrential downpours, rivers that devour bridges in minutes and freezing temperatures that can maim our human bodies.

I pass a fisherman who has been successful this morning; he guts the fish in front of a friend. His bicycle and fishing gear are parked next to him as he slides the guts out of the fish using an unusual gutting tool with a vertical blade some 200mm long. He looks at me with suspicion, "What are you doing here alone, Western man?" I try to be friendly and keep walking. There's a four-year-old boy playing with a phone on the step of his parents' shop; some game no doubt and it is keeping him deeply amused.

I'm nearly back to where I left Dilip and Poona and I pass a medicine shop where, if I had known, I would have extended my budget to buy enough pain relief medication for the people we would meet in the remote villages. I will do that for the villagers on my next trip. I'm at that stage of evolution in visiting Nepal where I want to offer any form of help to a people who have given me so much during my two short visits. I have come to love Nepal and particularly the mountain people of the Himalayas. It's the thousands of years of connection they have to these mountains and the richness I see in their eyes, particularly in those of the elderly.

As we head away from Beni, walking northwest, I look more closely at Poona's headband and the cord that runs away to the base of the cane basket. The headband ties off onto a five-millimetre cord just below his shoulders and spreads out to seventy millimetres of cloth that runs across his forehead, where a larger cloth prevents sweat falling into his eyes. It's a delicate balance that keeps his spine straight, along with strong muscle fibre; he's like a walking machine – except his smile is most certainly human.

On day eight, climbing one of the passes, the 5mm cord breaks and I offer Poona an 8mm climbing cord that I use to hang clothes at night. He is delighted and I'm happy for him to keep the rope – he will get many years of use from this climbing cord, which is equally as strong as he.

We pass a mother with thick black hair falling to her lower back; she is sitting on a step with her head resting on her knees while her seven-year-old daughter brushes her hair and checks her mother's head for mites and fleas. I see this ritual in many places and I smile at this mother/daughter bond that will help connect them for life.

There seems to be a greater purpose to fleas and this is most certainly something the Buddhists teach at Kopan Monastery – they must not be killed, not even a mosquito – due to the possibility of it being a mother from a past life.

These days Kopan does treat the beds for lice and fleas as the distraction and irritation from them is too great. In such cases killing is permitted, but then, even the Dalai Lama must at times eat meat; killing is permitted for necessary purpose.

On this trek we will be camping twelve nights as there are no villages in these remote parts, where bharal sheep eke out a living on steep rocky mountain slopes. I like these two men: Dilip for his attentive concern for me and his good English, although he is often apologetic, "My English only so good", he says, but we are to have many conversations on this trek. And Poona I like for his gentleness and the sense of rhythm he brings to this journey. I know I can rely on him. My task after ten days at Kopan Monastery is to 'love' these men no matter what. Their welfare is more important than mine – we are brothers as Dilip said from the start – every last step onto the plane at Juphal and the slow taxi ride back to Giri's office in Thamel, Kathmandu – we are brothers.

Giri is the owner of the trekking company who organised the Annapurna trip for me in December 2017, and who I contacted again in August 2019, explaining my plans. He had organised only a few trips to the Lower and Upper Dolpo as most Westerners don't want to go there – the guesthouses and tea houses are few and far between, there is no internet, and the landscape is positively barren most of the way. Perfect, I conclude, just what I need.

Within a few days he emailed an itinerary to me and a price tag in US dollars; I slept on the information and agreed the next morning. There were probably cheaper options, but Giri was a master of his trade and I liked him immensely. On my last night in Kathmandu he asks me to dinner; he refers to me as 'father' which I wonder about but eventually I took it as a compliment, and it is a role I love with my own three children, who are now in their twenties.

Giri had been very straight with me from the first time I met him at Kathmandu airport despite the problems Akash and I encountered from day 15 of the Annapurna trek. He had been a masterful negotiator and nothing was a problem for him. In hindsight the incident with Akash just required me being more willing to accept their guidelines of the journey, which didn't allow for me to head off on my own tangent to experience the wilderness of the Himalayas – which was all around me anyway.

The guides take their job of looking after their guests' safety very seriously, and the experience with Akash was more to do with me not appreciating that fact – and wanting to go off on my own wild adventure to the Tibetan border that would have certainly left me in deep icy cold water, or worse, a deep icy Chinese prison somewhere near the Tibetan border.

The important thing was the wounds and misunderstandings were open on both sides for healing, a better and more deeply shared future for us was certain. And with this new journey set to start, there was a genuine feeling of forgiveness on both sides. Akash and I did have a deep respect for each other; the experience on the Annapurna allowed us to reach the boundaries of respect which clearly drew a line in the sand of where our friendship could go in terms of guide and guest. I was now set to go on a 24-day journey – *In the Footsteps of the Snow Leopard* – with the professional help of Giri's good men, of which Akash is most certainly one.

CHAPTER III

Everything in the universe is within you.
Ask all from yourself.
RUMI

Our first night on the trail, more of a track really, was to reach the prosperous village of Tara Khet. We were walking six hours per day at an easy pace to assist with acclimatisation for the 5,000-metre passes we were to cross in the weeks ahead. Peter Matthiessen had come this way with his twenty-strong party, and he notes the mountains that soar to the north of this valley, where the mighty Myagdi Khola River roars in the thawing monsoon rains of March and April. Dhaulagiri I rises over 8,000 metres just 30 kilometres to the north of this valley, where the rice fields are now only weeks away from harvest.

We pass women carrying enormous loads in cane baskets just like Poona's; green fodder they have cut for their goats in the coming winter, and also firewood to fuel their stoves. They store the firewood on the roofs of their homes; everything is done by hand – the cutting, the splitting, the stacking. Winter in the Himalayas is a time to be prepared – fools and the unprepared perish. Countless generations of experience have taught these people how to survive, and how to respect their land; gas cookers are used, but the cost is not for everyone, and as we head further and higher both firewood and 12kg gas bottles become more and more valuable.

"These village folk own even less than those of Pokhara, yet they are spared by their old economies from modern poverty: one understands why 'village life' has been celebrated as the natural, happy domain of man by many thinkers from Lao-tzu to Ghandi." **(2)** Peter Matthiessen, p24

We stop in a family-run restaurant in Tatopani for lunch and look down on the turquoise green Myagdi Khola River flowing to the southeast; the whitecaps roll with the large stones that creep ever further down-river every monsoon. The hot springs, called Tatopani in Nepalese, are 50 metres below us with many locals stripping off to their shorts or sari to bathe. It's very tempting to join them but it's only day one and very few body parts need soothing. Our focus is to keep heading up this valley and gain elevation.

I see a threshing machine made of cast iron, the wheel a metre in diameter, heavy and able to grind corn, millet, and oats to flour. It is then distributed amongst the villagers, another staple diet for the winter. I see an elderly man with a traditional Tibetan instrument that looks like a crude lute painted bright blue; it's called a dranyen. He plays for me and I am delighted; I offer with gratitude 100NPR as we keep moving up the valley; I wished I had given him more as he carries an instrument passed down through the generations of his culture.

I feel enchanted to be here in the foothills of the Himalayas. I've always enjoyed travelling throughout my life whenever opportunities have arisen – coming to Nepal and in particular the Himalayas is indeed a blessing beyond words. And now that I have spent ten days in quiet meditation at Kopan Monastery I am beginning to understand the deeper, more spiritual aspects of this ancient culture; being from the West, I have so much to learn.

"In what became known as the Four Noble Truths, Sakyamuni perceived that man's existence is inseparable from sorrow; that the cause of suffering is craving; that peace is attained by extinguishing craving; that this liberation may be brought about by

following the Eight-fold Path: right attention to one's understanding, intentions, speech, and actions; right livelihood, effort, mindfulness; right concentration, by which is meant the unification of the self through sitting yoga." (2) Peter Matthiessen, p27

I photograph Dilip by a shining new Royal Enfield motorcycle, a design left over from the British Empire in Colonial India some 120 years ago. It is a reliable machine that I see whole families, mum, dad and several children, riding on this track. An excellent way to get to Beni or even Pokhara if the journey is necessary. I see a motorcycle workshop on the side of the road near Beni, a whole motor spread out on the oiled dirt workshop floor. I am impressed to say the least. These mechanically inclined men can strip a motorcycle down in a workshop with little more than a corrugated iron roof, no walls, just basic tools, and apply the 'gentle art of motorcycle maintenance'.

Further along this trail of discovery – and it's only day one of our journey – we see another mother with her two young daughters assisting with the grooming and flea removal from her hair. She looks at me knowingly as a parent – a huge smile on her face – and I smile back with the words, "How beautiful you are." Mum is sitting on the front step of their shop; her leg is stretched out onto the lower step, her daughter is behind with her little seven-year-old legs outstretched so she can really lean into the job at hand, her little feminine hip outstretched as she cranes into the task of flea removal. Mum probably has twenty things she needs to do but she endures the inspection, and I think she likes the attention I give her. She must guess I'm a parent too. Namaste!

IN THE FOOTSTEPS OF THE SNOW LEOPARD

We both laugh out loud as I keep moving up the valley; Dilip and Poona are at least 100 metres ahead of me. It is a beautiful moment of mutual appreciation. I remember my own daughters brushing their mother's hair – a ritual of mother and daughter – a life affirming appreciation passed down through the generations, from country to country – a global phenomenon.

My father, son and I would drive to far Western Queensland, camp in dry river beds, and hunt feral pig, goat, rabbit and fox with high-powered rifles; our aim was always for a clean shot at 100 metres; no animal should suffer; however, feral animals don't belong on the Australian landscape. We would cook damper in the coals and boil the billy to make tea, and stay a week or more if the feral game were plentiful.

The temperature is warm, at least 18 degrees Celsius. I wind up my long pants and roll up my sleeves. I have clothing in my pack to carry me through minus 15 degrees Celsius and I am most certainly prepared against finger frostbite with a good quality dual system of gloves. I really didn't need that experience again from the last trip with Akash when my fingertips burnt off in the freezing cold at Thorong La Pass. It was a lesson I surely learnt and on this trip the passes were just as high.

I was lucky though; despite the excruciating pain it was only the top two or three layers of skin that were lost, and the nerve endings did eventually grow back. It was a wake-up call to the power and unforgiving nature of the Himalayas. How people go above 8,000 metres is beyond me – the 'death zone' as climbers describe it – not for this Western man who's more interested in understanding Tibetan culture and staying alive with fingers, toes and face intact. Thank you.

I think about Peter Matthiessen's trip in 1973 and the very basic heavy gear he would have carried – leather boots, thick heavy woollen socks, a steel framed canvas pack, canvas tent, cotton blue jeans and shirts which, in wet weather and wind, can lead to hypothermia. Not surprising they had fourteen porters and four Sherpas. He talks about having to stretch his leather boots at the start of his journey so they would not cause blisters – they most likely weighed nearly a kilogram when dry.

How grateful I was for the extraordinarily comfortable equipment I carried. Perhaps in another fifty years there will be someone tracing my footsteps with a silent drone. Not sure how well they would deal with the powerful wind gusts in this region where I was to see half a school roof ripped off and thrown to the ground. Fortunately, no one was injured – but more on that when we get to Dho Tarap, where a local man is jailed for stealing Buddhist relics.

We pass buffalo tethered under buildings or in barns. They are used to plough the fields and to provide meat when the need arises. These animals look at me suspiciously, wondering if I have a knife or a wooden plough to work the fields. The buffalo generally are not happy to see me; humans are not to be trusted. However, they look healthy and well fed.

An older lady carries firewood in a cane basket stacked well above her head; I estimate it would weigh thirty kilograms. She wears rubber thongs, and she will make many such trips in preparation for winter.

The houses are painted with an earthen red clay, an ochre

colour they paint halfway up the walls – including the floors – to give a finish that looks part of the landscape; the buildings belong here. Above this layer they use a white ochre which enhances the earthen red. And in many places – wherever there is a hot place in the sun – grains are drying in preparation for the winter. Many types of beans, lentils and corn spread out on cloth so they can be easily gathered in for the night. Flat rooftops were a favourite for this necessary enterprise of preparing food for the long months of the coming winter.

Potato plots are also being prepared, a second crop before winter. I see several vegetable stalls with potatoes for sale. I am to learn a funny story further up the valley that Dilip tells me after our stay in Dhule; something to do with comparing the size of this year's potato harvest with a man's family jewels. Raucous male laughter abounds through the valleys when he tells me this story; but we also learn of a Frenchman the previous winter travelling alone and perishing in the mountains, lost!

It's in Beni that I first see a huddle of eager teenage boys around a board game. They stop briefly to look up at me, their eyes glowing with enjoyment and fun. It's so wonderful to see they are happy in their young teenage years, connected to a culture as deep as the valleys through which we journey. Some of the boys have dyed their hair with henna, several are plugged into earphones, some wear big chunky watches with lots of dials; jeans are a favourite, track pants with jackets, sandals or bare feet. I love most seeing their happiness, their enjoyment of each other, and the fact that the warm sun is shining down on them – that's what I see.

> **"For centuries, the Hindus have come up along the river valleys from the great plain of the Ganges, while Tibetans crossed the mountain passes from the north: the Tibetan-speaking Buddhist tribes, which include the Sherpas, are called Bhotes, or southern Tibetans."** *(2)* Peter Matthiessen, p29

When we reach the town of Tara Khet mid-afternoon, Dilip finds a guesthouse for us on the north-west side of town, where we will be heading the following day. I drop my pack in the room and head back through the town for a closer look. Dilip and Poona have to find a cobbler to stitch their boots and make running repairs on the basket. It's another prosperous town, and I see a man chopping goat meat on the pavement; crunching the bones with a heavy butcher's cleaver. He is amused by my need to photograph him and he would possibly realise that in the West we hide the killing of animals, and the processing of meat is almost sterile. Some might argue the West would see many more vegetarians if these places we call abattoirs were frequented by those of us who buy meat from our supermarket shelves in neat plastic containers, not a drop of sheep, pig or cow blood anywhere.

I head to the large suspension bridge, which spans one hundred metres across the Myagdi Khola River. On the other side of the river is another small village which needs to connect to Tara Khet for trade and medical help. I see a man who has a nasty wound, his shin is heavily bandaged and I can only guess it was some farming accident. He looks to be in much pain, and it's quite obviously a deep wound. I dig out a 500NPR note (AU$8) from my wallet, walk over and give it to him. It will keep him in food for at least a few weeks. I want to help but I don't hang around for applause from the group of people gathered around him. It's the least I can do for a man unable to work for some weeks at least.

I walk over to the little shop that sells all manner of chips, lollies and boxes of drinks that don't belong to this agricultural village. I use the precious greeting that connects our souls to the universe – I find it has gravitas – 'Namaste'. There is a friendly grandma, mother and daughter who are pleased to see me – 'Namaste,' and I begin to feel the meaning within me.

To the Buddhist deities to which I am learning to connect – thank you for this precious greeting that connects the world, and connects the universe: we are one, breathing the same air…I'm beginning to leave my Western culture behind me.

I try to tell these people – this grandmother – that I am from a world that created World War One and World War Two, which killed and wounded millions of people with such devastating force; their souls scarred for generations to come. Talking of suffering, we in the West know so much of this, but we cover it with pills to desensitise the sensitive who cry out for understanding, who write books to tell the world of their suffering in some hope that the message will get through. This planet – this Earth – demands that we change course. The world we create in the West is just that; and you precious Nepalese people here in the East have so much 'wealth' with which to educate us. Don't be fooled by my expensive trekking clothes, please don't. They are a facade to my wounded soul.

There is happiness in these people, a connection that binds them that I don't find in the West, my home. In the West we madly rush around in our cars, making a living so we can buy more things that we often don't need and feel less and less connected to our family, friends and community. I crave to come back to these remote places in the Himalayas and see just that; a grandmother, mother and daughter connected with an honesty I find hard to find in the West.

Maybe it's the enhanced feelings of being out of one's comfort zone, and the culture that I see before me, here in the Himalayas. I'm more gracious in these mountainous regions, more sensitive to the beauty I discover here, especially to the people, but also in the Himalayan mountains and these massive river systems: the fertility of the soil and the people's ability to grow healthy produce, as they have done for generations. I love myself when I come here, when I let go of 'my home' where Western marketing skilfully manipulates my every breath.

"I hear again my own wife's final breath. Such sights caused Sakyamuni to forsake Lumbini and go in search of the secret existence that would free men from the pain of this sensory world, known as Samsara." *(2)* **Peter Matthiessen, p31**

My professional life as a building estimator back in Australia was challenged ten years ago when I was diagnosed with bipolar disorder, an inherited illness that causes the mind to polarise with moods swinging from great sadness to extreme exaltation in some people. Not so with me. I remain more on the sad side, possibly due to a family tragedy when I was just 13 years of age in which I witnessed my sister, Heather Jan Easton, fall to her death on the western razorback of Lost World, Lamington National Park. But there is more in my Western soul, much more in the generations of suffering from European wars – World War One and World War Two – going back many generations. Suffering of our own making, our own stupid making that has – alas – cost our Earth in more ways than I can write in this book. We are, after all, searching for snow leopards – one or two would be wonderful – and seeing bharal with their large horns that blend into the Himalayan landscape like moving rocks. *(s)*

But more of my struggles – my Samsara: bipolar disorder, if left untreated, can cause mayhem for family, friends and career. The destruction of my marriage just may have been prevented if I had known of this in my twenties; if I could have unravelled this madness earlier. After a painful and confused ten-year period I found the help of an intelligent, intuitive doctor who prescribed lithium, and I have been taking it ever since.

My mind is now stable and the confusion of polarising is minimal so long as I keep my stress levels in check, find solace in the wilderness, and keep myself physically fit with healthy foods. I long for deeper connection with my family and friends, and I manage to do this most of the time. Perhaps this is a healing journey I seek; my father and grandfather both served in the British Army in World War Two and World War One. God, do I know their pain and their suffering, and those close to them. There is no escaping this fact and it is the same for many others who have experienced a similar history.

This inner journey starts with an ability to open myself to these feelings that lie so deeply bound within, wanting to come forward whenever I can muster the courage. But maybe it is better to keep the lid shut, to keep the lithium pumping through my veins for fear of a total collapse and need for hospitalisation. Travelling to the Himalayas and writing this story is a very healthy pursuit for me. Good god, we have all seen enough war footage, real or created, and yet so much of my short life has been an internal war – perhaps the experience of my father and grandfather coming to the surface; they had to bury their experiences: "Stiff upper lip and all that!" – "Just get on with your civilian life now; career, marriage, children, the next generation, all simple stuff really!" Forgive my sarcasm, I found none of those things easy; but my children are here, they hug me, they love me. They know my vulnerabilities ...my samsara...and they still love me.

My children know of this medical condition – this mental illness. I have grappled with it for over twenty years, something my parents would never have disclosed, "Stiff upper lip son, keep marching – we're British!" There is little chance my children will inherit the illness, as their mother does not have this particular genetic code; however, the next generation might. There is a ten percent chance according to medical science; the odds are therefore good.

Importantly though, it is not something to fear, but it *is* something to take action on with the help of a good doctor and a willingness to find a way of living that will sustain me mentally, physically and most importantly, spiritually. These travels, while I am still strong enough and my mind able enough, sustain me with a productive purpose that offers something to others, to help others on their journey through this often precarious life.

Outside the shop I see another tabby cat with the same markings as the little fellow at Kopan Monastery who would come during the day to sleep on my bed. I was very touched that he chose my bed out of some twenty beds in our men's dormitory – I took it as an omen that we would see a snow leopard, or at least know we were on the right journey of the snow leopard – and here he was again, sitting on his haunches on a rock wall at a convenient height to pat. But he was having nothing to do with patting: "Who do you think you are, touching this puddy tat from the Himalayas?" I may be able to charm a grandmother, mother and daughter but there is no way this 'snow leopard' was going to be patted by this human.

I walked back to the bridge and gave the injured man a wave – Namaste! – before heading across this elegantly engineered structure that is so simple in design yet so brilliantly effective in spanning these very long distances. It is a Swiss company we have to be thankful for; I describe their design in more detail in *21 Days in the Himalayas*.

There was an elderly woman sitting on the steps of a shop front with a large gold nose-piece. It seemed to dominate her face, a symbol of marriage and not ownership I hoped. It is called a bulaki and is often made of gold and red stone, and because of its size has to be held up while eating. At the time of death, it is often removed and placed inside the mouth, on the tongue. It is often complemented with a gold 'little flower' pierced into the left-hand nostril. It's called a phuli. (4)

Another elderly woman was happy to be photographed; she had a very sublime, knowing look on her face as if to say: "I've seen it all before, Western man visiting the Himalayas to find himself – pass me the spittoon." Well certainly, I did love it here and the experience is enriching beyond words. Thank you, I wanted to say as I continued up the valley. I nearly forgot; Namaste and thank you for being the people you are – villagers living in a very fertile and rich valley where a close community exists that enables healthy lives – something we in the West could do with more – honest connectedness.

I saw tool shops and men making and sharpening scythes in preparation for the rice harvest in the coming month – now that will be a community event of epic proportions – with much opportunity for celebration. There were other steel tools for digging, and big bladed knives for tree felling; spoons and ladles; hammers of several sizes; axes and other tools of which I was unsure as to their use, but most were made in this small shop and served the village well. This was the man to see for farm implements and the like. He had a small timber-fired furnace that he used to pump hot air onto the coals, and he probably did this most of the week, especially with the pre-winter harvest coming. He wore shorts and thongs and gave me a big smile, Namaste!

Two elderly women sit on a timber bench waiting for a man to sew fabric for them; they are happy to be photographed, and offer big smiles as they wait patiently for the sewing job to be done. Behind them are bean plants growing on trellises; agriculture and the land are never far from these people's lives. They wear bright-coloured clothes and have a shawl wrapped over their shoulders. Both of them have a bindu on their forehead, and the older lady has a little gold flower or phuli in her left nostril, symbolising marriage. The man sewing, using a heavy black steel machine operated by pedal power, works methodically, and is enjoying our interaction. I thank them – Namaste! – and a glowing bubble surrounds us: "Western man has a delightful interaction with the locals and catches the moment on camera". I keep walking, eager to keep up with Dilip and Poona who are very patient with my distractions, which make this journey so worthwhile – the Tibetan/Nepalese world I want to reach out and touch on this journey.

I see timber beehives strapped to the side of houses; they are made from a timber log, 300mm in diameter and about 900mm long. There is a small slot, fifty-millimetres wide, and a five-millimetre opening on which the small black bees can land. They remind me of our native Australian bee, but somewhere in these Himalayan regions there is the world's largest bee with a ferocious bite and an industry of extraction that only the bravest will cope with. I describe these bees and the brave people who gather the honey in *21 Days in the Himalayas*.

In a number of places, I come across large round stones that can be held in the hand; underneath is a flat stone some 300mm in diameter which is used for grinding chilli, among other things. They put four or five chillies on the flat stone at a time and gently pound them, allowing the weight of the stone to do the work. In time it becomes a paste and then they are ground to form a more fluid paste, ready for the table – delicious with boiled potato and salt – but beware, the chillies can be as hot as a furnace.

I see potato plots being prepared for planting. A man rests in the late afternoon sunlight with a cigarette in hand, and looks over his day's work, an area of some three hundred square metres he has dug – two-hundred by two-hundred-millimetre divots, eighty millimetres deep. Tomorrow, he will plant the potatoes from last season in the sandy light-coloured loam; this crop will be grown for the coming winter food supply.

There are all manner of legumes drying on sheets of plastic or hessian sacks: lentils, soya and other beans. I find Dilip and Poona in a cobbler's shop. Dilip is not happy with his new boots; he wants them stitched all around, and the cobbler works with a hand-stitching tool and a black linen thread. Eventually, we walk back to our guesthouse just a few doors up.

That evening I am introduced to the rice wine that is made in the village and which is about 15% alcohol. One glass was enough for me. I was ready for bed and the opportunity to listen to the soothing fast-flowing stream just outside my window. There were several other Nepalese men staying at the guesthouse who were drinking the rice wine by the glassful. They were quite possibly onto their eighth glass when I headed off to bed. For Dilip and Poona, their room was right next to the dining area and these men decided to party on with the rice wine flowing until the early hours of the morning.

Needless to say, Dilip and Poona were not impressed with the landlady the next morning, while I had blissfully slept through, thanks largely to the sounds of the flowing stream just outside my window. In Buddhist terms this was simply some past life Karma where Poona and Dilip had to balance the natural flow of energy by enduring their past life misdemeanours. It amused me because I had left my home in Australia during an eight-month battle with neighbours who made all manner of industrial noise to suit their commercial business. It was a challenge beyond measure, but I persisted using local council help, and I contemplated my past-life wrongdoings at the same time, Karma.

David, the Australian monk I met at Kopan who had decided after thirty years to leave from the monastery, advised me to get the authorities on board and deal with the issue legally, if necessary. He was very clear with his counsel and encouraged me not to be frivolous with past lives; what's more he had originally trained in Australia as a lawyer. Just the advice I needed from a clear, quietly spoken and highly intelligent man who wore Buddhist 'civvies' for his meditation practise with us. "Breathe out Western impurity, breath in Kopan Monastery teachings...repeat...repeat..." Thank you David.

CHAPTER IV

Close your eyes, fall in love, stay there.
RUMI

When we headed out of Tara Khet we came across a block works factory which consisted of five men, a massive pile of fine sieved gravel, a large cement mixer, bags and bags of cement, a machine to crush the concrete mix into shape, and a large drying area where the new blocks were carried on a flat wheelbarrow and laid out to harden in the sun.

Further up the road several elderly women were breaking fist-sized rocks into smaller gravel using a tool with a small metal loop to hold the rock in place while they belted it with a large steel hammer until they had made the required size of gravel. They did not look happy and I wondered what they had done in their past life. I wanted to help them – offer rupees – but thought it best to just keep walking...think snow leopard!

Then we came to a large retaining wall project with perhaps ten men working; the rock retaining wall was already at three metres high. The men worked from a bamboo scaffold. I find these projects vastly interesting having come from the building industry. The young man operating the huge cement mixer gave me the finger just as I took the photo. Hah, I thought, I'll be showing that to the Karma gods tonight, cheeky young pup with dyed red hair. Typical attitude of the 'building industry' I thought as I walked away; maybe he was Australian in a past life or maybe he was a mirror of me at that age?

Across the small bridge where a twenty-tonne excavator had been preparing ground for the next retaining walls some seven metres high, I could see a metre thickness of rich alluvial topsoil where the rice in this wealthy area grew so well. Little wonder this valley is so fertile and prosperous; food grew in abundance and the rice fields were now becoming terraced as we gained elevation.

In many of the smaller side creeks there were large clumps of bamboo rising twenty metres, and these were regularly harvested for building projects, bamboo being an excellent material for many purposes in this predominantly rural area. It most likely was sold to the local towns for scaffolding and other decorative projects.

The Myagdi Khola River is some one hundred metres wide, a fast-flowing current with lots of whitecaps. At one major bend in the river we saw men fishing in the deep currents that flowed down to Beni and eventually to the plains of Nepal and India. Dilip believed they most likely fished for trout, which had been introduced by the British in the nineteenth century. With a little research I discovered it is the brown trout that has taken so well to these cold waters up to 3,000m in elevation. Anything above that, they would need a down jacket, high altitude fin gloves, and a good measure of Diamox to stave off altitude sickness.

"...since they come from the Tibetan Plateau, these rivers are much older than the mountains, and the Kali Gandaki forged its great abysses as the mountains rose." [2] **Peter Matthiessen, p.37**

It is along this leg to Dharapani that we stop for lunch in a small village; a friendly, hospitable lady cooks our dal bhat and while she is preparing it, I go off to photograph the bright orange noodles that dry on racks in the warm sun. They are formed in circles about the size of a small dinner plate and just as thick, a woven matt that dries semi-hard, made from ground corn, Dilip tells me. They will be a crucial food source throughout the winter, and bags and bags of them are made.

A young woman is distracted from her television programme, which she watches with her father while her child sleeps between them. I ask how to get onto the roof where these brightly coloured noodles dry, both white and orange. She leads me through a dark attic space and shows me the door to the rooftop. I thank her, and she pauses momentarily to be sure there is nothing else I want to see. Food and its sources fascinate me in a land where not one single supermarket can be found – praise be to the Buddhist gods. *(28)*

In this prosperous village, baskets of fresh vegetables – cabbage, beans, cucumbers, tomatoes, garlic, onions, ginger, squash, and other long white vegetables I cannot name – are found. Healthy banana trees grow on the sides of the trail with large bunches of fruit that are still green but will provide good food in the winter. A large wasp, some forty millimetres long draws moisture and sugars from the purple head. There is a vibrancy to this land made rich by the mountain air, huge rivers, and thousands of years of fertile soil that produces rice, maize, lentils and many other types of bean. It is indeed a 'Garden of Eden,' but no reference intended to a man-made bible from another part of the world.

Back at the lunch spot I wish I could talk to a middle-aged lady who doesn't wear a red bindu on her forehead, which most likely means she is a widow. Our eyes connect and I see such peace and wisdom within her...I ask for a photo, she agrees. I know there is much more to her life story as she sits before me with such ease and grace – Namaste – thank you –

IN THE FOOTSTEPS OF THE SNOW LEOPARD

I wish I could stay and learn more of your wisdom.

It was over this lunch that Poona referred to me as 'grandfather'. I assumed it was my silver-grey beard that put a good ten years onto my complexion. However, I did find it an endearing term as with Giri referring to me as his 'father;' although I would much prefer a night out on the town in Kathmandu as his friend. He's such an incorrigible and naughty man, I like him immensely. His business acumen is targeted; he plans to visit Indonesia, Germany and Australia as part of his marketing and expansion plans in 2020 – the reason he likes to be paid in $US cash. He has charisma to soothe the Buddhist gods, backed by his honest dealings with me.

He spotted me at the airport in Kathmandu in December 2017, when I arrived from Australia for the first time. He was wearing a grey business suit and had an offsider with him to carry my bags. I had no intention of doing business with him at that point as I had already made plans, but his impeccable manners, very good English and most of all his trekking knowledge was all too much to ignore. He still has my business and most certainly my friendship. To be referred to now as his 'father' is respectful – but I would prefer to be his friend and be taken out on the town in Kathmandu – now that would be a Giri adventure.

He is also very good at 'reading' his customers, which I witnessed firsthand at the end of this trip when a young European woman came to his office and asked about a trek. He spent about an hour with her and later concluded that she was on too small of a budget for his company. But he remained patient and helpful the whole time he worked a plan out for her, always polite, always the gentlemen....and most certainly always the businessman.

At Darbang, a well-stocked trading village that boasts the end of the road and the start of the mule teams that service the route to Tara Khet, we stop at a police checkpoint and are greeted by five men wearing neatly pressed blue uniforms with dark blue trousers, lighter blue shirt, polished black boots, and polished black belts. They seem too distinguished and distant from the local dress code for this small trading village and gateway to the remote Dolpo region, which also has a hunting reserve where tourists' pay exorbitant US dollars to shoot bharal sheep using helicopters and many local 'foot soldiers' to 'carry out the dead' so to speak.

Several of the police are carrying semi-automatic weapons and as I am the only tourist within miles of this village it all seems rather excessive; however, Dilip assures me these men are here to help and our whereabouts needs to be protected – or a lot more is going through this village than meets the eye. They looked like they'd just been airlifted in by helicopter from Kathmandu wearing their efficient and clean, neatly pressed uniforms. The senior policeman asks me many questions about Australia; where I lived, what I did there, was I married. It started to feel more like an interrogation, and his English was just a little too good for my comfort.

I began to wonder if this checkpoint had a much more important purpose than to check the permit of one tourist, his guide and porter. Perhaps there was a drug trade through these parts connecting China and Tibet, then heading down into Nepal and India. Or there were poachers not paying the correct $US dollars to hunt bharal. That would certainly explain the significance of these very smartly dressed policemen, who spoke exceptional English. Dilip was not forthcoming with comments on any of my theories, only saying that they were here to help us – "and Nepal was the one true Buddhist nation, which Western man needs to remember and stop asking so many questions." "OK Dilip", I reply humbly. My suspicions as to their real purpose only increased, but no answer was forthcoming so we kept walking, Dharapani being our destination for the evening.

We stop for lunch at an isolated farmhouse and the lady cooks us dal bhat, which I'm rapidly realising is going to be the standard meal for the entire 24 days – breakfast, lunch and dinner. It is nutritious, if already becoming monotonous. The lady cooks over a wooden fire with a steel frame to support her pots. I am alarmed at the smoke inhalation she must endure, cooking several times per day. While we wait for lunch, I explore the farm building and discover a large copper urn, some 700mm high and 300mm in diameter, with a wood fire underneath.

Dilip explains that this is the rice wine cooker and we are to see many of them on this journey. It's almost a staple part of their diet and helps with the cold weather and with aching joints – or so the story goes. I find it delightful after a day's trekking, soothing to the soul, but one or two glasses in the evening is quite enough for me. Its alcohol content seems to vary considerably depending on the person entrusted with its distillation. It can also be made from maize, another crop I see ready for harvesting with 'fingers' of brown seeds.

Dilip and Poona love to share a cigarette at every opportunity; it's like a bonding of their brotherhood on this journey– to care for this Western man – and they do this ritual every day.

I ask Dilip how many cigarettes he smokes per day and he gives me a slightly quirky and embarrassed smile and says, "Twelve, maybe". They are both strong walkers and tobacco does not seem to inhibit their abilities – but I would like to tell him the warnings on the packets are real. It's socially accepted in Nepal, especially amongst the men despite the warnings on the packaging of rotting limbs, eyes and throat – but still people smoke.

It's a steady climb from here to Dharapani, nearly five hundred metres in elevation, on a series of switchback trails which pass through pine forests with views north to Dhaulagiri, a massive white mountain rising 8,167 metres above the oceans. The views are fleeting on this section of the trail because of the oak, pine and rhododendron trees growing ten metres tall.

I'm distracted by a Hindu ceremonial arena some five metres square, with a square boxed concrete pelmet on four sides rising two and half metres from the concrete floor. From this pelmet hang the heads of goats, sheep and ducks. In the centre of this small arena is a large stone with shaped corners to take the animal's legs. Their bodies are stretched out, so the throat can be cut; its head, dripping with blood, is then hung on the concrete pelmet above.

The blood is still fresh on the large stone and concrete floor from the past month of Hindu celebrations across Nepal, during which thousands of animals are slaughtered. I walk away shaking my head and muttering, "Barbaric, just barbaric." I agree with the Buddhists that no animal should die for human gratification, and this shrine situated high in the remote hills near Dharapani was just such an example.

But then I am not Hindu and these are ancient practices connecting the people to the gods; the deep red colour of blood represents honour, love and prosperity.

"On a corner of the trail is a weird shrine where horns of many slaughtered goats are piled in a kind of alter, with red ribbons tied to branches of the trees. At this time of year, people pay homage to Durga, a dread demoness of ancient origin, who emerged again in the first centuries A.D. as the black Kali, the dreadful female aspect of Lord Shiva and embodiment of all horrors of the mortal mind." (2) Peter Matthiessen, p.43

This ceremony connects the ancient practice of applying a bindu to the forehead of women and some men. They use a dye made from red turmeric, and it is applied either as a dot or a long strip using a wax to adhere the red paste to the forehead in ceremonies from Hinduism, Buddhism and Jainism. It signifies the third eye chakra where creation begins and perception is found beyond ordinary sight. The red turmeric is made into a paste called sindoor and applied to the forehead of women to symbolise marriage, and men to symbolise the healthy qualities of life. (5)

A prominent Hindu festival called Gadhimai is held on the border of Nepal and India; it lasts three days, and was banned in 2015 because it was estimated 250,000 animals were slaughtered at the 2009 festival alone. I find this practise barbaric, to say the least. (6)

In places along this route are large clumping grasses growing over two metres tall; Himalayan-sized grasses in full seed, with seed clumps as long as my arm. I stop for a closer look and discover a spider's web built between the stems forming a raft of web the size of a small dinner plate, thick, and white in colour. The small black spider, some thirty millimetres in diameter, comes out to check the vibrations – a skilful hunter eager to feast – but discovers no tasty lunch, just a small stick with which I have prodded his trap. He gives me the 'finger' for disturbing his web, then retreats into his lair. I am a little shocked by his behaviour.

We arrive in Dharapani mid-afternoon – 1,550m above the oceans – and find a guesthouse with views of the snow-capped mountains of the Northwest Himalayas. The Himalayan peaks to the north are shrouded in thick, white clouds – Dhaulagiri I (8,167m), Dhaulagiri VI (7,268m), Churen Himal (7,371m) and Gurja Himal (7,193m). I'm beginning to feel a part of this landscape now; this time-honoured landscape that I share with Peter Matthiessen, who passed through here some 50 years ago.

Dilip wants to explore the village with me; I find him to be a very patient man and he speaks with a deliberate tone that is most endearing. He tells me of the work he has done over his lifetime – painting high-rise buildings in Qatar and Korea. He is a man who has provided well for his family by leaving his home shores. He has one daughter, age nine, who he loves very much, and I feel great warmth towards him. He also has great respect for his father, a retired Gurkha now living in England as part of the rights he earned through his British Army service of over 20 years.

This agriculturally-based village is prosperous, with much of the produce growing in their backyards – fields of rice, maize, lentil, millet – an array of vegetables and chillies by the basket. I ask a lady if I can photograph her holding a large basket of bright red chillies she has just picked and will sun-dry for the coming winter. They use their rooftops and a large cloth sheet to spread the chillies out, or they tie them together with cord to hang in the sun or over the cooking fire.

This lady proudly holds the cane basket up for me to see, and there are literally hundreds of large fleshy red fruits that grow so easily here and are often used to spice up the nutritious yet somewhat bland dal bhat. Further up the trail, in towns like Tara Khet, we enjoy boiled new seasoned potatoes and a chilli paste is made to dip the potatoes in, a delicious meal in itself. However, I needed to be cautious with the chilli as it can take your 'head off' if the seed count is too high for my Western palate, not forgetting touching my face with 'chilli fingers'.

The stone houses in this village are beautifully crafted, with timber windows and doors painted bright blue. The familiar red earthen ochre is painted on the windowsills and where there is no render and paint, I can see the skill of the stonemason who has kept neat rows of natural stone. On one of the blue doors I see a small carving of what looks like a snow leopard; 'Stone the crows!', I say to myself as I make my way back up to my room.

We find a covered pen with tethered goats. They have a tasty bed of grasses and seem very content with their lot; they obviously haven't read the memo about the ceremony held just a half day's walk to the south. There is a post and rail gate nearby; the stone post is as high as my waist, three-hundred-millimetres wide, fifty millimetres thick with three eighty-millimetre holes drilled neatly to take the timber rails. I wonder how they drill stone in such a remote place – perhaps with a small steel punch and much patience.

Deep purple flower-heads as high as my waist grow in many places. Their colour is intense, and they line the pathways to the fields. Marigolds are also in abundance, growing to a similar height. I just love this bright gold and maroon flower that connects to Buddhism. On my return to hot, dry, fire-ravaged Australia – a summer of extreme proportions where millions of native species lost their lives; but apparently, it's still not climate change, just coincidence, with coal mining to resume as soon as practical – I soothe my soul and need for climate acclimatisation by planting more than 50 marigolds. Their flowers help heal my transition from East to West – but only just.

The most conspicuous crop in the fields surrounding the town of Dharapani are four-metre-high marijuana plants with seed-heads the size of my fist. Their colour ranges from a deep green to a rustic brown – they exude health and vitality and provide the village with medicinal qualities and cooking oil. I wonder who is the 'local dealer'? I discover there are two hybrid strains in the Himalayas; cannabis sativa and cannabis indica. Sativa grows to four metres and provides less of a high than indica. It is a plant integral to the locals' lives, and of great interest to western backpackers. (7)

This area of the Himalayas has both strains of cannabis: the very tall sativa with long leaves and buds and the bushier, shorter indica. Both have medicinal properties and a distinct difference between the two plants in terms of a high. Sativa is a more cerebral high which is uplifting and vivid, while indica tends to be more of a sedative with higher levels of THC (tetrahydrocannabinol), which is the principle psychoactive ingredient of cannabis. Peter does not mention rolling a reefer here, but then he did prefer more hallucinogenic substances not found in these mountains. *(7)*

I have only enjoyed cannabis baked into cookies – smoking it when I was sixteen had dismal consequences mostly due to the peer group pressure of the time. These were not healthy choices for me at a vulnerable time of life, and thankfully my parents had the strength to step in and pull me out of what could have destroyed my final year of high school. It is not a time in life I look back on with glowing feelings of accomplishment, despite the pleasure many seem to find in smoking this plant; it was simply not my cup of tea. I am forever thankful for my parents' wisdom at that delicate time of life.

There are large crops of finger millet growing with thick bushy heads, ripe for picking; it is ground into a powder, and used for making a type of thick bread. It stores well in its seed form, but once it is ground into flour the high oil content makes it difficult to store for long periods. It is also made into a beer which is an important part of Hindu rituals, and which I was offered back in Kathmandu. The grainy seeds float and a straw is inserted to consume the warm and potent liquid below; the alcohol content is more than Western wine – maybe as much as 20%.

I like its rich taste and the chewiness of the fermented seeds. On the Annapurna trail several years ago I was offered maize wine which I prefer over the rice wine; it had a richer colour and flavour. Millet is originally from Africa but was soon adapted to India and the Himalayas. It self-pollinates which makes for high production rates, and it thrives in these mountains. *(8)*

The villagers' companion-plant millet with maize – otherwise known as corn – and it grows two metres high with one metre spacing. One plant complements the other in its growth. There are trellises of legumes, long green beans that they dry and thresh by hand to release the small seeds to sun-dry. There's no need for gyms in these villages with so much manual work to attend to and prepare for the winter that is fast approaching. I come across what look like soya beans growing in rows through rice fields; whether this is for companion-planting or to stabilise the rice field's bank of water, I do not know.

The guesthouse has freshly painted bright blue handrails which I try not to grasp; they weren't expecting anyone tonight. I climb the narrow timber staircase to my room remembering to duck as I go through the low doorways. It's a delightful room with timber shutters that I open with views to the north, and the Himalayan Mountains are shrouded in thick white clouds. Dilip says it will snow in the mountains tonight. I drop my pack and walk back down the stairs, getting blobs of oil-based blue paint on my hands. It wipes off with an old rag when I go to wash by their only water source, a 150-litre black plastic tank fed by a thirty-millimetre black pipe that is fed by a local stream. I fill my three-litre water bladder, and treat it with three chlorine tablets. It seems a shame to pollute this mountain water but the thought of getting sick due to a buffalo turd or a dead goat in the stream is enough for me to remain vigilant.

The water is very chilly to say the least. I strip to my underwear, fast-drying clothes that Peter Matthiessen did not have the pleasure of utilising. It's a speedy and chilly wipe-down with a small, light towelette. The owners don't seem to mind my almost naked body; they probably think I'm a little crazy. I quickly pull on thermals made of lightweight Australian Merino wool – made in China though –– another comfort Peter Matthiessen didn't have in 1973. *(c)*

Peter talks of his blood-stained feet being ground by his heavy leather boots, which he tried to stretch in Pokhara before they set off. Thankfully trekking gear has come a very long way in the past 50 years; I wear a lightweight, tough, waterproof boot developed by an American company but most likely made in China. They are superb in terms of durability and they fit my foot like a glove – in twenty-four days of rigorous trekking I have no blisters and certainly no blood. I use two layers of lightweight socks that move and protect my feet. Peter Mattheissen would have used thick woollen socks that are nearly impossible to dry in this cold climate and sit heavily on the skin, creating the opportunity to grind the flesh of the feet to a bloody mess – especially after sixty-four days with plenty of rain and snow.

There is deep-fried egg on offer tonight with heavy bread made from local millet. It's a welcome change and I gobble it down with gusto. There is another grandmother, mother, and daughter crew on duty in the kitchen; they must be a prosperous family as they cook on the luxury of gas. The air in their kitchen is clear with only the smells of what they cook, free of timber smoke.

I sit with Poona and Dilip and invariably they drift into conversation with the owners; no doubt there is much to discuss being in the same industry of catering for travellers – not that there are many tourists to be found. In Dhorpatan we meet a French couple in their early sixties, and a younger German woman trekking with them. They are planning to climb Sonjo Lek, 5,922 metres in elevation to the east of Dovan, some five days trek from our current position. Our paths cross for several days – their party is large, with two guides, four porters, eight mules and two mule handlers. They travel at a slow but steady pace and they must carry all the food for the sixteen-strong party, including climbing equipment and grain for their mules.

I am grateful we travel light; we can move quickly when required and no animals are put at risk of injury from the narrow trails ahead of us, which pass close to the fast-flowing rivers where one slip will see an animal fall to its death, or be so seriously injured it must be left to the vultures. That fact doesn't fit comfortably with me – seeing animals put in such danger. The mule-men we walked with were very patient with their animals, and the mules were well fed on the grains they carried.

It is a peaceful night's sleep in Dharapani; the high mountains of the Himalayas are in view and the air feels crisp. For me this is the purpose of such a trip, to experience the rich and ancient culture of these people, their connection to the land, and the backdrop of some of the highest mountains on the planet.

"The holy grail is what Zen Buddhists call our "true nature"; each man is his own saviour after all. The fact that many a man who goes his own way ends in ruin means nothing...He must obey his own law if it were a daemon whispering to him of new and wonderful paths..." (2) Peter Matthiessen, p.50

CHAPTER V

You have escaped the cage.
Your wings are stretched out. Now fly.
RUMI

The following day we will venture to the Magar village of Lumsum (2,150 metres above sea level). The Magar are the third largest indigenous ethnic group of Nepal, making up 7.1% of the population. They are found in these north-western regions of the Himalayas, west of the Gandaki River which flows south from the Annapurna Mountains. They have a written history going back to 1,100AD and they form the oldest tribes of Nepal. They are known for their prosperity and many struggles for leadership and power over the centuries. *(9)*

The Magar language is still strong to this day, and has its roots in Tibetan linguistics. Tibetan Buddhism is their founding religion; however, animism and shamanism form part of their religion, where faith healers operate using places, objects, and creatures as part of their spiritual essence and social fabric throughout the generations. *(9)*

And to this day, Magars provide the highest number of recruits for the international military regiment known as the Gurkhas. They contribute strongly to folk music, dance and festivals; the largest festival is known as Maghe Sankranti and it is held at the end of winter, usually mid-January. It celebrates the animal stock coming down from the high mountain pastures from the previous autumn. It is a time of prosperity for the people with spring before them. They make a bread from black lentils, salt, pepper and turmeric deep fried in oil; it looks like a western doughnut – delicious! *(9)*

"As Buddhists, they know that the doing matters more than the attainment or reward, that to serve in this selfless way is to be free. Because of their belief in Karma – the principle of cause and effect

that permeates Buddhism and Hinduism (and Christianity, for that matter: as ye sow, so shall ye reap) ..." [2] **Peter Matthiessen, p.40**

It's a beautiful walk through this country with many smaller villages built of stone and painted up to their windowsills in a red earthen ochre. Hundreds of corncobs hang in bunches wherever they can dry under open roof areas, under window awnings, in the house, in livestock barns, in guest bedrooms. Marigolds grow wild with bushes a metre high, their gold and maroon flowers too prolific to count.

There's electrical wiring as thick as my finger coiled up in large bundles waiting to be installed as part of a local hydroelectric project. A transformer also waits to be connected to the flow of wires that will reach the many villages in this area. Two women are threshing millet and legumes to remove the seeds for winter, an essential process. I wonder what the next generation will do with their laptops and university educations – but they will still need to eat.

The trail rises into a dense forest of oak, rhododendrons, and birch. It feels cool within this open treescape, lush dark green leaves of the oak with fungi and lichen growing on the bark. As we come down the other side of this ridge, we meet a young girl with her sister; they are maybe fourteen and twelve years of age; they have been entrusted with a herd of goats and a buffalo, and no doubt seek the lush grasses that grow on the periphery of these forests.

The older girl is confident in her role as head herdswoman; she agrees to a photo, and I wonder what her future will be. Will she have access to education or will herding livestock for her village be her life? The bullock takes the wrong path so she heads off yelling commands that seems to do the trick; the bullock obeys and forms part of the herd again. The photo I have of this wild mountain girl developing into a young woman has her hair tied up in a bun to show her slender feminine neck. She carries an air of confidence; perhaps it is her Tibetan/Magar heritage and I wish her well on her journey. I know from this brief encounter she is a young woman of great service to her village.

Further along, as we approach smaller villages, there is an elderly woman cracking stones to make gravel. She holds the stone in that same loop of metal, forty millimetres high and a hundred millimetres in diameter. She then belts the rock until it reached the gravel size needed, ten to twenty millimetres in diameter. There's a pile near her, about half a cubic metre, which will be picked up to make concrete or track base in the village. She looks quite elderly, in her sixties at least, and seems to have resigned herself to this occupation as the best she can do for her village. It is a merciless task, but someone has to do it.

She works under the shade of a tree and her views to the mountains are unsurpassed, but I doubt she has really noticed the mountains; she most likely grew up here and knows the stories passed down through the generations, and she knows the mountains are a part of her. Perhaps the rock-breaking forms a type of meditation, the flowing movement and cracking of the stone, repeat, eat, sleep, repeat – maybe eight hours per day – or until her elderly body says enough.

At one small village we pass two big domestic pigs – black in colour in a wire pen, their noses deep in a trough of household leftovers – much the same as pigs anywhere in the world. Although this region is predominantly Buddhist that does not mean they don't kill for meat. Even the Dalai Lama will eat meat when his body requires it. They believe that in such cases animals may be sacrificed to assist human beings to maintain strength; however, that does not mean a wanton destruction or killing without necessity, like the Hindu sacrificial site we passed.

These villages are richly diverse with healthy produce, made so by fertile soils and ample waters straight from the Himalayas. As we walk, I talk with Dilip about the alternatives to reach Shey Gompa and Crystal Mountain on another trip. There are two options, the most challenging and more expensive is to fly into Jomsom and cross the eight passes, many of which are over 5,000 metres above sea level and, as there are no villages due to the harsh terrain and weather, it's necessary to carry all your own food and camp.

So, with the excess gear comes the need for mules, which expands the party even more. A thirty-day trip with passes could easily extend to AU$10,000, somewhat less with one or two friends to share the cost. I think of the factors with the additional challenges, but there is time to plan this next journey.

The second option – and by far the most efficient in terms of time and cost – is to fly into Juphal, trek up to Phoksundo lake and then onto Shey Monastery, all within thirty days, where time could be spent exploring Crystal Mountain and environs to Saldang and the Tibetan border. Peter Matthiessen and George Schaller explored this area extensively, but the Tibetan border was not their agenda – it was the elusive snow leopard they sought!

> "I would like to reach the Crystal Monastery, I would like to see a Snow Leopard, but if I do not, that is all right, too. In this moment, there are birds – red-billed choughs, those queer small crows of the high places, and a small buteo, black against the heavens, and southbound finches bounding down the wind, in their wake a sprinkling of song. A lark, a swift, a lammergeier, and more griffons: the vultures pass at eye level, on creaking wings." *(2)* **Peter Matthiessen, p.93**

Poona has done this trip twenty years ago with seventeen French people and fifty porters. Personally, I cannot think of anything more frightening than such a big party with all that could go wrong. At that time Poona was carrying over fifty kilograms which I find a little hard to comprehend; he is a stocky man but his overall weight I would guess to be ninety kilograms maximum, so that would mean he was carrying more than half his own bodyweight, mmm, maybe a tea house story?

There is a blue butterfly on the trail, sixty millimetres in diameter. Its wings are outstretched as it drinks from the muddy waters. The blue is almost iridescent and matches the blue colour the villagers paint on their doors and windows. Black surrounds the blue which makes for a striking contrast, and as the butterfly opens its wings the blue looks like large eyes focussed on me from the trail: "Hello Mr Easton, we wondered when you would arrive." I walked on, not realising butterflies could talk.

We are ascending a trail to reach Lumsum – 2,150 metres above sea level – and cross a fifty-metre suspension bridge with a large waterfall pouring out of the rocks almost eighty metres high. I go down to the fresh pool to fill my water bladder and I treat the water out of habit. The surrounding foliage is a lush dark green, a mixture of bushes and medium sized trees. The spray from the waterfall is tempting me to swim but I'm too much of a 'wuss,' preferring my 'landlubber' ways, not forgetting the water is probably less than five degrees Celsius. In my homeland water temperatures start at around eighteen degrees Celsius and go up from there, hence my 'wuss' factor. *(r)*

The trail winds up at a steady pace to the village of Lumsum; we pass a woman carrying an enormous load of cut grass for her livestock back in the village. The villagers take this process of caring for their livestock very seriously; their animals are an integral part of their own survival in this remote and often harsh climate.

We find a guesthouse very close to the entrance of the village and a group of teenage boys are playing a board game that requires them to slide small discs across the board's surface aided by talcum powder to keep the surface slippery. It creates shrieks of delight in the boys as they compete for dominance; it looks similar to soccer in its play. I love to hear their happiness and the connections they have to their village – they are healthy and loved young men.

There is another group of boys, some years younger than the main table, playing a type of draughts. It's a much more serious game; the competitors must concentrate to move their pieces around the board. The guesthouse seems to be the place to hang out in Lumsum. Bunches of red chilli and corncobs hang from the roof beams and veranda posts – just about anywhere really; winter is approaching and food must be dried and stored.

I'm shown to my room; a narrow and very steep set of timber stairs winds up to the second level at the back of the building. There are bags and bags of grains stored in the stairwell, behind the stairs, and in the small corridor to my room. There are three beds with mattresses like stone. I lay out my sleeping mat and bedding, then head down for a cup of tea and to see if a 'birdbath' is in order, with the possibility of washing some clothes.

They are burning timber to heat water, so it's a precious commodity. I settle for a pot of warm water to bath using my towelette to wipe over my skin. It's refreshing to say the least in the private back area of the house next to a very smelly toilet and chicken roost built off the ground with well-fitted doors to protect the birds from prowling wolves that lurk in these regions.

I hang my washing in my room using a length of six millimetre climbing rope. Even though the temperature will drop below three degrees tonight I expect my clothes to dry; they are light-weight and just the material for such a trip. Peter Matthiessen is unlikely to have had the luxury of washing clothes; most likely, being made of cotton and wool, they would have taken days to dry. What's worse wet cotton can make the human body vulnerable to hypothermia.

The husband of the guesthouse returns home late in the afternoon. He makes his living with seven mules and transports whatever he can, hence all the bags of grain that they must grow somewhere nearby. He is a wonderfully pleasant man and I admire the respectful way he treats his mules; they are given shelter under a tarpaulin held up by two-metre-high stakes and ropes pegged to the ground. He ties a nose bag on each of the mules with a mixture of grains. The mules look at me while they chew; they seem most content with their world and as we sit on the timber benches on the stone veranda above the boys playing board games, we enjoy tea together with Dilip interpreting the conversation for me about life in Lumsum. The mules delivered cement to a construction site today, a profitable exercise I am told.

The young daughter, about twelve, is beautiful; she has rich, black Tibetan hair and light brown skin but most of all it is her wide-eyed beauty of youth and her two parents who obviously love her very much, despite Nepal's not so distant past of girls being sold off to slave traders from India. This young girl is empowered, and it is so beautiful to see her health and vitality; a combination of Himalayan Mountain air, food, water – and no internet access or social media.

"Finally, I remove my watch, as the time it tells is losing all significance. In the rain, all day, the Tibetans come to look at us, and again I am struck by the resemblances between our Native Americans and these Mongol peoples." *(2)* **Peter Matthiessen, p.57**

In many ways this trip is like a silent retreat for me. Dilip is the only access I have to conversation and we conserve that conversation; we don't want this journey through the foothills of the Himalayas to be a talkfest, but rather an opportunity to walk in silence and connect to our own heartbeats, away from the distractions of the human world – that other world of the internet, marketing, corruption, greed and global warming – the greatest threat known to our planet – where human beings have forgotten we are 'beings' and the deeply spiritual connections that exist, and have existed for millennia.

We are a species at the helm that our planet does not need – she only tolerates us, and could easily flick us off with one natural disaster after another – gone within three generations. But there is hope and the opportunity to build a world that is in balance with this precious Earth that has known the human species for only 100,000 years. She's tolerated us for the last 200 years; and we know this Earth is speaking to us, only quietly now; she will roar if she must, and millions of us may perish – until we hear the message of this life creation and life source, Planet Earth.

The lady of the guesthouse cooks dal bhat for our dinner on an open fire with a steel frame that sits over the flames which lick at the blackened pots filled with rice, vegetables and chicken. I feel for her working conditions as this is a daily practice, for most of the year. There are health consequences to breathing in fiery wood smoke every day, not forgetting the impact of deforestation surrounding their village.

"...Nepal has the most serious erosion problem of any country in the world, and the problem worsens as more forests disappear in the scouring of the land for food and fuel; in eastern Nepal, and especially the Kathmandu Valley, firewood for cooking (not to speak of heat) is already precious, brought in by peasants who have walked for many miles to sell the meagre faggots on their backs. The country folk cook their own food by burning cakes of livestock dung, depriving the soil of the precious manure that would nourish it and permit it to hold water. Without wood, humus or manure, the soil deteriorates, compacts, and turns to dust, to be washed away in the rush of

the monsoon." *(2)* **Peter Matthiessen, p.31/32**

A man holding a Nepalese flag flying on a two-metre cane arrives with three other men. One of the men looks very official in his grey suit and formal dark-coloured traditional hat; he carries important books that look like ledgers. I am told he is the tax collector. I nearly fall off the bench; a tax collector up here in the remote Northwest Himalayas? He asks the lady of the house where her husband is – obviously women are not trusted with such important matters. She tells him he will be home later, so he goes.

As we finish our meals and the night sky is forming, I go for a short stroll into the village which clings to this Himalayan hillside. I marvel at how close these people live to nature, the fields and crops that they depend on grow right up to their homes. Behind the fields and disappearing up the hillside is the native forest which I'm told still has red pandas, a rufus-red coloured animal that lives in the trees. It is some six hundred millimetres long, weighs less than ten kilograms, and has a big bushy tail almost the length of its body. In 2008, it was entered on the international endangered species list due mostly to deforestation and lack of natural habitat. *(9a)*

There are small patches of stars in the heavens tonight; the clouds are rolling in and out of this hillside village. I can barely recognise the constellations with the Himalayas so close to the Northern Hemisphere. I stroll back and retire to my smoky room, but do not dare complain as I am only here one night. My thoughts are with all those who have to cook on these open fires day in and day out.

The morning brings the 20th of October, the fifth day of our trek. Today, with the help of the gods, we will reach our first pass, Jaljala Pass at 3,390m, but first we dine on fried eggs and chapatti. A small crowd of musicians arrive carrying a variety of drums made of timber and cow hide, and a long trumpet made of brass which one of the musicians demonstrates for me; then he wants me to dance – which I do for a few brief minutes – my new friends are impressed.

The tax collector returns, and he says hello to me in very good English. He looks the part of an efficient bureaucrat and I wonder what he does with everyone's taxes once they are collected – does he use electronic cable to transfer the money to head office? I doubt that very much. He must have a secret wallet stitched into his very official jacket. The husband offers him keys on a metal ring and he walks away with phone in hand, which surely must be for show unless it is a satellite phone. And what are the keys for? The village vault?

The husband fills the mules' nose bags with a mixture of grains, wheat and corn. He squats on a plastic sheet as he mixes and scoops the grain into the bags. There is much talk between the landlady and a group of ladies who have gathered. There is to be a local political dignitary visiting this morning to open the hydroelectric plant that will give this village electric light and hopefully another form of fuel to cook on – anything is better than deforesting their land and clogging their lungs with burnt timber sap. Hence the musicians – there is much to celebrate; it's not every day a village in the Northwest Himalayas gets its own power source... hence the tax collector.

We are camping in Jaljala Pass tonight, so Dilip and Poona are stocking up with food. I am keen to stay and experience the festivities, but Dilip assures me we must keep moving. I am offered a neckband of purple bougainvillea flowers which I surely would have accepted, but our journey is calling us on. I'm pleased for the people of Lumsum to be receiving hydroelectricity and for the forest timbers it will save. As we leave, I give a NPR300 (AU$5) tip to the wife of the guesthouse owner; they work hard and I want to thank them for their generous hospitality, and I hope they will soon have gas and hydroelectricity with which to cook and heat.

As we head through the village, we meet the husband with a tray of twenty-five eggs; he poses for a photo, so very proud of his chickens. This industrious couple seem to have their hands in many 'village pies' – the issuing of keys was still playing on my fertile imagination. Dilip could throw no light on the subject and besides, he was rather busy purchasing goods for our first camp.

The trail rises steadily all morning through forests of oak, birch, cedar and rhododendron. A man comes towards us carrying an enormous basket of grass on his back – I guess the weight to be thirty kilograms. As we draw closer, I see he is wearing 'heavy duty' rubber thongs – nothing stops these people, they do what they have done for countless generations, before they even had rubber thongs. And they never complain. Their livestock need the grass, winter is coming; this is how they survive by getting the job done.

We stop at Moreni for tea; a little boy is playing nearby. He is sharpening a stick using a blunt scythe and wears a green cape over his head that reminds me of the character from Robin Hood. He is curious about this white man and is gracious in offering to be photographed. His parents seem very busy with guesthouse renovations. There is obviously a tourist trade here as English signs are fixed to the external wall even though precariously spelt. There are magnificent views to Gurja Himal (7,193m) and the rest of the Himalayas behind. It is starting to feel that we are getting into the high country, and I'm excited to be camping on our first high pass tonight.

We steadily keep climbing through forest on a dirt trail well-used by mule teams and villagers. I ask what weight Poona is carrying and after some consideration Dilip tells me twenty-five kilograms. I know this is the answer he wants me to hear and I'm very sure it's more like 30kg. He is certainly earning his living and I make a mental note to give him the same financial tip as I will give Dilip. These men are doing their very best to ensure this journey goes well for me and I am so very thankful for their kindness.

We stop for lunch in an open grassy area. Dilip and Poona work well as a team; Poona sets up the kitchen with a shelter of sleeping mats protecting the flame from the fresh mountain breezes. Dilip goes to get water. They want no help from me so I go off to explore the forest nearby. Dal bhat is the order of the day and it tastes very good, cooked on a small pressure cooker over a gas flame; the other vegetables are cooked in a saucepan on the same gas flame. I offer to wash the dishes – but no, they insist! I feel like an honoured guest, a 'grandfather guest' according to Poona...cheeky bugger. But I'm flattered by his affections.

There are some very tall trees in this area, some thirty metres high and a metre in diameter. They have few branches, perhaps the impact of high winds; they are a type of oak, native to this region. There are rhododendrons growing everywhere around the perimeter of this open grassy area. The colourful displays of this beautiful tree in spring – April/May – must be a sight to behold, especially with the Himalayan Mountains as the backdrop, somewhat different to Kew Gardens.

The pasture is now fading in colour to a deep rustic red with winter so close, but every March and April the locals head up to these higher plains with their goats and sheep to feed on the natural pastures. On this day the clouds are hanging onto the high mountains to the north, and Dilip believes it will be snowing at Thorong La Pass (5,416m), 100km to the northeast of here as the crow flies. The air feels heavy and quiet, like there is snow falling close by.

We are packed and ready to climb the last section to Jaljala Pass where we will set our first camp and hopefully enjoy the high Himalayan Mountains to the northeast, free from clouds – Gurja Himal (7,193m), Churen Himal (7,371m), Dhaulagiri VI (7,268m) and Dhaulagiri I (8,167m).

I watch Poona as he carries his thirty-kilogram basket, his right hand on a single walking stick, his left hand tweaking and adjusting the headband that holds the rope that carries the full brunt of his load. He walks steadily and deliberately, his basket overflowing with two sleeping mats, an empty ten litre water container, an empty jug, green vegetables for our dinner, and his toothbrush tucked into one of the sleeping mats so it will dry. This man is doing the lion's share of the grunt work needed for this trip. He does it tirelessly and never complains.

> "Tibetans say that obstacles in a hard journey, such as hailstones, wind and unrelenting rains, are the work of demons, anxious to test the sincerity of the pilgrims and eliminate the fainthearted among them. George Schaller has certainly been tested: still three days short of Jang La, we are now stranded in heavy rain, with no help to be had from the only settlement between Dhorpatan and Tarakot, which lies on the far side of the Jang." **(2) Peter Matthiessen, p.87/88**

The trail continues upward through the forest: the trunks of tall oak trees are covered in small ferns and mosses that add to this beautiful temperate forest. We don't see red pandas, and the elevation is beginning to be too high for them. As we near the pass I see a small Hindu temple off to the left with a dam next to it. This must have been built to cater for the livestock that comes this way every spring and summer.

> "The snow cone of Great Dhaulagiri, five miles high, rises from the clouds behind and is quickly misted over; though far away, it fills the whole north-east. Ahead, a valley of yellow maples descends gently to the west, on one side a wall of firs, on the other a rampart of bare rock...." **(2) Peter Matthiessen, p.53**

We head to the new and small hunting shelter with a bright blue roof near the edge of this large open plateau. We are now on the southern border of the Dhorpatan Hunting Reserve; helicopters land here to set up camps for international hunters eager to shoot bharal for their curly horns so they can mount them on a wall in their homes far, far, from here, and so their ego can claim to be 'big game hunters'...sounds so very hollow to me.

IN THE FOOTSTEPS OF THE SNOW LEOPARD

Dilip and Poona insist on pitching my tent – I'm really not used to such gracious luxury – but they give me no choice. They see this as their job, and I really do appreciate their kindness. I head off to explore the small timber abodes that have been constructed for the spring and summer months. They are simple shelters made from slabs of timber for roofing and walls. There is a fireplace in the middle with an arrangement of larger stones to place their pots and the very cosy sleeping areas consist of slats of small canes. The ceiling is black from many fires that would burn day and night when people come to stay and tend their livestock in the warmer months.

The natural materials for these abodes are sourced locally unlike the hunters' shelter with its concrete slab, stonewall perimeter, and a bright blue corrugated iron roof. Outside the abodes are areas penned off for livestock; goats, chickens, and mules. They are completely self-sufficient, and I wonder what they think of the helicopters that land here and the hunters who come to kill for sport. Most likely there is an opportunity for work carrying out the dead, but are the men in this high camp more focussed on their livestock, their families, and the way things have always been, as opposed to the 'elite' few who come to hunt? I hope the latter.

I explore the small ridge that faces the Himalayas to the north; rhododendrons grow with their trunks close to the ground, bending and following the Earth. The winter winds must howl here as these plants would otherwise grow to twenty metres. There is a curious groundcover I have seen in several places; its green and purple leaves span out across the ground the size of my finger, covering an area of half a metre or more. The leaves are crinkly with a soft, fur-like texture. Another pink and white coloured wildflower grows 100mm vertically along the base of a root for half a metre. There are light purple daisies and another deeper purple flowering bush. It's like these plants are pushing their last growth for the year; snow will fall in just over a month.

I find Buddhist prayer flags tied around the branches of trees and a large stone rising over a metre out of the ground. In all there must be hundreds of these flags sending their prayers out into the universe – messages of love, compassion and peace. Buddhists are eternal optimists for our planet and the ability we humans have to save ourselves. And as I cast my eyes to the northeast and the very large Himalayan mountains, I see a number of beautiful golden trees glowing in autumn colours in the late afternoon light and I sense the Buddhist optimism; I know we will triumph over the very difficult future ahead of us. It will be a future of great changes like we've never faced before, but we are an intelligent species despite our list of failings – this time we will head to a cleaner, more sustainable future because we simply have to, our planet demands this.

Dhorpatan Hunting Reserve covers 1,325km2 over three regions – Rakum, Myagdi and Baglung – and serves a greater purpose, preserving many species of plants and animals which otherwise may have been claimed for farming. It was created in 1985 with a long list of impressive animals preserved here – bharal, musk deer, red panda, Tibetan wolf, jharal, Himalayan tahr, Himalayan black bear, deer, wild boar, rhesus macaque, langur, mouse hare, musk deer, cheer pheasant, danphe, and 137 species of birds. *(10)*

IN THE FOOTSTEPS OF THE SNOW LEOPARD

I come face-to-face with a Tibetan wolf on the exit track to one of the smaller villages close to Dhule. The animal had been strung up at least a year ago as a warning to other wolves – or perhaps to bandits and thieves – not to enter the village and kill the livestock, or possibly a small child. The wolf's jaw is wide open baring its teeth, and most of the fur had rotted off making it look ferocious, to say the least. Its large black body hung with its paws outstretched, its black bushy tail still intact. Despite its appearance, I doubt it would scare off another hungry wolf in the middle of a cold winter; most likely it was there to warn off bandits.

It is possible to hike for up to fifteen days with an organised group in Dhorpatan Hunting Reserve, so one hopes there is sufficient coordination for the hikers not to become the accidental hunted. Conservation does seem to be the centre of attention based on the information I could find, while killing animals for government revenue is more the drawcard for wealthy Western visitors.

Back at camp, Dilip and Poona are cooking dinner within the protection of the shelter walls; steamed rice and tinned fish from Thailand. They offer me a cup of sweet mint tea and I chat about the remarkable finds I had made in these open pastures. Dilip always seems interested in what I had discovered, but then I suppose it was part of his job, poor fellow. I wandered over to my tent and pulled from my pack; thermals, down sleeping bag, liner, down jacket, sleeping matt, thermal head gear, two layers of gloves, head torch, and a *giraffe*! Where did that come from? I don't remember packing a giraffe!

I stripped off my day gear and dressed for the cool night. The sun was almost setting. It must have been only a few degrees above zero; fresh and exhilarating, just like the view before me. I simply love these mountains and the people that live here.

"...like the Buddhist Mind, like Tao, the Great Spirit of the American Indian is everywhere and, in all things, unchanging. Even the Australian aborigines – considered to be the most ancient race on earth – distinguish between linear time and a "Great Time" of dreams, myths, and heroes, in which all is present in this moment." (2) Peter Matthiessen, p.60

I find the dinner tasty and appreciate that Dilip and Poona have worked hard to accommodate me. I have nothing but grateful praise for their efforts. I'm simply not used to having my tent erected, dinner cooked and utensils washed up – I feel grateful – and they do it all with a cheerful smile and a few cigarettes. Bed!

CHAPTER VI

If you want to win hearts, sow the seeds of love.
RUMI

I awaken early to a clear morning; the Himalayas to the north are looking bigger and clearer than ever: Gurja Himal (7,193m), Dhaulagiri VI (7,268m), Dhaulagiri I (8,167m), and Churen Himal (7,371m) behind. They are snow-covered and their size is powerful and awe-inspiring. Gurja is a massive snow-covered peak facing south with a sharp point at its summit. Dhaulagiri I, stands more alone, and nearly 1,000 metres higher than the others. It too has a sharp point at the summit. They form a range with other mountains in the background; they are covered in brilliant white snow and stand resolute, part of the Himalayas. I'm blissfully at peace sitting up on the southern rise near our campsite to gain the best vantage point. How beautiful it feels to be a human being in the majesty of nature so far from my home, immersed in a culture in which I find solace. Namaste!

The mountains ask why I came, and I answer as humbly as I can: "To hear the Earth, to listen to her wishes away from the noise of the human species." They seem happy with this answer, but I know they seek more. "Why have you come?" I try again, looking out to one of the most beautiful mountain wilderness scenes I have ever seen; "To hear your wishes, to serve you." That seems to satisfy them for now; the mountains, the wilderness before me rising to some of the highest points on the Earth, fifty kilometres from the 'Roof of the World' – Tibet. Is it any wonder these answers come? The spiritual dimensions that belong to this planet and universe of which we as a people are so fortunate to experience with ancient wisdom…alas though in 2020 we seem to have lost that connection. That Earth connection the Indigenous peoples the world over knew to the core of their being.

I am reminded of the inherent natural beauty that is this planet, and for tens of thousands of years it has been protected by *homo sapiens* who lived within the natural laws and boundaries. The name *homo sapiens* is Latin for 'wise man'; it was chosen in 1758 and I believe needs to be upgraded to reflect an equal gender balance so we can move forward on a more equal footing: "*et mulieres sapientes*" translates to: "wise men and women" with particular emphasis on the 'wise', as our planet has seen enough of our bullshit! *(11)*

I think we were once wise. We understood the natural boundaries and the sacredness of this Earth, and we lived within her means. Our population has grown since traditional times; there are now 7.7 billion of us. How are we to find solutions with such a crushing number? I can still only think the closer we connect with the Earth and its natural boundaries of clean air, clean water and wholesome food, the more apparent the answers to our survival will become. This, combined with a lot less "real time, on-line" and returning to an Earth connection, should be our quest again.

The more we disconnect from television, social media and news feeds – which perpetuate self-doubt and sell goods and services that separate us more than connect us – the healthier we will become, and so will this precious planet begin to heal. I see hope in this way forward, of disconnecting from the human noise we have created.

It sounds so simple in a world with nuclear armaments, water and ocean pollution, sanitation services to only 45% of our population, desertification, air pollution, threatened species, global warming – the list goes on. Why does our planet put up with us? She's been so patient – but the cracks in her patience are showing – God forbid if she truly loses patience with us; this fragile species that looks everywhere but within for answers could be brushed off the face of this Earth. *(11)*

And as I sit here looking out onto the Himalayas – in a natural setting that has been visited by *et mulieres sapientes* for thousands of years – I hear the 'silent heartbeat' of Planet Earth. This has occurred a few times in my life, most notably when I was nineteen. I rode a motorcycle to Cape York Peninsula in Australia where I travelled and camped in so many wild places; it was easy to see how the Indigenous people of Australia lived with such connection and respect for the land, which is deeply ingrained in their black-skinned souls.

In these places I could hear the 'silent heartbeat' of the Earth and now, here in the Himalayas nearly forty years on, I feel that connection again – the Earth's 'silent heartbeat', a connection to the Earth, found in wilderness away from the 'maddening crowd'. That, to me, is the real challenge we as a species face – connecting more to each other and this living, breathing Earth.

The traditional peoples of this Earth had that connection; they lived within her natural boundaries and so must we learn to do that again in 2020 – all 7.7 billion of us! Now that's a challenge worthy of a collective effort.

I walk back down to meet Dilip and Poona who have done the dishes, pulled down my tent, packed the gear, and are now enjoying their morning cigarette. I see that Dilip has filled a plastic bag with our rubbish and placed it in the adjoining herders' hut which just adds to the already considerable rubbish dump. I don't have a solution as carrying it anywhere here will most likely only result in it being burnt, so I reluctantly accept this dilemma which is now prevalent throughout the Himalayas – but disposal wells are emerging in many places and we are to see one before we reach Ringmo village, on the shores of Phoksundo Lake.

Dilip and Poona are ready to go. I look forward to spending the day with them as we head to the large village of Dhorpatan. Within an hour we come to another large open grassy area with several more of the herders' huts built into the landscape. This one has a slab stone roof, gathered from the river we are about to cross. I hope the timbers supporting the slabs are sound; it would be challenging at night to sleep wondering if one of these large rocks might fall through onto a delicate human body below – they would inflict far more damage than a headache. There are a set of timber slab doors just one and half metres high that I am able to squeeze my way through.

I find these huts fascinating; their low roofs, timber-slatted earthen beds and central fireplaces lined with stones, complete with larger stones to place cooking pots and a channel for the air onto the fire. The ceilings are blackened with soot. These are simple abodes; it's certain that these peoples' impact is minimal compared to us in the West with our cars, oil refineries, appliances, wi-fi, supermarket chains, and high-rise industries. Outside there are pens, built of timber canes, for sheep, goats and cows. They must tether them at night and remain vigilant, as hungry wolves prowl these lands and kill at any opportunity.

I sit quietly inside while Dilip and Poona enjoy a cigarette and most likely discuss my weird enthusiasm for these abodes: "I thought he was from the West, with two motor cars in every garage". I close my eyes and imagine these people, the families who come to these mountain places with their worldly possessions to sustain life. I imagine them sitting around this fireplace eager for the warmth and closeness they would feel as a family. The whole space is no more than twenty square metres. I imagine the fire smoke permeating this place and I imagine the men going outside for a smoke; I never see women smoking. The people are safe in this place knowing their goat herd is just outside, and perhaps they lay traps for the wolves who visit on the coldest of nights.

These people are from generations of herders; many are Tibetan and some are from as far as Mongolia originally. Poona tells me his ancestors are Mongolian and this rings true, for his face is round and his skin is a deeper brown. He says his ancestors travelled this way several thousand years ago; he speaks with pride for his people. I continue to sit in this little hut where so many stories have been told of the Himalayas, what the tall mountains mean and what it means to be Tibetan or Mongolian, just like the stories my father and grandfather told me of what it was like to be English, originally Mercia – now that's another book – *England, My Parents' Birthplace*.

I climb my way back outside and the views to the northeast are inspiring to say the least – the Himalayas rising to the Tibetan gods. These mountains provide such a striking backdrop that makes me feel humble, yet so inspired and appreciative of this precious planet, so threatened by *et mulieres sapientes*. We walk on through large pine forests with trees soaring thirty metres, their trunks one metre in diameter, a characteristic dark brown and tessellated bark, vibrant and powerful – part of this planet's life-force. Many thousands of cones are formed on the branches, holding their seeds till next spring...and so the cycle goes.

The trail winds through these forests at a steady downhill pace. We meet a family of goat herders with some thirty fat, healthy goats in tow. The husband carries a large cane basket which overflows with blankets; he walks in rubber boots. His wife carries a basket on her back with a two-year-old baby's head popping out of the top. A five-year-old walks next to her, half jogging to keep up. They are walking at a strong pace, eager to get their goats up to the open grass plains from which we have come.

But why, with winter coming? Dilip cannot explain but he tells me they are a wealthy family to have so many goats. I ask, "Where do they park their motor car and 140cm surround sound colour TV?" How could they watch the footy and the cricket? These people are connected to the Earth, they watch the weather patterns, they know where to find food and clean water, and they are connected to the Buddhist gods, to the universe; their ancestors are with them every step of the way. 'Footy and cricket' simply isn't on their radar – they are tuned to *Om...Mani...Padme...Hum* – Mother Earth connection.

There have been some extensive wild fires in this area, perhaps two summers ago, and the damage is evident as large tracks of the forest are severely burnt, and many of the trees have died. Dilip explains that these forests burn explosively being pine, and there is little to no fire control used here. It burns until there is nothing left to burn, hence the acres and acres of destroyed forest.

Wildflowers along the trail abound, a blue ground cover is my favourite as it looks almost iridescent, a delicate beauty. In another clearing near a creek I see a fence some fifty metres long made from large river stones just like the roof slates. The intensity of labour for this wall is quite remarkable but it serves the purpose of keeping the sheep in and the wolves out – with some luck.

Around mid-day we come to a small village where most of the inhabitants have headed south for the coming winter. We find a place open for business, willing to cook us lunch – dal bhat. I smile pleasantly and say, "Thank you, that would be delicious". Every chef cooks it differently. It is nutritious, so I mustn't complain, but I do enjoy the deep-fried egg with chapati for a change when available.

The kitchen ceiling is dripping in black soot; perhaps he burns green timber as the sap drips from the ceiling in small black lumps. There are various sausage meats hanging from the rafters, drying and being flavoured by the natural timbers that burn gently 24/7. I feel for the man as he toils for an hour or more to prepare our meal in the smoky kitchen, but when he has finished, he goes outside for some fresh air and a cigarette.

He tells us that last winter there was three metres of snow in the village. It's hard to imagine with the sun so strong but in one month it will be a very different story; our elevation is close to 3,000 metres. It is little wonder the people who live here head south for the winter to soak up the sun's warmth and help their livestock fatten.

I go outside and find all sorts of interesting things with which to amuse myself, including a timber hammer and Viking-style axe that needs a good sharpening. I notice a woman heading towards us from the same way we have come. She is carrying a large cane basket, and is dressed beautifully in a red turban loosely holding her rich black hair. She wears a green long-sleeved shirt, blue pants with large white stars, and 'trekking grade' rubber thongs on her toughened bare feet. She places her cane baskets down very near to me; she squats down and shows me, running her hands through her produce.

The baskets are full of mushrooms, but no ordinary mushrooms according to Dilip. These are dark in colour with golden tops, not unlike our 'gold tops' at home that can send people off on psychedelic trips, rendering some people psychotic with vomiting, diarrhoea and seizures. Dilip walks away muttering to me that she's a complete 'nutter'. And I was just starting to like her – besides she had a beautiful red turban. I needed Dilip to interpret some more... but he buggered off!

"...the Tibetan *Book of the Dead* which I carry with me – a guide for the living, actually, since it teaches that a man's last thoughts will determine the quality of his reincarnation. Therefore, every moment of life is to be lived calmly, mindfully, as if it were the last, to insure that the most is made of precious human state – the only one in which enlightenment is possible." (2) Peter Matthiessen, p.89

There are small creeks and a river to cross, we remove our boots; it's wide but less than knee deep. My feet feel like they have been frozen numb – that aching numb feeling like a mild frostbite; we push through the fast-flowing waters as quickly as we can. In Peter Matthiessen's time there were few bridges so this is just a taste of what his large trekking party endured in cotton shirts, blue jeans, heavy woollen socks, leather boots, woollen jumpers and waxed cotton jackets – no wonder they had eighteen porters.

We were on fairly level ground from this point and the pine forests – with trees growing over thirty metres tall with thick bases, some several metres in circumference – were simply enchanting, with a moss-covered forest floor. I was waiting for Robin Hood and his merry men from Mercia to ride into view but it remained quite definitely just Dilip, Poona and I. As we draw closer to Dhorpatan the trail follows a string of small villages with stone dwellings, timber trellises drying rice, some five metres tall – no one is likely to starve this winter.

There are red apple trees that are difficult to resist. There are timber post-and-rail fences, mixed with the labour-intensive vertical stone type I saw in Dharapani. There is little livestock to be seen; maybe they too have been herded to the lower plains before the arrival of winter. Mules are the main animal corralled here by the look of the saddles and blankets hanging on timber rails, drying in the sun after a hard trek to source produce.

I find a white-coloured flat stone about the size of a small table near one of the creek crossings that looks remarkably like a piece of the ancient sea floor. It had the characteristic patterns of sand from the ocean floor. Some 66 million years ago the Himalayas were, in fact, in an ocean connecting North Africa to Australia. It was the Cenozoic Era during which fauna and flora had almost finished evolving in the continents that exist today. *(12)*

The Himalayas were part of an Afro-Asian bridge in a sub-era called the Neogene, 23 million years ago – hence the rock that looks like the sea floor. I have seen these rocks in central Australia, deep red in colour. They reflect an ever changing and expanding planet with much disruption and chaos. Goodness knows what Mother Earth has in store for us with the era, Globaloic Warmingene coming our way! *(12)*

Dilip tells me there are trout in these mountain rivers that are descendants from 'European times.' Trout are well-suited to the cold waters that flow in abundance, and with all the huge pines one could mistake being in North America, Canada, Scotland or other parts of Europe. I photograph Dilip and Poona with the forest surrounding them, a sandy white trail weaves through the trees and mossy floor of this most picturesque place in the foothills of the Himalayas. I'm sure Robin Hood and his merry men are near or King Arthur from *Monty Python's Holy Grail*, clip clopping along with coconut shells instead of horses. It was an enchanting place of merriment.

We arrive in Dhorpatan late in the afternoon. It has been a big day and especially wonderful to see so many interesting things and this superbly beautiful forest. The last five kilometres passes through a succession of villages with many Tibetan flags flying high on five metre timber poles. The people are proud of their culture and religion. It's like they stake a pole in the ground with a five-metre-high Buddhist flag flowing, to say: "This is what we believe, and there's 2,500 years of history connecting us." Namaste!

> "Among Hindus and Buddhists, realisation is attained through inner stillness, usually achieved through the *samadhi* state of sitting yoga. In Tantric practice, the student may displace the ego by filling his whole being with the real or imagined object of his concentration; in Zen, one seeks to empty out the mind, to return it to the clear, pure stillness of a seashell or flower petal." (2) Peter Matthiessen, p.90

Dilip and Poona choose a guesthouse, one with a large open grassy area in front and a stream that flows to the mighty Uttar Ganga River draining this long valley to the east. Dilip wants us to have a rest day here, a day to acclimatise: with an elevation just less than 3,000m it is an ideal place to do so. What's more there are Magar settlements here and many Tibetan refugees from the Chinese invasion of Tibet in the early fifties; and the Chinese Red Army is still there – to 'keep the peace' apparently.

It is one of the world's unexplained mysteries – the Chinese Red Army's invasion of Tibet to 'keep the peace'. It almost seems incongruous for an army to be needed to 'keep the peace' in a country like Tibet which is so strongly Buddhist, and for there to be a need to re-educate the people who have fallen prey to traditional Buddhism.

However, the real reason for this Chinese invasion is most likely to be found in the rich mineral wealth located on the Tibetan Plateau...and then there is the enormous rail line that has been built to Lhasa. Somehow I don't think it has anything to do with tourism; maybe it is to assist with re-education, but most certainly it is there to carry the rich mineral wealth back to the heartland of China to keep the burgeoning dragon that is China alive and powerful for the rest of the world to quake at. I personally do not see the logic in such a quest – continually proving it can increase its GDP – but then China was at war with the British over tea in 1839 and Japan invaded China in 1894 and again in 1931. Perhaps they have reason to grind an historical axe of expansionism.

The sooner we follow the lead of countries like Bhutan – which has a happiness factor built into their GDP – the healthier our world will be. What's more, Mother Earth may honour us for being *et mulieres sapientes* instead of our squabbling behaviour over the last 2,000 years or more.

Three young men are enjoying rice wine when we arrive at the guesthouse. They seem harmless enough but they are loud like most young men the world over. Dilip looks at me, and I shrug my shoulders. The guesthouse is lovely with a small shop where a lady sleeps at night. I hope it is not the guesthouse owner's wife. I ask about the possibility of some hot water to bathe. The owner looks at me strangely but realises my white skin must be 'precious'; NPR300 (AU$5) for a bucket of warm water and a place out the back to 'do the job.' Thank you.

There is a small concrete room next to another concrete room that has a 100mm hole in it for 'dumping'; I figure the one and a half metre square concrete room is the bathhouse. I enter carrying my precious bucket of warm water with clean thermals and nightclothes under my other arm. This is going to be quick; ice is already forming outside and the sun is low on the northern horizon. The concrete walls do nothing to retain any heat from my small and expensive bucket of warm water. There is a door to close behind me; I strip off and dunk my towelette in and wipe it over my body – repeat, repeat. With washing complete in a new record of ninety seconds, I scramble to put on my thermals, down jacket, socks and sandals. Why do I bother? There is a certain afterglow from the warm water and wipe down...and of course the fresh clothes are a treat.

I wash my walking clothes; we are now in day five of our trip and hopefully tomorrow will provide a hearty burst of sunlight to thoroughly air and dry them. With the bathing and washing complete, I find a clothesline on which to pin my clothes.

I head back to my room, just big enough for a bed; it has a plastic sheet for a window and four steel bars the thickness of my finger across to prevent wolves in the night. I put on some outer layers of clothing, complete with beanie and head torch. I'm beginning to feel warm again... now where's that cup of tea?

Dilip and Poona are in the opposite room talking guide talk; they have shooed away the rice wine drinkers, much to the owner's dislike. It seems Dilip has some sway here but then he is bringing three men for two nights and this is a guesthouse, not a drinking house. The hot steaming tea is brought to us and nothing tastes more delicious at this point of the afternoon with the daylight fading. I go outside to see what all the commotion is; a team of seven mules has arrived fully loaded with food and equipment.

There are four porters, two guides, two mule handlers, six mules, a French couple and young German woman. I wonder where they can be heading with all this stuff. I decide that tomorrow will be a good time to find that out – for now I want to find a quiet place to meditate that is not too cold. I decide my room is the best option with the noisy young men gone.

I had started taking Diamox back in Dharapani, 100mg per day. It is a Western medication to assist in the prevention of altitude sickness. It worked well for me on the Annapurna trail where we reached altitudes over 5,000m, and in a week or so we will be at those heights again. It takes preparation, and half-day rests to acclimatise, but I find Diamox just one more insurance to combat altitude sickness that most certainly can be fatal. "Diamox works by acidifying the blood, which stimulates breathing, allowing a greater amount of oxygen to enter into the bloodstream". (13)

It is by no means a 'cure all' for altitude sickness, and allergic reactions are possible; however, I have found it useful to date so will continue to use it. Dilip and Poona occasionally found it fun to take a tablet to amuse the tourist, but I sensed they were so used to these mountains they didn't need to take it. However, it amused me that they went along with the Western 'pill taking ritual', and I stopped offering it to them after a few days.

With my meditation complete for now – a lifetime of spiritual practise to go, with much to unfold and unpack – I head out into the world. Dilip and Poona are rustling up some dinner – dal bhat; the food is nutritious and sustains these people. I find it challenging to watch the locals eat with their hands; I always look away out of respect. It's been their traditional way of eating for countless generations but my Western palate is challenged; hence my polite offering to look away. I enjoy the option of a light pancake with jam, omelettes cooked in oil, and chapati...anything for variation. Fresh apples appear on the radar at times, and I buy them in half dozen lots, some large, others quite small, red in colour. They are fresh from the tree and tasty.

In the night the mules near my window continue to graze, moving around on their tethers and stamping their hooves. I drift in and out of sleep; I'm thankful I can't smell or hear the rear end of their anatomy. After dinner I had brought in my drying clothes for fear of them becoming mule fodder; also, the night is icy cold so I rig up a line inside my room where my breath and body heat would offer a better chance of them drying.

CHAPTER VII

Silence, gives answers.
RUMI

The new day arrives. Dilip and Poona go off to find the Dhorpatan Hunting Reserve checkpoint, as there is an entrance fee to be paid. I take the opportunity to explore the village and the huge suspension bridge over the Uttar Ganga River to the east of the village. I wander along the main route through the village and buy a handful of sweets at a small shop along the way. I stuff them into my pocket and keep walking. There are many places where bundles of rice are hung to dry; there are more of the five-metre high timber trestles for drying the rice behind the main buildings. These people are unlikely to go hungry this winter – the gods have been kind to them, and they certainly work hard.

I hear a small boy screaming in protest up ahead and discover his grandmother is trying to bathe him under the cold water tap on the main trail. I think the little boy has every right to protest...but then he probably needs a bath. I wander over and with the grandmother's approval I offer the little boy a sweet. He goes very quiet and I don't hear a peep as I head further along the route. As a 'hands on' father of three children I've heard these protests before, but then we did have hot water in the West, my children had no reason to scream, but a bribe nearly always worked. Some parents would refer to 'bath time' as 'arsenic hour', and wine was the parental panacea – gallons of it!

Another little boy of about five is brushing his teeth with his two older sisters nearby. The toothpaste is frothed up around his mouth; he has worked hard to clean his teeth. I ask permission to take a photo and they line up like little soldiers – not quite what I had in mind – with the little boy's mouth covered in toothpaste. Further along an older brother and sister, age around twelve, stand to attention for a photo; the girl is more relaxed. She looks almost North American Indian with her dark Tibetan skin, and jet-black hair set in long ponytails, one over her shoulder, the other in front. She is a proud Tibetan girl on her way to becoming a proud Tibetan woman in 2020. I want to honour her and wish her well in this life but then I remember, Namaste!

This has not always been the case for Nepalese women. Traditionally their place has been very much at the mercy of their husbands and fathers. However, being a predominantly agriculturally-based economy, women have played a significant role in decisions relating to farming practices. Women generally have had less access to essential services like healthcare, education and local government services. Malnutrition and poverty have always affected women first, due to their position on the 'food chain'.

Literacy has been the greatest obstacle to women gaining equal opportunity; in the 1990s education was made available with equal access. In 1975 property rights were made available to women – meaning they could legally inherit property from families or a husband. In 2002 women gained the right to divorce, abortion was legalised, and the punishment for rape was greatly increased – including marital rape. Even with these improved gender equalities, the husband can largely control the opportunities available for women. The significant male in the household still holds the key to a girl becoming a woman with freedom, education, and independence. *(14)*

Dowries are still common in Nepal, although the practice is illegal as domestic violence is often related to this custom.

Child marriage for girls less than 18 years of age still occurs, especially in areas of low economic status, and domestic violence is more prevalent; women can end up virtual slaves to their husbands. In research conducted in 2009, 46% of women surveyed across Nepal claimed to have been sexually assaulted, and 25% physically assaulted. *(14)*

The Hindu practice of Chhaupadi is where women must move out of the family home every month at the time of menstruation, as it is considered by some men to be impure or unclean. There is usually a small building provided for the women, but they aren't allowed to leave this small building. The practice was outlawed in 2005 but it wasn't until a woman died in 2016 inside one of these small buildings that harsher punishments were imposed. *(14)*

Witch hunts are possibly the most alarming concern, and still occur in Nepal among the lower castes. Superstition, lack of education and public awareness, illiteracy, male preference, and women being made dependent on men for financial support are all factors which allow this barbaric medieval behaviour to remain. Thankfully, that is changing in 2020. *(14)*

Nepalese women in 2020 feature in all levels of government – they defy cultural traditions as community leaders, politicians and business owners. Since 2015 Nepal has enjoyed a female president, Bidhya Devi Bhandari who, in 2016, was voted number 52 on the world stage of most powerful women. Anuradha Koirala is the founder of a not-for-profit organisation called 'Maiti Nepal', which translates to mean, "Home of the girl's birth parents". The organisation has a rehabilitation home in Kathmandu specifically for female victims of sex trafficking, an alarming industry still prevalent in 2020 and which is by no means restricted to Nepal. *(14)*

Pushpa Basnet is known for her entrepreneurial skills in not-for-profit organisations. She is the founder of the "Early Childhood Development Centre (ECDC)" which specialises in helping children who are incarcerated along with their parents, something unheard of in the West. She was nominated CNN Hero of the Year in 2012, and Anuradha Koirala was nominated in 2010 – a prestigious honour for anyone doing extraordinary humanitarian work the world over. *(14)*

Pasang Lhamu Sherpa was the first Nepalese woman to climb Mt Everest (8,848m) on 22 April, 1993 at just 22 years of age. Tragically the weather deteriorated as it does at those very high altitudes and, on their descent, two of the party died from altitude sickness, including Pasang. The King of Nepal awarded her the 'Nepal Tara' (Nepal Star) for her bravery, and a life-sized statue was erected in her honour near Boudhanath Stupa, Kathmandu. A postage stamp was also created in her honour. The statue is constructed in such a way as to honour her bravery, skill and determination but also to show other young women the way forward to strength and self-determination. May it also show husbands and fathers the way forward in their own self-determination as men helping women. *(14)*

Mira Rai is an international Nepalese name, now in her early 30s; she is known for her extraordinary trail and 'sky' runs, over 2,000 metres above sea level. In 2017 she won the 'National Geographic Adventurer of the Year' award for setting new records for the 'Ben Nevis Ultra' and 'Mont Blanc

80km'. From 2014 to 2017 she competed in 20 international events, taking first place in 14 of those events, second place in another four events, and third place in the Dolomite 'sky' run. The women of Nepal have much to be proud of with this young lady's ability to step above and beyond any conditioning caused by traditional norms. *(14)*

Phupu Llamu Khatri is a Nepalese Judo competitor and gold medal winner in the 2016 South Asian Games. She is a role model in the art of self-defence. Sushila Karki is a Nepali jurist, former Chief Justice of the Supreme Court of Nepal and, in July 2016, she became the Chief Justice of Nepal, the lead role in Nepal's judicial system. She is known and respected for her zero-tolerance on corruption. An impeachment motion was submitted to the Federal Parliament of Nepal by the Maoist Centre and the Nepali Congress, but it was withdrawn due to public pressure. She holds gravitas with the people of Nepal. *(14)*

These examples of remarkable women doing remarkable work give great hope to the young people of Nepal. I thanked the young brother and his beautiful young sister and walked away hoping, praying they would become anything they wanted: carpenter, doctor, builder, farmer, truck driver, nurse, engineer, business owner, teacher, lawyer, Gurkha.... The privileges of choice we have in the West are often taken for granted; to choose one's career and fulfil that choice to the best of our ability over a lifetime. It's most certainly up there on the list, after clean air, clean water and organic soils in terms of importance in fulfilling our role in life.

I reached the far end of the village and came across a building project led by a Tibetan woman. She tells me in very good

English that Nepal gives land to Tibetan refugees so long as they develop it in an appropriate way. She and her husband are building a guesthouse and Buddhist study centre which no doubt gained a tick of approval from local authorities. They offer me tea from a pot of water heated using a large solar collector a metre in diameter, that can be moved with the path of the sun. I'm impressed as this project is being done with few expenses spared; the tradesmen are doing fine work. The centre has an air of permanence and certainly an excellent Tibetan Buddhist base. I look forward to returning one day when the work is complete and the ideals, they most certainly possess are available for all to discover.

Women hold the portal to new life; and they have been doing this extraordinary and physically dangerous task since time immemorial. Men have done the hunting – and we've waged war, spread our seed, colonised – outwardly we behave 'tough', or so I've learnt growing up in the West. It is only now, approaching sixty, that I'm realising there is no need to be 'tough' but rather to love, to understand, and to connect are the most valuable tools. Hopefully I still have another twenty or more years to perfect these simple human needs, Namaste!

"...this mantra may be translated: *Om!* The Jewel in the Heart of the Lotus! *Hum!* The deep, resonant *Om* is all sound and silence throughout time, the roar of eternity and also the great stillness of pure being; when intoned with the prescribed vibrations, it invokes the All that is otherwise inexpressible. The *mani* is the "adamantine diamond" of the Void – primordial, pure, and indestructible essence of existence beyond all matter or even anti-matter, all

phenomena, all change, and all becoming, *Padme* – in the Lotus – is the world of phenomena, samsara, unfolding with spiritual progress to reveal beneath the leaves of delusion the *mani* jewel of nirvana, that lies not apart from daily life but at its heart. Hum has no literal meaning, and it is variously interpreted (as is all of this great mantra, about which whole volumes have been written) ...." *(2)* Peter Matthiessen, p.102/103

I turn east, towards the fast-flowing Uttar Ganga river. On the fertile river flats there is a paddock of healthy cabbages growing, and further along there is a man ploughing his field using a large bullock and a handcrafted timber plough. His two small children have been brought along to help in preparing the soil for planting, harvesting and the supplying of essential produce for their village for the long winter ahead.

I stop to watch this organic process, with generations of skill woven into this man. One hundred metres to the north is their home and here I could see mother and baby – the family unit was complete – and perhaps within the home an elderly parent or two; a family connection and continuation of support and balance with the rhythms of our planet. It was all happening before me. I watched the rich, dark brown soil being turned as the man and bullock walked forward, the young children danced around as young children do – they were made even more dancy having this Western man taking an interest in their connected community.

The African proverb goes, "It takes a village to raise a child"; as a stay-at-home-dad of some seven years I understand this – anyone with children understands this proverb, this fundamental need we have. The mother of my three children was away on official Qantas business ten days out of fourteen. We were less than connected, mostly fragmented...and the healing continues.

The ploughman stops to say hello; what I found most extraordinary was the timber plough carved out of a local pine tree some 150mm in diameter, with a natural curve that dug into the soil to a depth of about 200mm. Various timber frames were added to run ropes up to the bullock and 'Hey presto' – a totally carbon-neutral piece of machinery equipped to help provide a variety of foods to the community...and dad was providing childcare for their mother who was attending to baby number three.

I don't find that connection in the West; what's more, 90% of us are connected to commercial television, iPads, laptops, mainframes, and our politicians are often out of touch with the needs of Planet Earth. Yet we are supposed to be the 'lucky ones' – the 'intelligent ones' – or maybe we in the West are the 'deluded ones' whose lives have become disconnected from the 'silent heartbeat' of this precious planet. The heartbeat that keeps us alive. I believe we are at the breaking point of that choice...that change...with human-created climate change on our doorsteps, now!

The man knew little English and you know about my Nepalese, but I wanted to embrace him and his children, offer him 100,000NPR, and tell him what a great job he was doing for the planet – but I figured he was in fact far wealthier than I being from the West, as he physically worked out in the clean Himalayan air for eight or ten hours per day. He was connected to his family, his community, and the soil he ploughed. The human psyche in the West has been damaging this planet for the past three hundred years – *et mulieres sapientes* we must aspire too. This man is part of a more balanced world; he is connected to thousands of years of survival and nurturing of the human soul. I believe our Earth will destroy us if we think we can ignore this responsibility, this ancient wisdom.

I waved goodbye to my new friend and inside felt very moved by what I had just experienced; this social study could be taken to the West so that US oranges don't arrive on Australian shores by plane while our best oranges fly back to Canada, all in the b/s name of international trade. Dr David Suzuki has been championing this call of global living for 60 years; our need as a species to be Earth-focussed being far more important than economic-focussed.

Dr Suzuki still waits for that call, along with so many of our great scientists who know this fundamental truth. Our own Professor Ian Lowe has, for fifty or more years, been calling for this need to change...but still in Queensland we talk of coal mining – in fact, the biggest coal mine in the Western world. God forbid, if it ever goes ahead...and what drongos we would appear to the rest of the world. *(h)*

I'm walking east towards the river and the massive suspension bridge that spans 150 metres with two twelve-metre high steel towers end to end to carry the forty-millimetre wire ropes that are tied back from the bridge into large concrete footings and gives the bridge its ability to suspend – simple engineering brilliance. I walk across it and notice the bridge connects Dhorpatan to an entirely new part of this region. I read later a road can be found some two days walk to the south via the village of Bobang, hence the importance of this bridge.

After admiring the concrete footings as only a builder can, and the dozen or more forty-millimetre steel cables bolted to it, I walk back to the Dhorpatan side of the river and find a space in the Himalayan sun just below the bridge to the west. I take my boots off, wind up my pants, take off my shirt for about three minutes – but decide it's not that warm; back on goes the shirt. I relax on the gravelly bank and start to meditate on how I love this country, the Himalayas, but most of all the people who I have met in my two extended visits here. I find much gratitude in my meditation; gratitude for my privileged life in Australia but also for my ancestors, my mother and father, grandparents on both sides, the list of appreciation goes on. And here I am feeling privileged to be doing this twenty-four day trek, to have Dilip as guide, Poona as porter, but all the while I have this Achilles' heel that I want to share as Peter Matthiessen shared regarding his grief in losing his wife.

In life there is great tragedy and from that I don't think we can escape. As Buddhists say: "There is much to be gained in understanding suffering". In fact, it can be our reason for living when undertaken in a healthy way, to unpack the levels of deeper pain only to find deeper understanding and more meaning to one's life. Preferably away from 140cm TVs, the concrete, the neon lights, social media and commercial invasions of 2020 that try to cheat us of our precious humanity. It is easy to forget the magic of this planet and the universe when we are immersed in a commercially created human world.

Bipolar is a difficult illness to come to terms with. For

years I pretended nothing was wrong. I was very good at 'laughing things off', and avoiding what was really going on inside. I worked hard to make sure everything looked 'fine on the outside'. However, on the inside I had this screaming confusion of rushing thoughts, many of which were most unhelpful. I had no understanding as to its origin or why I simply couldn't solve the problem myself. It wasn't until my marriage ended in January of 2003 that I had to look more deeply for answers, to take more responsibility for what had happened in my life.

This was not just about depression or witnessing my sister fall to her death in a bushwalking accident when I was 13; this was my mind polarising and not able to operate in a stable way. Everything in life became a struggle. Thankfully I have maintained good relations with my children who have insight into what I have experienced. And it needs to be acknowledged, this is an inherited illness that possibly stemmed from my mother and father's sides of the family – but it was never spoken about due to the limited understanding of those times and the stigma. "British, you know, we don't talk of such things" – never mind feeling these deep broken emotions – "it's simply not cricket, old boy."

Rest and retirement from work were the solution of the day – and tell as few people as possible; these were the recommendations of the 1880s moving forward to about 1990. I'm fortunate in 2020; there is real help available with evidence-based science backing the treatment – but still, it's preferable not to discuss bipolar disorder on your first date.

Up to 2012 I had been in and out of hospital several times; another doctor had tried a cacophony of different antipsychotic drugs over a three-year period, but none of them sat well with me. I certainly do not blame him; in fact we recently connected by email – I wanted to apologise. He understood – it was OK – he was another good doctor doing his human best.

It was simply that I had become very good at masking the symptoms which raged on the inside of my mind and often forced me to withdraw from the 'happy reality' on the outside. My mind was playing tricks on me and to this day I need to be vigilant in my mind's process of chaos, made so much better by the balancing effect of lithium.

In 2012 a friend recommended a doctor who believed I needed to try lithium, an age-old treatment for bipolar. I was at a desperate stage of being willing to try anything to bring some sort of normality back into my life. I couldn't hold down a job in the building industry where I was trained as an estimator; I also held several building sales positions – jobs that I loved in theory with my long history and knowledge of the industry starting as a carpenter's apprentice. This was another job I greatly enjoyed in my early twenties for its physicality and the camaraderie amongst the men I worked with. I loved those men, a bunch of scallywags who enjoyed a bit of fun on the worksite.

In my treatment for bipolar, lithium has helped greatly in the past ten years to stabilise my mind, and certainly doing physical activity like this extended trek is a good thing. I manage to keep a healthy balance; writing about the journey is another healthy pastime for me, away from the pressures of a building estimator. The thought of going back into the building industry no matter what the salary package is really a distant dream for me – my mental health is my priority.

With good health I can manage the other important things like my relationship to my now adult children who I see regularly, and a network of male friendships through a grassroots organisation called *menswellbeing.org* based in South East Queensland. It is an organisation dedicated to the welfare of men, their partners and families. Men being 'real' and open about their life rather than some 'parade' dictated by a marketing fever of insatiable dreams displayed on 140cm televisions. What's really going on inside is what I aim for – in this I find understanding; and by sharing this journey, I hope will be of use to others.

I feel fortunate that my life is well supported, and for the medical assistance offered in Australia – without it, I most likely would be dead – unable to cope with a polarising mind. I am grateful for this support and I would never be complacent about this – it takes vigilance to not become isolated or sidelined from society. I am at times amazed at how my mind can still work in a spiralling, destructive way, but these days I am far more aware of what's really going on – by being objective – and I will call out for help; either to my doctor for an appointment or possibly the need for hospital – although this has not been necessary for over twelve months now. I don't see hospital as a burden but more as an opportunity to rest an overworked mind made confused by bipolar disorder. Hospital can be a place of sanctuary where every nurse, every patient, and certainly every doctor knows what it's like to live with this illness. It is a sanctuary, and an opportunity to keep my life on track.

I no longer have to face this illness on my own. Denial and

isolation are very real factors – an illness we would rather keep quiet, but in my very real experience calling out for help is the most important thing. I wish my forebears could have had this support – this understanding, but then they faced two world wars firsthand; the fallout from those times, I believe, is still with us, within me. I have heard it described as intergenerational trauma – it certainly feels real for my mind especially when not 'treated'. *(s)*

Trekking in these remote locations is hugely beneficial for me – the exercise, the simpleness and beauty of being in wilderness - Mother Earth - she resides in my soul like nothing else I have experienced. The feelings of connection to a greater universe is most definitely enriching and then being able to turn these unique experiences into a readable story for others is indeed a great joy for me.

While Peter Matthiessen was grieving for the loss of his wife to cancer – I have grieved for the loss of career, but most of all the loss of my marriage. It's almost inevitable with most people diagnosed with bipolar disorder who chose to make the most of their life in a productive way that they will go through some destructive phase that can derail careers and important relationships. It's been a wake-up call for me, a call for healing, a call for responsibility, a call for understanding – medical understanding – and the need to find purpose in the best way I can.

It's interesting to note the following list of people who have suffered bipolar disorder and in many ways have gone on to do worthwhile things, despite the illness. They certainly offer inspiration to me: Mel Gibson (actor/director), Ernest Hemingway (author), Mariah Carey (singer), Vivien Leigh (actress), Frank Sinatra (singer/actor), Sinead O'Connor (singer), Jimi Hendrix (musician), Winston Churchill (British Prime Minister, WWII), Stephen Fry (comedian/actor), Dusty Springfield (singer), Lou Reed (musician), Graham Greene (author), Vincent Van Gogh (painter), Amy Winehouse (singer), Catherine Zeta-Jones (actor) and John Cleese (comedian/actor) to name a few. *(14a)*

The inherent weakness of bipolar disorder lies in the brain's nervous system where the circuits do not connect as efficiently as they need too – lithium is the bridge between weaker nerve cells within the brain. The rasping dry mouth for much of the day is a small price to pay for stability of mind. I sometimes get a slight tremor in my forefinger but nothing really to be of concern. Alcohol is best in small amounts; binging is a destructive license to die. *(15)*

Of more concern is my kidney function later in life but even if my kidneys do fail, I will at least have had more than twenty years with a stable, productive mind producing stories of this kind. I am fortunate to have an intelligent and intuitive doctor I can trust, an excellent Australian medical system and as for my kidneys, all is well to date.

I do these extended wilderness trips because they thrill me but they also educate me about our Earth; to share the story and hopefully motivate others. May I be carried out in a box and cremated on one of these high passes – with half of my ashes being scattered where my sister, Heather, fell – a place my children know well; they have climbed Razorback many times with me. That to me would be a successful conclusion – a grand exit to a life well lived – accepting of the suffering we all must endure and embrace. Samsara! *(m)*

These experiences enlarge my view of the world in a way I hope, as readers, you too will understand our need for action, a global action of change. These glimpses into the wilderness that I travel and describe using photography and the written word are somehow helpful in the healing process of Planet Earth. This is my contribution, and may 7.7 billion of us join in this march forward with the cooperation our planet needs from us as a species, a human species: *et mulieres sapientes*.

Due to the lithium, I also have blood tests four times per year to ensure the balance is correct. There is a narrow window with lithium; too much becomes toxic, too little and it doesn't work. I also take thyroxin, 50um, to assist the thyroid gland affected by the lithium and 200mg of another mood stabilizer, Seroquel.

All in all, my mind is held together by pills and 'bandages'. If this were to be played out in the form of a physical injury like a broken leg, bandages would appear on the whole of my leg – thick protective bandages. I would need to continually tweak the tension of the bandages to ensure things are running well and then include a monthly visit to my doctor who further ensures these tweaks are in fact correct.

Coincidently, my doctor did in fact give 'glowing gold stars' for this trek and my ten day stay at Kopan Monastery, where I found the monks to be loving, funny and attentive to our Western ways. Secretly I wondered if they kept a private report card on each of us, but they were always content if we just became 5% Buddhists. This, they believe, will still serve the planet in a healthy and nurturing way.

Some years back I was interested in a ten-day Buddhist retreat called Vipassana in South East Queensland – my doctor strongly recommended I avoid such brutal manifestations of the mind – meditation ten hours per day, silence for ten days, and a whip in case one felt too comfortable – the last bit was, in fact, a lame joke. I didn't attend the retreat; my mind would probably not have been strong enough. It possibly would have imploded – yet a twenty-four-day trek, out here in the wilderness, is just pure delight and of great inspiration to my mind, and hopefully those who read this account.

Apart from these adventures to wild places, what sustains me is my love for my children and their partners' wellbeing, and my connection to community – all the while managing the absurdity of a mind tempered greatly by medication. There is the ability for me to be creative in this process of writing which is indeed a panacea for my condition, but something Ernest Hemingway or Graham Greene would have never shared in their public writing. It is now 2020 and I am open to sharing this, and feel the humanness in doing so is helpful for other people coming to terms with the really difficult 'stuff' that is this illness. The really important thing to know, especially if your partner is supportive, is that there are answers even if it is necessary to work hard at it and limit the booze, rock 'n' roll and drugs...but not the sex! These pleasures are healthy medicine.

However, one cold, concrete fact is that bipolar is a life-long partnership. No pills will fix it – there is no quick fix – but there is a lifetime of commitment to oneself, to do the best that one can. To help my children whenever I can and produce these stories of wilderness and Earth connection – these true stories – and bring inspiration with a deeper understanding of our Earth which is understood for the reality of what it is rather than through a television or internet screen, with advertising and sales agendas.

There are always five factors that govern our life on this planet: clean air, clean water, healthy soil to produce food, shelter, and clothing – anything after this is in fact a luxury. There was a saying I learnt at Kopan Monastery which is pretty much a universal truth for Buddhists; the simple phrase, "love and compassion". There are times, especially when at home, that this phrase doesn't always resonate for me but when I use it – even at times through gritted teeth – it does work; it helps to quieten my mind, especially in relation to the 'battle' I was having with a neighbour over industrial noise... 'love and compassion'...'love and compassion'. I find this a helpful phrase with the opportunity to look within when it doesn't resonate. There is possibly a lifetime of teaching just in that simple phrase. Just maybe World War One and World War Two could have been averted. If only it was that simple, Samsara! *(s) (m)*

Buddhists also believe that if we don't get it right the first time or second time – or however many times – we can always have another go and be happy with ourselves as we keep trying. I have shed a tear with the knowledge of these universal Buddhist realisations. Shedding tears is not something that comes easily for me, being the son of a British Army lieutenant and whose grandfather served five years in World War One, and an extra year in Afghanistan because he wanted to serve the British Empire, as one did in those days, for King and Country.

At Kopan, I bought a copy of the Fourteenth Dalai Lama's book, *The Power of Compassion* so there is more for me to study. And recently I finished reading his autobiography and in that there is most definitely a lifetime of understanding and the search for inner peace; especially in regards to CHINA'S BRUTAL INVASION OF TIBET – just in case anyone missed that particular piece of history starting in 1950 – and the Chinese Red Army's despicable treatment of the Tibetan people, especially many of the monks who were rounded up, thrown into re-education camps where they were tortured and often killed, similar to what happened in Nazi Germany with the Jewish people just sixteen years earlier. The Dalai Lama aimed to keep peaceful negotiations open with his adversaries who he saw as the Chinese Red Army, never the people of China. In fact, he has great hope for future generations as Buddhism in China is on the rise. It is an extraordinary book written by an extraordinary man, now in his mid-eighties.

While sitting by the Uttar Ganga on this particularly warm sunny afternoon, the rapids are flowing, the breeze is cool, the birds are calling; three ladies cross the suspension bridge carrying baskets laden with grass and fodder for their livestock. I find truth and peace and love here. There's no television or computer telling me this. I am feeling at peace here, next to this river in the foothills of the Northwest Himalayas. There truly is peace to be found on the inside of my soul. It just helps in this process to TURN-OFF the external noise created by our human world. If only I could take this home – market it – make millions of dollars and then buy an exotic island somewhere to live a hedonist life…but this is NOT what I learnt in my ten days at Kopan Monastery. Buddhists focus on helping others, on serving others, giving,

giving and more giving of one's particular skill-set. I can feel our planet relaxing – our Earth breathing deeply – as I write these words. Namaste!

"The Dalai Lama, when asked what surprised him most about humanity, he answered: Man, because he sacrifices his health in order to make money, then he sacrifices money to recuperate his health. And then he is so anxious about the future that he does not enjoy the present; the result being that he does not enjoy the present or the future; he lives as if he is never going to die, and then dies having never lived." (His Holiness the 14th Dalai Lama)

A quote from my diary at the river, 22nd October, 2019: "These are the sounds of nature that the twenty-first century lacks, where the majority of Western people are stressed trying to make a living, where corporations get richer and more powerful at the expense of human wellbeing and indeed, the natural world's wellbeing. This must be turned around if we are to survive."

I walk back into the village and come across a woman with twin babies, about 12 months old. The mother is trying to knit and doesn't look happy. I hope she is just tired from looking after her babies, a huge task in any culture. There appears to be no other family around and I wonder if the father is still part of her family. Or the babies are girls and the father is not happy at this gender 'shortfall'. I can feel her pain...but ask for a photo and she grunts a 'yes'...when I get out of sight, I decide I want to offer 500NPR (AU$8) which would buy baby goods or knitting wool...but would it put a smile on her face? Probably not.

I head back and she's sitting with her babies who are now playing in the dirt, and when she sees the money, she says no. I decide to drop it in her lap and depart the scene back to the guesthouse, as quickly as possible. My mind wonders: would her husband be suspicious? Is she already in enough trouble in producing two girls? I know none of the answers and I innocently only want to help, because I can and money is a useful tool; nothing else but that.

Two women are doing their weekly washing next to the guesthouse where a small stream flows and carries all their soap suds down to the main river, and I wonder if it's biodegradable. The pair of them are having a great time together, working hard in the sunshine, not a care in the world as they chortle away to each other, a chance to catch up on the village gossip. "Did you see that 'Western man' by the river last week? Huh! He was fair haired, fair skinned with a great big bushy grey beard". "Yeah, he must have been nearly 60; do you think he can still get it up?"

I meet up with Dilip and Poona who have had a day of drinking tea, smoking, talking with the locals and the men who own the mules. They too are enjoying the acclimatisation day. The French couple are in their sixties, from Chamonix next to the French Alps. They are planning to climb Sonjo Lek, 5,922 metres above the oceans and just five kilometres west of Dovan. I sit in the afternoon sun and enjoy the tea and company, but not the cigarette smoke.

It has been good to rest today; my body is saying thank you. I was reminded of another Buddhist skill I learnt at Kopan which went something like this: Watch your thoughts when you're alone, watch your words when you're in company, and watch what you do with your body as this determines what you do. In doing this we can lead a healthy life of happiness. Something I'd like to add to this in terms of giving – act on it when it comes from a deep, genuine place within.

A Nepalese man with very good English asks me if I am a writer as I'm catching up on my notes for the day. I tell him I am aiming to be, having published my first book on the Himalayas in April 2019, but I have no delusions of grandeur in this arena. I write because I enjoy it – to tell a story – it does not so far sustain me in bread and water, but I do believe doing what one loves brings love to others, and so I will continue to write.

There is another Nepalese man with equally good English; he has been to Toowoomba, a significant town an hour's drive west of where I live in Australia. He tells me he is a documentary filmmaker and is in Dhorpatan to make a film about the families that migrate south every winter to avoid the icy conditions. Ninety-five percent of the people migrate, which explains why so many of the houses in this village are boarded up, doors bolted. So why was the lady with the two babies still here, and why were the three elderly ladies carrying huge baskets of firewood? Perhaps the figure is more like eighty percent?

The afternoon sun is beautifully warm as we sit in the garden, come horse stable, come teahouse, come meeting area, come mountaineering-storage area, come clothes-drying area, come cigarette-smoking domain. The flow of the river can be heard quietly to the east and large eagles fly above looking for opportunities; they are silent and majestic.

The French couple are relieved to hear I am not a hunter; in fact, they are quietly impressed to see me out here with only a guide and porter. They want to hear about my writing of this trip, 'In the footsteps of Peter Matthiessen'. They know the story. The husband is the organiser of their expedition and there is much to carry, including food for the mules. I connect with the head mule man and head porter; they are both gentle men, very strong of heart.

The mules are decorated with a large metal bell tied around their necks in case they stray, and to tell people on the trail that a mule caravan is coming. They wear a decorative braided headpiece of yellow, red and green which connects them to Buddhism. Tassels hang from below their large ears in the same colours of red, green and yellow. Some of them have a string of smaller brass bells around their necks and they all have a wooden-framed harness strapped to their back with a 'drag line' connected under their long tails to stabilise the load going downhill. They look in excellent health and I see first-hand the respect the handlers show to these beautiful animals who carry the 'mule's share' of any expedition; their large ears directing the way like aircraft bombsights.

The Frenchman asks; "You travel alone?" And then his wife comes into the guesthouse where we are sitting and asks; "You travel alone?" I explain to them, in the words of Rudyard Kipling; "He travels fastest who travels alone." And as we become a travelling convoy over the next few days these words ring true as Dilip, Poona and I move off into the wilderness with much greater speed than their ten mules, two guides, four porters and three Europeans. I like to travel light and fast when required; besides, we had many more high passes to cross and for me, the less things to go wrong the better.

My addiction to internet Wi-Fi is apparent in Dhorpatan; I want to send messages home – and even though Dilip offers to hotspot for me, the signal is weak. I have wanted this – to cut off from the 'connected world' and connect to myself and the greater universe within. There is no need for the internet out here, I know this. Nor is there need for the distractions of a large expedition, a broken cooker, the need for more cooking oil, a broken mule harness, the physical and emotional wellbeing of all-party members, altitude sickness for the Europeans at least…the list goes on.

The following are the words of a good friend back in Australia, whose life-journey is parallel to mine; an affirmation that was gifted to him by a Peruvian shaman the previous year:

"I am the whole Universe having a human experience, so I always have access to the endless Joy and Love of the Universe". You are the whole Universe having a human experience. And it brings context to the notion that each of us has a unique gift to bring to the world, and the world needs all of these gifts. So, I have a responsibility to manifest my gift fully in service to the whole." (Mike Mee, February 2020)

CHAPTER VIII

There is a force within you that seeks life. Seek that.
RUMI

We leave Dhorpatan early in the morning as we have another pass to cross; Phagune Dhuri, at 4,061 metres above the oceans. It rises almost 4,000 metres above my homeland of Australia; being the oldest land mass on the planet our altitudes are minimal compared to the Himalayas, where the mountains continue to rise ten millimetres per year due to the forces of the tectonic plates. *(15a)*

The stakes are higher for this pass in terms of altitude, but I feel confident about the rest of the day's walking. I continue to take Diamox each morning; it helps to develop my blood into the rich mountain blood mixture that is naturally occurring in these parts – Tibetan, Nepalese, Mongolian.

The trail heads north and we weave our way through another ghost village – the people have migrated south except for a man driving a large, impressive farm tractor decorated in Hindu colours including streamers of coloured cloth attached to the large wheels. The driver pulls up, and asks Dilip for a cigarette. Dilip delivers and asks if we are on the right trail – the driver says yes and the tractor keeps going. It was a quick exchange – perhaps the driver had much to do before his own migration south, and there was urgency in his work...and his tractor was very impressive to say the least.

On the outskirts of Dhorpatan we stop at an army base to show our credentials, all part of entering Dhorpatan Hunting Reserve. There must be several hundred men in this well-established camp judging by the number of buildings. There are three men attending to our permits, and they take their job very seriously. Again, Dilip reassures me it is for our protection that the army knows of our whereabouts. I was starting to wonder again if there was some kind of drug trade in these parts, however Dilip was not forthcoming with any answers to my questions. "Nepal is one pure god of the universe," he sends via mental telepathy, "so stop asking questions Mr Tim...breath in the Himalayan air of the gods...breathe out your Western nosiness...repeat...repeat... repeat..."

He does tell me it costs US$500 to shoot a bharal in these parts. That sounds an excessive sum to me, especially as there would be expedition costs on top of that, including helicopter and labour fees. However, if the money goes back into the local region perhaps it's a useful source of revenue... but I would have questions around this enterprise, like where specifically does the revenue go? Do the locals agree with this sport? How is the killing monitored? And why is this large army base here? I can't help this flow of questions, especially when Dilip tries to use mind telepathy on me – I sense something else is going on here.

The trail begins to climb and there are views down to the Uttar Ganga River and the fertile Dhorpatan Valley. We are entering a largely uninhabited wilderness, through rhododendron forests which grow to ten metres. The higher we get the sparser the vegetation, and the foothills take on a brown hue that in places stretches as far as the eye can see. Mid-morning, we stop for tea at a teahouse clinging to the hillside at an elevation I guess to be around 3,000m. I wonder why these people are still here.

There is a timber stove inside the teahouse which is also her home; the lady makes our tea; smoke fills the room, goat meat hangs above to dry, turning it dark red/black in colour. I go outside for fresh air and see several eagles flying high, searching for an opportunity to swoop down on a food source. I find fresh cabbage leaves to eat – they go well with the tea. When it's time to go Poona refers to me as "boss". I prefer "grandad" or even better still, "Tim," thank you Poona.

It's this overflow from nineteenth century colonial times that I want to see gone from this trek. I want to explain this to Poona; I want to be his equal – not some privileged white man who they perceive to be superior. I simply don't think that way; just ask my 92-year-old mother, who was head girl at a Quaker school in Yorkshire. When my father would sound off about the Germans, my mother would remind him it was Hitler's Nazis with whom we were at war, not the German people. I think my mother would get on famously with the Fourteenth Dalai Lama; they would chortle and laugh for hours together.

I want these people to see me as another human being – on the same page – even if I can afford a better boot or trekking pack; that's quite superficial compared to being part of this Earth, connected to hundreds of generations on the same plane...*et mulieres sapientes*.

The trail climbs with many switchbacks, and the yellow/brown hills are emerging more and more – the pine trees and rhododendrons have gone. There is much ice in the small creeks we pass, and in a month or so there will be much snow in these parts. About half an hour from the top, at 4,061 metres above sea level, I begin to feel the altitude; my walking pace is slower, my breath is slower, desperate for oxygen. It's a pivotal point in my body learning to adjust to the altitude. I know I will be fine; however, when I reach the top I sit down, lean up against a rock, and begin to drift off...to sleep!

Dilip intervenes; he is well-trained in spotting these signs – I mustn't go to sleep, I need to allow my body to adjust to the new height, even if it is only 4,061 metres – God knows what 8,000 metres must be like. I need to acclimatise, so I take my pack off and walk around. I am grateful Dilip was looking out for me. He and Poona, of course, light up a cigarette the moment they reached the pass. As if it were a Sunday stroll in the Himalayas – it must be something to do with the rich blend of Tibetan/Nepalese/Mongolian blood they both possess.

Falling asleep is a big mistake as your body slows down – and literally goes to sleep – to the point that it doesn't make the effort to rise to the occasion so to speak. It's very important to keep the blood moving, even if slowly. After ten minutes, I feel fine and ready to head onward. The landscape is barren now and it's easy to see why no one has ever wanted to inhabit this land. In terms of trekking, with the wilderness, the mountains, and the good help of Dilip and Poona I feel truly blessed to be here, experiencing wilderness untouched by human settlement – there can be no agriculture here – although this has been a trade route from Tibet, China and Mongolia for several thousand years.

The French expedition is with us on this section and I notice the sure footedness of the mules, their small hooves just sixty millimetres in diameter. The trail is no more than an arm's width but they judge their load well. I love their big ears and alertness as they walk. I admire the head mule man for his gentleness towards the animals, and I can see the mule's confidence through this man's good treatment and guidance.

There are extraordinary vistas northeast, to several of the very high mountains – Churen Himal (7,371m) and Putha

Hiunchuli (7,246m). They are breathtakingly beautiful on the skyline that can only belong to the Himalayas. These brown/black foothills that we walk stretch all the way to the high mountains through a timeless wilderness – with no signs of human activity except for the trail itself.

We continue on for several hours heading in a north-easterly direction to Takur, which is more a location than village. We descend eight hundred metres through an oak forest with a series of switchbacks. I do love these forests, the very old and very large straight trees. They feel like an enchanted wood with those merry men – and sheltered from the strong sunlight and elevated cold exposure we had come from.

There is one family at Takur, and they survive with this passing trade of mule caravans, tourists and hunters. There is a small grassy clearing with one building for the family, a cookhouse, and another room behind in which we will sleep. I'm guessing it's used for livestock in winter as it is pretty basic, to say the least – but there are three beds. There is no electricity - they have a timber fire - coffee and chapatis are offered for dinner.

The French party arrive not long after us and they camp on the grassy clearing up from the main building. It will be a cold night, certainly below zero. The conifer forest comes right down to the clearing and rises all the way to the snow line and mountains beyond. I could be in North America or Canada or Peru, and I wonder if deer ever wander out into this clearing to graze. Back at the main house I go into the kitchen for some tea and I hear a woman coughing uncontrollably; it's another blackened room from all the fire smoke where she must work too often. I immediately think it must be the smoke from the fires affecting her health and I wonder if I have medication that would help her.

I carry Bisolvon which I find useful for chest infections while travelling. It may work, although I sense this is a far deeper medical issue, made worse every day by working near the smoky kitchen fires. Dilip tells me she is suffering pain in her joints from giving birth five years ago. She really needs a doctor, but I offer Panadeine and ibuprofen. I give her a strip of ten tablets for each drug. Dilip translates the dosage and I pray it helps to loosen her lungs from the congestion of the fire smoke.

There does not appear to be a toilet in this small settlement although I do find an outhouse one hundred metres away. It has a broken door and a large stone across the hole dug into the ground. I decide to use my standard issue tent peg to dig a hole and a little hand sanitizer to finish off the job, so to speak. God knows what the other ten guests are going to do – off with the bears, I guess.

CHAPTER IX

Be foolishly in love. Because love is all there is.
RUMI

The following day we drop in elevation through a conifer and oak forest, and cross a fifty-metre suspension bridge with a boiling white/green river below. What did these people do before the bridges were built? The waters are too fast and too cold to wade across.

We see small deer on a far ridge, brown in colour and about the size of a large dog. My nose bleeds along this section and I assume it's from the altitude change. I use my handkerchief to block the passage and the bleeding passes within half an hour. We stop in one small village of three buildings to buy fresh apples. There are large cannabis plants with huge heads bursting with ripeness. A brown, gold and black butterfly lands on the muddy track in front of me; I find its strong markings beautiful as it sits there. I ponder its impermanence in this life, not much different to our own really.

"We are visitors on this planet for ninety or one hundred years at the very most. During this period, we must do something useful with our lives. If you can contribute to other people's happiness, you will find the true goal, the true meaning of life." (His Holiness the 14th Dalai Lama)

The French expedition is carrying two large kerosene stoves that only just fit in the baskets of the porters. I am almost in disbelief as to the size of this expedition for just three Europeans; however, the men doing the work don't seem to mind at all. In fact, they are often very jovial at dinner time when they are preparing food; it's very lovely to witness. I photograph the head porter with his hands gripping his headpiece. He's such a relaxed man and obviously loves being in the mountains doing this work; tough to the core.

We stop for lunch in a dusty village called Khaim, two buildings in size, 2,890 meters above sea level. It sits on an open ridge with views to the south-west. A woman on the second level uses a phone with a wireless connection to communicate between villages, a government initiative to keep the villages connected, Dilip tells me. There was a group of a dozen men on the higher ridge as we walked down and into the village; they were waiting for a helicopter to arrive with a big game hunter, ready to kill bharal after having paid US$500. The men were there to carry out the dead, set up camp and, in some cases, guide the hunter to a closer vantage point.

This village had no water on tap so it had to be carried in from a local stream, five hundred metres away. Drying on the stone walls of the village were cannabis seeds by the kilogram; also legumes. Perhaps there was a trade for this cannabis, although there didn't seem enough to make a living – perhaps it was for local distribution. There were large pumpkins stored inside the buildings and the village could be corralled off with timber poles to be free of livestock and the many mule caravans that pass this way.

We walk through a series of small subsistence villages with four-metre-high cannabis, and crops of rice, corn and millet. On the rooftops of every house is a beautifully-made round grass hut with a pointy grass roof tied off at the top to hold everything together. These very practical drying huts were full of corncobs and other grains. I was sure at least one had a stash of cannabis to help bodily aches and pains throughout the winter. There are wildflowers in abundance, sliced apples sun-drying on large ground sheets, and pairs of stone grinding wheels three-hundred-millimetres in diameter, for use on the grains once they are dry.

In one village where we stop for tea there is an expectation that I will be carrying western medication that will cure all ailments from sore joints to headaches, and possibly even pregnancy. I offer a meagre supply of Panadeine, Panadol and ibuprofen, but I need to keep a small supply for my own bodily needs if something goes wrong. I decide I will bring more medication on the next trip; in the meantime, 'Dr Tim' suggests drinking much more of the fresh mountain water – it will stave off headaches and help with sore joints.

Dilip tells me, several times per year a government medical team passes this way and administers medication as required. For some reason the gathering of thirty villagers thought I was in fact 'Dr Tim'. I did what I could with what I had from my training in outdoor first aid; however, I made it very clear I was not, in fact, 'Dr Tim'...just a trekker very interested in their culture and the extraordinary mountains in which they live.

On the outskirts of one of these villages was a dead wolf, strung up by its neck; quite clearly it had been there for several years due to its rotting black coat. It was a metre and half long outstretched, an eerie sight to see with its large bared teeth, rotting flesh, legs dangling and bushy black tail. It was intended as a warning, being so close to the village entrance, but would a hungry wolf in the middle of winter be warned off by one of its own being strung up? Dilip could throw no light on the subject, or he just wasn't telling this foreign tourist that it was a warning to the bandits who lurked in these parts and who waited for the caterpillar mushroom trade to begin next spring – more on this lucrative trade later. I certainly wasn't convinced it was a warning to other wolves.

We walked on, the track winding its way down through deep dark forests of oak, birch and rhododendron trees. There was a large mountain stream that raged next to us, which we eventually crossed to reach another village by the name Tatopani (or hot springs). This was a one-building, one-family location with two raging streams coming together just below the building. We set up camp – or rather Dilip and Poona insisted again on setting up my tent – while I headed off with towelette, soap and a change of clothes to find the hot baths.

Unfortunately, the rectangular concrete bath had not been waterproofed sufficiently so the otherwise thigh deep, hot steamy water was reduced to toe depth with vast quantities of mouldy green algae, but there was a twenty-millimetre pipe oozing a good quantity of the steamy hot water into the concrete bath. I stripped off in the very chilly, late afternoon light and bathed to my heart's content, relishing the rich mineral waters splashing over me.

I was bathed and re-dressed within about three minutes as the outdoor temperature of this very lush green forest with the raging mountain stream right next to me was only a few degrees above zero. How this family was to survive winter here was beyond me, but then perhaps they were part of the migrations south and they just hadn't gone yet. They were in a strategic location for mule caravans so perhaps business was still booming. Tonight, they had our party of three and the French party of twelve. That's got to be good for business.

The owners have a five-year-old girl who at times dominates her mother's attention and has to be put in her place as the couple are preparing our dinner; as parents they are patient and caring. The kitchen area is another smoky room with a blackened ceiling. There is a store adjoining the kitchen where everything from cigarettes to beer, soft drinks and sweets could be bought.

I sleep soundly amongst the roaring waters of the two mountain streams. I trust in the fact that many generations of people have lived here and never seen a flash flood carry the building away – or our tents for that matter. I try not to think about such things. The sounds of the rushing streams are beautiful all through the night. Our tents are pitched in the only available space, a recently harvested corn paddock some twenty-five metres square. The French party and their eight mules are also sharing this space between the roaring mountain streams, teahouse and goat shed; a cold dark valley surrounded by rock.

Above our tents is another suspension bridge we will cross tomorrow; it spans fifty metres and there are great views up and down the rocky gorge. We have a leisurely start the following day but as the sun is still nowhere to be seen in this deep gorge, we decide to get moving. The owners stay here because they are hardened mountain people, most likely from Tibet, where people are well acclimatised with a strong spiritual conviction; they will endure.

There is an 'uncle' staying with these people; he's quite old, perhaps in his sixties, and has some deformity as he walks. In the early morning I find him washing a pile of dishes in the hot spring water. He carries the basket of clean dishes back to the house awkwardly; he squats near the fire to warm himself. He wears a big overcoat that looks European; God knows where he got it from. He waits patiently in that position until the tea is poured. I feel for his disability but he seems strong in himself and is obviously of great help to his family. He notices everything as he sits there and jokes with the little girl, who gets into trouble with her father for using his phone. This is a remote place where the sun shines for only a few hours per day. I wonder what the phone is for, out here in this valley of rock.

CHAPTER X

Wherever beauty looks, love is also there.
RUMI

It's a steady climb for most of the day, a thousand metres in elevation, and we pass through more small villages with grains drying on rooftops and corncobs tied together in bundles of a dozen, hung from anywhere they will dry. The round grass huts with pointy roofs abound in these parts, along with pumpkins and assorted legumes. The fields are terraced up the steep hillsides so they can grow grains such as rice, millet and corn. These people live in a fertile land – rich in produce – there is no doubt they will survive this winter with generations of culture and agricultural training behind them.

The corn grows to three metres in these villages, as does the cannabis. I find artistic drawings on one of the walls in a village. There is a grey-coloured mud wash as a background on the walls with drawings of trees, plants and flowers. The single line brushwork is elegant. There's a green and white vegetable drying that has been through some sort of grater. Another tarpaulin is spread out on the rooftop; it has buckwheat drying on it, and there are plastic buckets full of small potatoes, recently dug in preparation for the winter.

From the last village, we walk with a group of three elderly men wearing grey business jackets and traditional black hats. They walk with their hands behind their backs – they carry nothing but their elder wisdom – at a steady pace, and they look like they could walk all day, so gracious and with such purpose; perhaps village business needs attending to elsewhere.

We make it to Dhule mid-afternoon; it's another small village with an elevation of 3,340 metres. Dilip finds us a guesthouse run by a lady with a small girl about three years old. Her husband is away herding the livestock down from the higher mountains. She makes us tea and I enjoy sitting in her kitchen area, which has a chimney so the fire is far less smoky. They are a prosperous family as they have well-made pine furniture built by a local carpenter using local timber. We are to meet him near the end of our trek at the beautiful and prosperous trading town of Ringmo on the edge of Phoksundo Lake.

On the open shelves are rows of large brass dinner plates, cooking utensils, and a row of millet-beer mugs with aluminium straws poking out the top. I sample this refreshing beverage when I get back to Kathmandu. The ingredients consist of finger millets processed and fermented for months. There is a twenty-millimetre layer of millet seed on the top of the warm liquid, hence the large straw. It's a tasty and a warming brew with an alcohol content of about 15%. It is known locally as Chhaang or 'beer of the Himalayas'. "One with the mountains where the millets grow". It is traditionally served in bamboo mugs. (16)

There is a cylindrical drum, the length of my arm and a hand's width in diameter, hanging on the wall; it's made of timber with brass strapping around it. It has a plunger resting inside. I ask Dilip what it is and he explains; "A Tibetan tea-making tool". The ingredients for this tea are yak butter, eggs, salt, Himalayan tea leaves, water and milk – shaken up and down to distribute the flavours. It's then heated on the stove and hey presto, a nourishing hot healthy drink that nourishes the soul – just what one needs in these cold parts where temperatures plunge below zero for months on end.

After a dinner of boiled potatoes, salt and chilli paste washed down with another mug of nourishing Tibetan tea I head up to my room via a steep narrow stair case. The views flow down the valley and over the rice terraces that surround the lower areas of this village. The light is rapidly fading as I brush my teeth over the balcony that looks out onto the rice fields. Dilip and Poona stay downstairs for a little social chat with the owner. She is a strong woman, well-built and in very good health. Earlier I took a photo of her cradling her three-year-old sitting in her lap. I promise to post a hard copy to her and it takes her some time to work out the address. I dutifully carry out this gesture of goodwill when I get home, but I have no idea if it ever got to her. I did put a return address on the padded postage bag in case it ended up in no-man's land, so to speak.

I can see the French expedition camped on a neighbouring hillside, their torches going in and out of their tents. The porters work hard to make dinner while the mule men tend to their animals with grain bags; they tether them all in a row – strength in numbers if the wolves attack in the night.

As I stepped out onto the balcony, I could see the Tibetan flags flying throughout the village. There are men still working, preparing a building site; they labour by hand to dig and level a platform. It is hard, dusty work and they have been tireless in their pursuit, but soon nightfall will be upon them. It's a very cold night, at least zero degrees, and I just love the freshness of this mountain air and the sheer thrill of experiencing these Himalayan Mountains and the ancient culture that still exists here. I sleep soundly; the room is clean and the bed has some give. I feel at peace with the universe; this clear mountain air is good for my soul.

CHAPTER XI

I am a mountain. You call, I echo.
RUMI

We have Nautale Pass at 3,961 metres above sea level to cross this morning and our second high-camp at 4,000m. At breakfast Dilip retells the story of a Frenchman who died here last year, travelling alone in November – so close to winter, losing his way and perishing. His body was found in the spring of 2019 by the "caterpillar mushroom" people. It's a sad tale, but one which reinforces the need to never travel alone in these mountains, at least not intentionally.

As we leave the guesthouse owner's very organised life, I feel appreciative for her hospitality, being so warmly received and the way she manages her guesthouse but also for the way she treats her three-year-old daughter with such loving attention. Some of their furniture has hand-carved Buddhist symbols that remind me of the Nazi swastika when tipped 45 degrees. This ancient symbol was copied and modified by the Nazis for their own hellish purposes; it has nothing to do with the original – an ancient symbol belonging to Eurasia which encompasses 93 countries dating back to the ninth century AD. This tilted version can be found on the Snoldelev Runestone in Denmark, dating back to the Viking era of the fourth century AD. *(17)*

It has connections to Japan's ancient Buddhist culture where it symbolises the interplay of opposites such as heaven and earth, day and night, water and fire. It was also found in the ancient city of Troy, the Iron Age culture of Koban, pre-Christian Europe, Ancient Greece and the Native American Indian cultures. Jainism, Hinduism, Buddhism and Christianity all use this precious symbol for celebrations such as Puja, marriage and Vastu Shanti – a ceremony to cleanse the home. It is a symbol born out of the universe and is over a thousand years old. I find it fascinating that it emerged in so many cultures over this time, none of which were connected by the internet – just a universal knowledge. How then did the Nazis manage to use it for their destructive purposes? *(17)*

In all cases throughout the generations of *et mulieres sapientes*, this symbol was for good. It was not until the Second World War and the rise of the Nazi party that this precious ancient symbol was changed to represent the very opposite in the form of hatred and racial vilification unlike the world had ever seen. Unsurprisingly Hitler, in formulating the Nazi party, sought out people to promote his cause. A French woman of the time known as Savitri Devi proclaimed Hitler as an avatar of the Hindu God Vishnu – one of the most powerful Hindu gods – but in none of these ancient cultures were they given the right to kill over six million people, build armaments that caused untold destruction and killed millions more across Europe – not forgetting the overall contribution to greenhouse gases, the effects of which we are feeling today; over sixty years on. *(17a)*

Heinrich Himmler, head of the SS, a division of the Nazi Party, was another deluded soul who believed he was of the second highest caste – not sure what held his delusions back from being the highest; perhaps it was Adolf himself. Himmler carried a copy of the Bhagavad Gita with him, one of the holiest of ancient Hindu scripts on dharma. Clearly Himmler was a very poor reader, or someone had 'cut and pasted' his version of the book into Nazism. How heavy those wars feel in my soul and for millions more who are descendants of that dark, dark time. *(17b)*

I do join the march on Anzac Day wearing the service medals that belonged to my father and grandfather. It is only in the past five years I discovered the details of my father's military service and was able to request his service medals from the Ministry of Defence in England. He never felt proud to have been in World War Two, it was nothing to do with glory, it was about doing what he thought was right in defending England like so many other men and women from that awful time. Anzac Day and every other service we hold for that period is a time to remember the death and destruction not only to ourselves as a species – a heartfelt, soul species – but also for the damage we did to this Earth which includes the greenhouse gases lingering in the ozone from that time. There were also two nuclear bombs detonated at that time; such brutal devastation which may never be understood in terms of the human suffering caused to the souls involved. I'm in the process of writing another book on this; *England, My Parent's Birthplace*. Healing, so much human healing!

I can be sure this strong and healthy Himalayan woman with her little two-year-old daughter didn't just happen to have these ancient symbols carved into her furniture; they had been passed down through many generations to help them lead a good and prosperous life. In her case they are Buddhist symbols, as this Dolpo region is steeped in a rich Buddhist culture called Bon.

The shelves are marked with the swastika, that archaic symbol of creation that occurs everywhere around the world except south of the Sahara and in Australia. It was taken to North America by the ancestors of the American aborigines; in the Teutonic cultures, it

was the emblem of Thor; it appeared at Troy and in ancient India, where it was adopted by Hindus, then Buddhists. The reversed swastika is also here, in sign of the B'on religion, still prevalent in old corners of these mountains; since it reverses time, it is thought to be destructive to the universe, and is often associated with black magic. *(2)* Peter Matthiessen, p.131

As we were leaving, the guesthouse lady is carrying a twenty-litre water drum in one hand and holding her little daughter's hand with the other; they need water for the home and must fetch it from a communal tap in the centre of the village. Some years back it would have been from the local mountain stream with much greater effort required. We in the West simply turn on a tap knowing there will be water – treated water – but not knowing where is comes from or even how it got there in one of the driest continents on the planet. I believe most Australians are aware of the precious importance of water, but it still appears magically in our bathrooms, kitchens and laundries by the bucketful, simply by turning on a tap...then turning it off. Magic, but not really; our per capita water usage is far more than these village people, but then we are learning to recycle our own waste – to drink – now that is clever.

Dilip and Poona have stocked up on food for our camp tonight and as we ascend the ridge through mossy forests Dilip tells me a funny story; the guesthouse lady was playing a game with him and Poona after I had gone to bed. She was washing potatoes in a large bowl and as she pulled the potatoes out, she would ask Dilip and Poona whose testicle did the size of the potato fit? We were laughing out loud as only men can at such ribald fun. I do hope she received my photo of her cradling her three-year-old. We had such a wonderful experience in Dhule, and to see the village people in good health in a healthy environment was simply delightful.

The trail kept rising steadily and I was feeling more adjusted in terms of altitude. To the northwest, Dogari Himal (6,536m) looked massive and splendidly Himalayan. Nautale Bhanjyang Pass is 3,961 metres. It means 'nine steps', a reference to 'Bon belief' and a sign that the religious landscape is changing with the physical elevation. *(18)*

The Bon religion originated in central and western Tibet from the eleventh century; however, it shares the same teachings and terminology as that of Buddhism, two and half thousand years ago. Ancient Buddhist scripts are believed to have been created from the eighth century and remain 'esoterically hidden' by the people of that time. *(19)*

Deities are built into the home to keep out malevolent forces; a male god traditionally protects the home, and so the man of the house burns juniper to placate this god. Women also have protective powers – usually within the kitchen. There is a 'Sky God' or 'White Old Man' who is recognised in the interplay of these deities. The deity Zhangzhung is central to Bon religion and culture, and has influenced the philosophies and practices of Tibetan Buddhism over the centuries. The people from Bon were considered to be the original rulers of central and western Tibet, hence the connection in the mountains I now trek. *(19)*

With the invasion of Tibet by China in 1950 it is believed only ten percent of Tibetans now follow Bon – the destruction by the Chinese Red Army was brutal. There were over three hundred monasteries in Tibet at that time, and now Nepal has Bon monasteries emerging as the destruction continues in Tibet. God forbid if China ever invaded Nepal.

In 1987 the 14th Dalai Lama forbade discrimination against the Bon religion and now it is recognised equally within the philosophy and religion of Buddhism. And so I find the swastika, an ancient sacred symbol, carved into the furniture of the guesthouse in Dhule; it belongs to the Bon religion, a recognised part of Buddhism, and it is a symbol I would see shaped onto gompas and many people's pine furniture as we journeyed. (19)

We continued on through birch forests and black bamboo growing to three metres. There were deep purple and yellow wildflowers, one-metre-high bushes with bright red berries that begged not to be eaten. Bharal were well camouflaged on the high country in herds of a dozen or more. I hoped they would keep their heads down and not become the next US$500 bounty. There are high country views to the north and east of Dhaulagiri Himal, the snow crisp and white against the blue sky and, like so many views in the Himalayas, the depth, detail and distance of these mountains seems to go on forever.

We pass two Europeans, a father and daughter expedition; they have a guide and mule man for their four mules. I have many questions, but neither they nor I feel like talking. We smile graciously to each other and keep on our way; these mountains can be exhausting, too exhausting for talk. We pass in mutual respect. I guessed they were from northern Europe with their fair hair, blue eyes and long slim bodies.

We find a suitable high-country camp near a stream with many frozen chunks of white ice. This was Seng Khola, 3,820 metres above the oceans, and we are most certainly in for a cold night, well below zero. The landscape around us is barren; brown, ochre-yellow short grasses with many dried bracken patches. It indicated winter was close and soon this country would be covered in snow. In the higher country there are landslides and scree slopes hundreds of metres long, all part of a weathering process that grinds and groans every minute of every day.

Dilip and Poona insist on putting up my tent, cooking my dinner, and washing up. I didn't want to feel like the colonial 'trooper' but it was appreciated as I could write my notes from the day and savour the rugged wilderness that surrounded us. This is the reason I come to such places, to be inspired by wilderness in a land that has been travelled – but never settled – for thousands of years. It will forever remain a wilderness due to its remoteness and inability to be tamed into agricultural land.

I needed to change into my layers of warm clothing and prepare carefully for the very cold night ahead of us. It feels so very quiet – apart from the distant movement of rock, a trickle of water near where I dress and prepare for the night. By god, I felt alive – so fragilely alive in a wilderness high in the Himalayas – I could hear the gods talking to me in a whispered tone of gratitude, of being human and walking this Earth.

CHAPTER XII

*In the house of lovers, the music never stops,
the walls are made of songs and the floor dances.*
RUMI

It is day nine. My natural bodily functions have not adapted to the dal bhat with rice, vegetables, deep fried eggs, chapati, tinned fish and little fresh fruit. I'm constipated – I find this a predicament but know it will 'pass' sooner rather than later; however, the food sits heavily in my digestive tract and while I want to eat there is a certain discomfort that can only be fixed with 'movement', so to speak. I am rewarded the next morning with a 235mm turd that winds not so neatly into the inadequate hole I have dug for it. But the relief is bigger than Mt. Everest! The Buddhist gods cheer and a flock of fifty pigeons dip their wings in awe as they turn south for the winter. The bharal stamp their feet and rut with their horns – victory!

Dilip thinks the night temperature was minus ten degrees, and it surely felt it. I had on every piece of clothing I carried; thermals on my skin, trousers, shirt, jumper, outer rain pants, down jacket, outer jacket, beanie with a liner, two pairs of socks and two layers of gloves... not forgetting the giraffe. Dilip offered me his extra sleeping bag just to add to the protection against this cold night. I was able to sleep, even though intermittently, but my body was tired and certainly the altitude helped.

Dilip brings me a cup of hot sweet chocolate early in the morning. I'm very thankful as I strip layers off to prepare for the day's walk. The hot chocolate warms me as I emerge from the tent. Poona has cooked chapati, served with jam. I eat five of them washed down with milky sweet tea – such pleasures in this remote place. I notice frozen clumps of grass where moisture has oozed from the ground then frozen into hundred-millimetre icicle clumps, like a frozen flower.

And the stream that flowed a little yesterday on our arrival has frozen solid.

The oddest thing happened in the night around 9.00pm, of which I was only vaguely aware; two men visited our camp – one a Nepalese guide, the other a young Australian according to Dilip. They had bitten off more than they could chew and carried minimal gear. Dilip suggested they needed to walk down to where the French expedition was camped; it would be warmer there, and they were likely to have a spare blanket. Bizarre, is all I could think: why do such a dumb thing in minus ten degree temperatures? Was it poor planning or a thirst for adventure? Both possibilities are bizarre in these freezing mountains.

And there was another visit in the night by two Nepalese men who Dilip felt were up to no good. This was another reason to be thankful to have the security of Dilip and Poona, who would be a formidable force if things got out of hand. Thankfully nothing did.

We will cross the Panidal La Pass today at 4,540m. Our bodies, by this stage, are well acclimatised, but one can never be too certain. It's important to be 'awake' for the signs of altitude sickness, sleepiness, imbalance, muscle aches, loss of appetite, shortness of breath, fatigue, nausea, vomiting, headache and dizziness; like a hangover, but without the fun bit.

Poona digs a hole for the rubbish and we are nearly ready to go, just the morning cigarette ritual and Dilip announces, "May the battle begin!" He is referring to the elevation we must climb at a steady relentless pace where it pays to focus on my body's progress and how I feel, as anyone who has done this type of trek will know; patience and steadiness are necessary tools. The air is crisp and the sky a deep azure blue. It felt so beautiful to be alive. To be here in these remote northwest Himalayas, with two men I have come to greatly respect.

There's a flock of fifty pigeons flying on the horizon and an orange-coloured fox with a big bushy red tail traversing the skyline. The trail wanders from the ridge to a large open drainage system with a partially frozen lake some fifty metres wide. There are Buddhist flags, well-worn from last year, leftovers from the spring season annual harvest of the caterpillar mushroom. This has become a 'big-ticket item' for many hundreds of Nepalese and Tibetans who migrate to these parts for the lure of earning US\$25,000/kg – or at least that is what it sells for in China.

Ophiocordyceps sinensis is a fungus that grows on an insect – in this case a caterpillar – from the Himalayan regions between 3,000 and 5,000 metres above sea level. It has been used in Traditional Chinese Medicine for thousands of years; however, since 2016 Chinese health authorities have monitored this naturally occurring product for high levels of heavy metals and arsenic, which exist organically in these higher mountain regions of the Himalayas. [20]

The fungus germinates within the caterpillar – kills and mummifies it – and a dark brown stalk like fruit grows from the caterpillar's head. It is still classified as a medicinal mushroom and is used as an antibiotic, anti-inflammatory, anti-viral, and anti-oxidant; it is effective in the treatment of cancer, cholesterol and ergosterol synthesis, boosting immune-systems, controlling cell proliferation, natural fungicide; and is a psychotropic drug. It also helps with erectile dysfunction, hair replacement, and increases politeness... OK, I exaggerated the last few. *(20)*

It is now considered an endangered species due to the commercial harvesting throughout this region where it has proved to be a valuable cash crop in Tibet and Nepal. It is yellow and black in colour; forty to a hundred millimetres long and up to ten millimetres in diameter. The product is known as 'soft gold' in China due to its high cost and usefulness in Traditional Chinese Medicine. It can now be produced in a laboratory without using a caterpillar; so hopefully this will help alleviate the rubbish in these mountains and other less savoury activities related to this industry that occur in these deep Himalayan valleys. *(21)*

The Nepal Geological Society have been researching heavy metals for twenty years in the Nepalese Himalayas and while arsenic, zinc, iron, cobalt, copper and nickel certainly occur here, there is no proof that there is a direct effect on human health; research on this natural phenomenon continues. *(22)*

The rubbish from these camps is 'testing to the eyes' to say the least; Coke bottles lead the count, followed by Sprite bottles; plastic sheets, cigarette packets, chip packets, beer bottles, spirit bottles, the list goes on – in an otherwise pristine wilderness.

As we ascend towards the main pass, Panidal La (4,530m), we come across another very bizarre thing which I thought was caused by altitude sickness – from a distance I can make out a round metal shape, rusty in colour, standing ten metres high. And as I walk nearer and nearer, I can make out a Ferris wheel in the middle of the wilderness. As I head over the crest, I come across another large dumping ground for what used to be a caterpillar mushroom camp.

The Ferris wheel is almost five metres in diameter with small double chairs made of timber for children to sit on. It seems nothing is spared in these remote camps for the families who come here, including this awkward steel structure that must have been carried in by mules and bolted together for the enjoyment of the camp. However, there is no shortage of whiskey bottles, beer bottles and plastic wrapping which, fortunately, are contained in this relatively small sheltered area, a hundred metres in circumference. The Ferris wheel looks at least five years old with its rusty metal surface. It has six metal chairs spaced evenly around the wheel with two large triangle supports complete with drive axle. It's a 'work of art' and to see it here is most remarkable, but sadly it's seen better days. Perhaps this injunction on trade due to the fear of heavy metal contamination has stalled progress for the men and women who collect this natural phenomenon known as 'soft gold'. I quietly hope so; this mountainous wilderness is precious just the way it is.

The natural environment would certainly improve with this outcome; the natural beauty of this place far surpasses any 'big dollar' gain and their ability to install their own personal Ferris wheel, here in the wilderness. The sooner caterpillar mushroom 'mining' ends the sooner this wilderness can be protected in my humble planet-focussed opinion, but what other focus can there be with the wisdom we now carry in 2020?

We walk on slowly and ever up to the main pass. It's hard going – "Let the battle begin", Dilip so aptly said this morning – but it's more the battle within, the reason why

I do this – the challenge of it all. I could be at home in our climate controlled home, a lovely Australian native garden to attend with rainbow lorikeets visiting every day to the bird feeders and listening to Radio National podcasts as I garden, or visiting my adult children from time to time knowing I live in a mostly very safe country.

At nineteen, free from all the trappings of career, study, and family, I rode a motorcycle to the tip of Cape York, one of Australia's last great wilderness regions. My goal was to explore – specifically the wilderness areas of Lake Field National Park and the indigenous communities to the north. I wrote to five communities and received permission to visit Lockhart River Mission on the east coast, about half way up the peninsula, very near Iron Range National Park. If I am so fortunate to write this story, it will be part of a fourth book: *Australia, my place*.

Adventurous travel is in my DNA; it's when I feel most alive, when I feel most connected to the heavens, universe and self. For the indigenous peoples the world over, they lived in wilderness all the time – we in the West referred to them as 'savages' – yet they hold the keys to understanding the natural flow of this planet, this small Earth in this unfathomable universe – and tribal peoples have done this for thousands of years.

In Australia it has taken us less than two hundred and fifty years to severely damage our environment with our 'superior and splendid' white culture. I belong to that white culture; I'm one of the 'lucky ones' in our 'lucky country'... but something is missing. Something black. "There is a black history to our white privileged life" ... still so much more to be unravelled and much to be understood. I believe we are getting there...

but then I'm privileged and white. Our own Stan Grant has much to say on this essential topic of reconciliation. He wrote *Australia Day,* and he goes deeply into his Aboriginal beliefs; his anger that comes from our black, shameful history. I would not pretend to begin this discussion; I just know it needs to happen for the world to hear. *Et mulieres sapientes!*

Today , more and more stories are surfacing about the rich indigenous culture that currently stands at 65,000 years old, but it will most likely reach 100,000 years as research progresses. The Australian Aborigines are the oldest culture on the planet and they know how to nurture and protect her wisdom – to help bring us out of this crisis called climate change – CC for urgency! I'm very sure our politicians don't have these answers when they have to serve a people who want an economy and lifestyle beyond the boundaries of Planet Earth. Ask a black person – currently living in white Australia; there is much anger, deep anger – generations deep – two hundred and fifty years of British colonisation.

Now, where were we? Ah yes, on the last hundred metres of the ascent of Panidal La Pass at 4,530m; that's got to explain my exuberance on the current state of play. The views are breathtakingly wild, barren, and it is chilly to say the least. On reaching the summit we jump for glee, and pay homage to the gods – however, we kept moving as we wanted to make Purpang by nightfall. I picked up an eagle feather which reminds me of my sister Heather, who fell from the western razorback of Lost World, Lamington National Park; one of the world's most beautiful and unique national parks where my sister chose to depart this planet – in front of my eyes – and who should turn up while waiting on that cliff face but an

IN THE FOOTSTEPS OF THE SNOW LEOPARD

Australian wedge tail eagle. Bonza bloody bottler! (c)

Wherever I go in wilderness areas in Australia one of these majestic birds turns up, like: "G'day Tim, what's going down, good to see you." On the final day of Larapinta – a sixteen-day trek from Mt. Sonder to Alice Springs, in some of Australia's most beautiful desert country – I had one of these remarkable birds follow me for what felt like hours (but more likely about thirty minutes) on the last day, where the escarpment falls away to the south. It was as though this majestic bird knew my story and my place in the world, so aptly shaped by my sister, Heather – now my youngest daughter has Heather as her middle name.

The wedge tail continued: "So what's going to happen when you finish this walk, when are you going to work for us, as the indigenous people did; when are you truly going to join our crusade? You do know this is your one purpose in life; many will be there to help you."

This is the continuing conversation these birds have with me but perhaps some of you, many of you, may think I am rather barmy, a few screws loose. He did tell us earlier he had bipolar disorder – well then, case closed – bonkers. We can all get back to our normal lives again and not think too much about this burgeoning crisis facing us all, called 'CC' – sounds so much better, more clinical, more controlled. "The gods will fix it. Back to our happy hour with cocktails and schnapps in our own artificially controlled living quarters, thirty stories up where the sun never sets – not that we see the sun much these days, thing of the past really, nature stuff, nothing to do with us."

Walking north from the summit I think of my father who passed away on 1st October 2013, aged 87. I loved him, and with my own maturing years I understand the difficulties he faced, especially with his own father who didn't acknowledge him for over ten years because he left England without his blessing. There is a time for 'king and country' and all that... being 'English' – but really...ten years.

It was my feisty mother who wrote to the opposing team's mother and over the course of years my grandfather finally saw reason and came out with my grandmother to Australia to visit. They liked it so much they moved there permanently just two years later. There was a winning feeling all around, and much praise must go to my mother for "sticking it up those two British toffs." I am referring to the less than healthy behaviour between my grandfather and father. You'll find more on this story in, *England, My Parents' Birthplace*.

My mother was the antithesis of my very British father and grandfather. It's interesting that I have inherited her more universal view of the world, and certainly with more understanding and tolerance to races of people who just may not be British. God forbid! Especially those 'blacks' in the colonies. What can we exploit from their lands? Got to be a diamond mine, gold mine, coal mine or exploitable timbers here somewhere? Call it colonisation to improve the locals' education and 'Bob's your uncle', we've exploited – I mean nourished – the souls of those poor peoples who need our guidance, our gods, our education, our poisons, our – 'whiteness'.

The Australian Indigenous peoples' need for healing goes deeper than any white person will ever understand however a good place to start, is reading the history of the Nazi concentration camps; Dachau, Auschwitz and Buchenwald, to name a few; extermination camps with the intent of 'improving' the human race. We all have suffered from this method of thinking, yet it still happens in the northwest of China; unspeakable atrocities to the Uyghur people. This seems to be our collective 'dark side' of humanity which no god will cure – it takes human action and intervention.

Reading *Forgotten War* by Henry Reynolds, *Dark Emu*, by Bruce Pascoe and, *Australia Day* by Stan Grant are excellent sources to begin understanding the need for reconciliation on black terms in Australia. They have a 100,000 year head start on us, with their inherent ability to nourish this Earth.

CHAPTER XIII

Our greatest strength lies in the gentleness of our heart.
RUMI

My father did truly love me; he tried in his own way to steer me in a direction he saw fit. However, trying to sign me up for officer training to the Royal Australian Navy at age fifteen was perhaps not his best idea, especially as the exams were designed for those who had finished grade twelve and I was still in Grade 10. The maths paper may as well have been written in another language... however, he meant well and I believe he was trying to move me away from the family sorrow of losing Heather; something he could not fix or understand in his own saddened way. I love him for that gesture of good will which I could not fulfil for him but then I had my own path to follow, unique from my father.

From the age of ten we would go off on early morning motorcycle rides; they were a blast of fatherly love for any boy. He would ride me out to the tracks around Brookfield at dawn and let me ride to my heart's content while he read the newspaper, and then he would often let me double him home. My father was not someone that played by the rules; if a locked gate had a sign on it that read, "Keep Out. Trespassers will be prosecuted," he would walk straight past as if it read, "Welcome, John Elliot Easton, we have been waiting for your honoured arrival".

Perhaps that was all part of growing up in the West Country in England and breathing the same air as Sir Francis Drake. Now there's a man for queen and country; Queen Elizabeth I, I do believe. Drake was a master plunderer for the British Empire...and himself.

Other memories I have with my father include watching James Bond movies in the days of Sean Connery and Roger Moore playing 007. It was the swashbuckling fun in those films that I enjoyed sitting with my father. I also loved helping him on weekends clearing the lantana from our Brookfield property. Lantana is a noxious persistent weed originally from Mexico and grows with massive entanglements many metres high if allowed. It was introduced from England where it grows in neat little hedgerows; however, in Queensland's tropical climate, it grows out of control especially if it has a tree or shed to grow over. We used to dig it out with a 'grubber' – like a pickaxe but with a flat steel blade for wider digging – and by the end of the day we were done; it was 'hard yakka'. I was sent up to the house to get a 'tallie' from the fridge and two glasses from the freezer – beer in Australia has to be drunk icy cold which means even the glasses have to be frozen – and there we would sit looking out over our efforts for the day bathed in sweat, watching the afternoon sunlight change the landscape. I was probably about ten at that time – golden moments with my very British father. *(22a) (k) (q)*

We also did many day trips together to Lost World in Lamington National Park where I helped him secure the brass plaque with these words for my sister, Heather Jan Easton:

> ON 10 DECEMBER, 1974
> HEATHER JAN EASTON
> AGED NINETEEN FELL TO HER DEATH
> FROM THIS CLIFF WHILE ON A
> FOUR DAY TREK WITH HER BROTHER TIM,
> KARL STAISCH AND FOUR FRIENDS
> WHO ALL SHARED HER LOVE OF THE GREAT OUTDOORS.
>
> MAY HER SPIRIT WATCH OVER THE
> BUSHWALKERS WHO PASS THIS WAY

I don't know exactly how many trips my father made to this site, but I do know how much he loved the expanse and beauty of South-East Queensland, and there are no better views than from where Heather's plaque is bolted to black basalt rock. My last visit was in March 2019, and to this day I have not needed to do any repairs or other maintenance – he secured it well with mortar made from the local creek packed in behind the plaque. Perhaps it was the place my father grieved for all the difficult things he had faced in his life; perhaps it is where he made peace with himself in the presence of his lost daughter, Heather.

I will never know for certain. I was a young teenager at the time and threw myself into rugby as a physical, combative outlet – loved it! My grieving came much later, in my late thirties, when I faced a deep depression that I needed professional help to unpack. The answer was simple; the traumatic loss of Heather with no real understanding or counselling at the time to unpack her tragic loss...just physical combative rugby to soothe the hurt and pain. I would recommend the unpacking method first; as wonderful as rugby is for a physical young man.

These days I have a much greater depth of understanding around the loss of Heather and the impact on our family; but as I write about this family tragedy tears flow down my cheeks, and it is not often this happens for me. "Men, just don't cry" But cry we must – not too much though – especially at kick-off for a game of rugby. Traditionally, feelings don't come easily for men. We are wired to get the job done; it's part of our genetic coding which perhaps needs further exploration...*but don't ask us to change! Huh!*

Another wonderful thing I used to do with my father as a young boy was to hunt rabbits and foxes with a .22 rifle around Stanthorpe in South-East Queensland. Mostly it was just the two of us, but my mother would come sometimes; we would drive in our big Holden Kingswood station wagon, a car built in Australia for Australian conditions. We'd camp out under the stars on canvas stretcher beds, make a fire, and cook jaffles with bacon and cheese. In the morning we would leave camp before dawn and drive till we found the bunnies. There was no shortage in this country, another legacy of the British.

On returning to camp my father would boil the billy and make damper while I skinned the bunnies for their fur. I loved to tan them using a traditional method of salt and alum combined with lots of elbow grease. Sometimes we would keep a carcass but one had to be vigilant for myxomatoses, a horrible human-made disease found in feral rabbits. The liver had to be clear of white spots, the tell-tale sign of this horrid slow death. A .22 calibre in the right hands was a humane way to kill a bunny but, of course, not feasible for the numbers they breed.

My father taught me how to use rifles and to understand their ballistics; when fired the projectile could travel two kilometres, so I needed be sure to know where I was aiming – always safety with my father. Rifle down when walking; beware of water, the bullet could skip. And never fire into the air. These simple rules apply even more to the larger calibre rifles. My father was a lieutenant in the Royal Horse Artillery so he knew about guns; big 25-pounders that could fire very accurately for miles and kill and maim many hundreds of people with just one shell. Just brilliant really – excuse my sarcasm – God, are we as a species ready to STOP and focus on the majesty that is this planet? Not all planets have oxygen, water, and soil – rather a good point for looking after this one to the best of our *et mulieres sapientes!* This one is special; we need to treat her with more respect before she shakes us off! And the gods cheer at this revelation.

My father had a very good friend who lived on the outskirts of Stanthorpe, on Amosfield Rd, who had served in the New Zealand Army at El Alamein in North Africa during WWII. They got on like a 'house on fire' and we would spend weekends on their forty-acre farm learning how to tan rabbit skins and sight in a rifle. We would also help Matt slaughter a cattle beast on Friday nights – the head and lower limbs were removed, and the carcass was lifted up onto two four-metre-high timber trestles with a timber crosspiece and chains strong enough to lift the 900kg bullock using a tractor. We would then remove the skin, gut it and leave the carcass till morning so the meat would 'harden' overnight. This was always done in winter when the fly population was minimal. The following day, beginning at dawn, Matt would show us how to butcher and cut the meat into the many parts ready for the kitchen.

For me as a young boy it was all good 'swashbuckling' male bonding working with my father and Matt. I still have the scar on my right thumb from cleaning one of the razor-sharp knives with a cloth. The blood flowed from the wound like water and all Matt said to me was: "Well, you won't do that again." And he'd walked off; boo hoo, me. Lesson learnt young fella.

Another time my father – and mother – helped me was when

IN THE FOOTSTEPS OF THE SNOW LEOPARD

I was sixteen and looking to test the boundaries of domestic life. I had become caught up with two cannabis smoking teenagers who took it on themselves to train me in the gentle art of smoking a reefer and being cool. It had the reverse effect on me – I felt dreadful most of the time. What's more it affected my school studies incredibly. Fortunately, my parents confronted the parents of one of the boys and demanded their son not to see me again. I was so relieved, as drugs just weren't my cup of tea and the peer pressure was broken. To this day I feel great gratitude to my parents for getting me off that particular misguided adolescent route I had taken. Thanks to my parents, it lasted only a few months. I was later able to repair my English results, which gave me entrance to university to study journalism, as a mature student, graduating in 2000 from Griffith University. Victory!

Saturday mornings when I was eight or nine, my father would bake us scones and raise the Union Jack as the sun was rising over our deck, which looked out over our very beautiful two-acre property in Brookfield. He would play British Army military music, which I am sure my mother only just tolerated. I still remember the call of the Sergeant Major: "Band and drums by the centre, MARCH!" Luckily there were no close neighbours. I still have the Union Jack and wonder what on earth I am going to do with it? Surrender it to the British Empire is one possibility.

I cringe at the thought of this now but that was who he was, British to the core, just like Sir Francis Drake, five hundred years earlier: just give me a British monarch to serve. My mother on the other hand was most certainly very different with her 'English' gypsy blood running through her veins and

Quaker values that align far more with my own.

About an hour from the summit of Panidal La, 4,530 metres above the oceans, we stop for lunch – a light snack of biscuits and tinned fish. The French porters catch up to us which begs the question, "How?" Not that it really matters as I feel so very content being with these men. I just wished I could speak the language, but as Dilip points out, he has trouble understanding the local villagers as they speak a different Nepalese dialect and some only speak Tibetan.

So, I just look as affable as I can, take their photo, and somehow try to convey that I really do appreciate their work and we do share the common interest of loving these wild places. Some of the porters are young, barely eighteen, and they have that eagerness and 'fruitiness' of youth. I hope they are carrying no more than thirty kilograms despite the stories of old, where whole 'elephants' were carried to the top of Mt Everest...before morning tea!

The porters carry two large kerosene cookers that look very clumsy and heavy, and belong to the days of Sir Edmund Hillary; perhaps that is testament to the reliability and sheer cook-ability of these large cold clime stoves. I want to ask them so many questions as we share the excitement of this adventure to wild places, but for now glowing in each other's company is rather excellent, to say the least. I feel accepted and equal to these men. I couldn't do this trip if not for them leaving their families for weeks on end. We bath in the sun close to the Himalayan Mountains that rise over 5,000 metres; Dogari Himal to the southeast rises 6,536 metres. It's remarkable to say the least, and it's not surprising a religion such as Buddhism has flourished here for a thousand years or more; the mountains offer a backdrop of spirituality so easily lost in our Western metropolises.

However, in the West we do build some of the most extraordinary structures – cathedrals – that most certainly hold an awe and spirituality as is found in these mountains. I find the human spirit remarkable when I ponder such thoughts, surrounded by these massive heights of icy white peaks...Planet Earth!

"At the fire, we cook rice before dusk falls; and afterward, I climb the hill and sit under a pine and watch the stars appear over Tibet. Then the planet Mars, bright orange-gold, rises swiftly overnight snows in the north-east. How clear it is! How imminent! An owl hoots, deep in the black needles. *Whooo-ooo.*" (2) Peter Matthiessen, p.111

The views to Dogari Himal, rising six and a half kilometres above the oceans, are just astounding with a raft of barren mountains, ridges and valleys in the foreground. The barren foothills are brown/black in colour; scree slopes fall away from the trail with large greyish-white stones bigger than footballs. Three men on horseback come towards us with cheerful smiles. They look like they are returning to their homes after many weeks away working. Dilip thinks it could be the guesthouse owner's husband from Dhule. No wonder he looks so purposeful in his ride, he wants to get home to his wife and family.

Pine trees are beginning to show on the landscape as we descend to Purpang. There are apple orchards and holding yards for mules, as we are soon to join the main trading route from Juphal to Ringmo and Dho Tarap. We purchase small red apples and keep heading down to the river. There are Buddhist flags flying in many directions and a large yellow flag signifying the arrival of the local lama tomorrow – there is a Buddhist festival planned, and people will arrive from around the district. Unfortunately, our journey does not allow us to partake; winter is coming and there is much country to cross before reaching the village of Ringmo, our turning point for home.

There is cannabis growing to three metres with large purple heads the size of my hand. A small boy is on one of the ladders going up to the roof; these ladders are characteristic of the Himalayas and most of Nepal. They are a single trunk of pine with steps carved into them, very durable but not so easy to move around the village.

The whole village is terraced back up the ridge from where we came; it blends into the landscape like a bharal. The houses are made of the natural materials found here: stone from the Thuli Bheri River below, pine timber from the forest above, and thicket thatching from the fields around.

It was as though the houses were piled on top of each other; children stood on open balconies with a five metre drop below. Piles of winter fodder are stacked on the roofs one metre high, and Buddhist flagpoles rise four metres waiting for the religious festival in winter which just happens to be starting tomorrow. It is no wonder James Fisher found it so difficult to map the villages and discern who lived where, for how long, and for what purpose. But somehow in 1968 he did, with the help of his wife, several guides, and many porters. *(22b)*

We weave our way down through the stone-built village; the path is rocky, with much mud created by the natural water course trying to reach the river below. There are surprisingly few people about given the size of the village. Dilip thinks many have moved to lower altitudes for the winter.

We see many walls of Mani stones, I feel so drawn to them – their age, their shape, the carving, the Sanskrit, the meaning, the artwork – all in rock – Tibetan in origin, the word Mani meaning jewel. They date back at least three hundred years and originally just had the four-word Tibetan mantra, *Om Mani Padme Hum*. In more recent times whole Tibetan texts can be seen carved on the stones with the most intricate of design, love, and devotion to ancient roots.

It could be described as an altruistic practice of love and compassion; but so many walls of these stones drown out my Western scepticism – there were walls of Mani stones on the trail, walls of Mani stones near the chortens, walls near rivers, and sometimes even *in* the rivers. On the mountainsides some of the walls were over five metres long, several metres wide, and a metre high; real sweat, blood and tears made these stones. Human beings created them; they were capable of ignoring their gods – but they chose not to. They chose to toil and sweat and bleed and cry to tell what they knew – for people like myself who searched the planet for human grace, dignity and spiritual connectivity. These stones, the size of a briefcase and larger, were weathered with moss and algae, which gave them a mystical and spiritual depth. *(22c)*

"...and just above this bridge, in the roaring waters, is a boulder that was somehow reached by a believer. OM MANI PADME HUM has been carved there in

mid-torrent, as if to hurl this mantra down out of the Himalayas to the benighted millions on the Ganges Plain." (2) Peter Matthiessen, p.135

I don't pretend to understand these stones of carved scripture, but I do know they help to connect me to the heart and soul of this planet...because they are connected to thousands of years of ancient, traditional history of a people who have lived in sync with the Earth. That's history you may say, the dark ages, the past but like so many of us living in this modern world of cyber-connection I feel we are missing the point – something these ancient cultures knew to the core of their being, the core of the Earth's being and the reason for existence.

In Australia, it is the indigenous peoples who I believe hold the key to our survival, as do the North American Indians and other ancient cultures of Africa, Arabia, South America, and Europe. There is a revival we need that incorporates the efficiency of our modern world, yet digs deep to find the wisdom and soul of our ancient past. With this combination we could survive as a species, within the enormous biological web that connects us, but try and tell that to a politician vying for votes in a predominantly 'white fella' culture of less than two hundred and fifty years. Let's leave the coal in the ground and step forward into a new era, with science and our human soul to guide us.

In the late sixties an American anthropologist, James Fisher, came to this region to study the people, their economy and culture. He spent a year in this village which he calls by a pseudonym, Tarangpur – my map and guidebook refers to it as Sahar Tara. In those days, he concluded there was a population of 367 people with three dialects of language; an unwritten mother language of Tibeto-Burman called Kaike, Nepali and Tibetan. *(22b)*

In the surrounding area there are twelve smaller villages each speaking one of these three languages. This area is strategically located in terms of trade with Dunai – a regional centre –being a solid days' trek to the northwest, Dho Tarap is two days to the northeast, Jomsom several weeks' trek to the east and Beni – where I had come from – was twelve days' trek if the weather is kind.

According to Fisher, Buddhism, Hinduism and a collection of indigenous deities are all synchronised into daily life throughout the thirteen villages. Fisher describes this synthesis of religions where "all the gods are the same". And then there are differences between villages as to what crops they grow: wheat in most villages, corn in some, and cannabis; it seems to grow in all the villages. As Fisher describes, "Even such a basic fact of life as death is dealt with differently from place to place." In some villages it is a three-day ceremony, in other villages it can take seven days, yet in Sahar Tara there is no such ceremony, and the people keep on working. This mix of cultures, as Fisher describes it, is not homogenous; the people retain their language, religion and trade within villages as well as engaging in export and trade from afar, despite the topographical remoteness. *(22b)*

We come to the large gompa in Sahar Tara, nearly eight metres square, three layers high; an overall height of seven metres; it is painted white; there has been plenty of weathering over the generations. Inside are paintings of the Buddha in bright blue, yellow and green; over one hundred are painted on one wall, high up to protect them from weather and human touch. I don't pretend to understand what it all means but I am fascinated and deeply moved to see these paintings with such delicate lines in such a remote place. Whoever painted them knew what they were doing, similar to the new Buddhist gompas I saw on the Annapurna near Manang. They were professional Buddhist builders and these were professional artists who had a deep love for their religion.

The structure is several hundred years old and most likely has been replaced several times as natural forces wear them down. Depending on the economics of the time they keep

re-building. This region has been made prosperous by the abundant farming land and ancient trade routes running through India, Tibet, and China.

The heads of cannabis growing nearby have a rich bluish-rust colour – just begging to be smoked – I mean, cooked into a wheat bread or made into cooking oil. I am often offered rice or millet wine but unless I bring the subject up with Dilip, dope smoking is never mentioned. Maybe it is just us in the West that have this bad boy fascination with dope smoking; the locals here in the Himalayas just treat it like wheat or corn – it grows well and is a good trade item.

Fisher only mentions cannabis as a popular oil for cooking where the seeds are ground, but it seems like the 'elephant in the room', and in some places taller than an elephant! These plants grow nearly four metres high, and have burgeoning heads of seeds that they make into cooking oil. I'm definitely a long way from the West – or there is a flourishing ganja trade not mentioned in the tourist brochures that developed after Fisher's studies in the late 1960s. *(22b)*

Dilip wants to keep moving as he likes to keep to schedule. There is a place he knows down near the river where we will camp the night. After about thirty more minutes I'm feeling tired; Dilip is fussing around in a goat paddock trying to find a suitable place to set my tent where it is flat and also free of goat poo. I would normally be touched by his eye for detail and care for my well-being, but it has been a long day crossing Jangla Bhanjyang Pass and I just wanted to make camp, eat and ...sleep!

A characteristic white canvas tent from the caterpillar mushroom trade has Chinese characters above the doorway. It is a teahouse run by a husband and wife; they offer us dinner and Tibetan tea. While we are waiting for our meal to be prepared by his wife, the husband talks to me in broken English about a treasure he has, and asks if I would like to see it. Above our heads are slices of freshly killed goat meat being smoked and dried in this spacious tent some five metres square.

I am intrigued and show great interest as to what it may be; however, he is cagey and careful not to give too much away. I guess he is trying to gauge my trust that I won't tell anyone of his secret treasure. Either that or he is a very clever salesman carefully watching my response to his unfolding sales presentation in a Chinese tent not too far from Tara Khet, close to the Tibetan plateau on Planet Earth. He takes a string necklace from around his neck with a yellow/amber-coloured stone the size of my wristwatch. When we first came to sit in their tent, he was licking the stone, taking it into his mouth like it was a good luck charm.

Dilip interprets whenever possible, but he too is wondering

what this man is going to show us. Half an hour goes by and he brings out a dark round stone the size of a large marble that he keeps in a box amongst the many boxes and bags of produce that surround the interior of this Chinese-made calico tent. Dilip is either unable to interpret the Tibetan dialogue of this man, or he doesn't want to for fear that he will share too much of this man's stolen secret.

He pulls a left-winding conch shell wrapped in cloth from a packing box. These shells most likely come from the oceans off India, the Bay of Bengal, or the Arabian Sea. Other cultures and religions have used these shells; the Aztecs, Hindus and Christians. The conch is important to Buddhism as it represents the direction of the sun, the path of Buddhism, the voice of Buddhism, and the truth of Dharma. (23)

It holds an esoteric wisdom, a spiritual symbol that forms part of the eight auspicious signs of Buddhism: 1/ umbrella, 2/ yellow fish, 3/ vase, 4/ lotus, 5/ white conch shell, 6/ glorious peu, 7/ banner, 8/ Dharma chakra. The white conch shell represents priests, the red conch represents warriors, yellow represents merchants, and grey represents labourers. The shell I am shown seems to be none of these; perhaps a red/brown colour, but certainly spiralling left from the top of the shell's centre. With enough polishing and attention, I am sure this shell could be turned into the prized smooth white colour of a priestly standard.

In ancient Tibetan Sanskrit, the conch has a Shankha meaning of a shell holding water, wisdom realising emptiness, a truthful speech and strength. In relation to creation the conch represents the beginning of existence, shown by its spiral pattern representing the universe. The sacred chakra found in our abdomen – where we can summon our strength and courage – is symbolic of the conch; where we find our gut feelings, our innate sense of the world. I think we could do with a few dozen of these in the West where less 'head solving' could be replaced by a greater innate sense of our world, our Earth. *(23)*

It is known as Dung Dkar in Tibetan – and as Shankha in Buddhism and Hinduism. In ancient times of battle, it was used like a bugle to summon the troops. It is an emblem of power, authority and sovereignty to this day, and when sounded will banish evil spirits, avert natural disasters, and scare away poisonous creatures. *(23)*

Left-spiralling conches are the most common; right-spiralling conches do exist and are considered especially sacred, representing the celestial motion of the sun, moon, planets, and stars across the heavens. It appears on statues of the Buddha – on the head, forehead, throat, limbs, breast, palms, and soles of the feet. *(24)*

I'm left with a mixture of feelings as to what he was showing us – fascinating yes! But he was not a man connected to Buddhism so the only likely explanation for them being in his possession was that they were stolen from a Buddhist temple anywhere from here to Tibet. The fact he kept his contraband wrapped up and hidden in bags at the back of a Chinese tent did suggest they were not for general viewing, but this Western man who just appeared on his doorstep could possibly have meant a sale. But no extortionate price was offered; perhaps he knew I was an unlikely buyer, or perhaps he could sense that I was not that impressed with the fact these goods belonged to a Buddhist temple somewhere.

They certainly did not belong in the back of a Chinese tent wrapped up in cloth waiting for a potential buyer. It just felt so very wrong to me, and to Dilip.

Dinner is served and we enjoy a tasty meal of potatoes with chilli paste, vegetables and some dried goat meat, washed down by more Tibetan tea that could almost be described as a soup with the richness of the yak butter added. This depends greatly on the tea-maker, their budget, and the ingredients available at any particular time of year. It is always rich in flavour and very nourishing; ideal in this cold climate from which it originates.

CHAPTER XIV

*At the end of my life with just one breath left,
if you come, I will sit up and sing.*
RUMI

The following morning, we headed east along the Thuli Bheri River for several hours and came to a large suspension bridge that would take us north to the famous village of Dho Tarap. We stopped for tea in another calico-coloured Chinese tent that was nearly seven metres square, with a dirt floor and small benches to sit on. The lady who prepared our tea had a brimming smile; she was large-framed and as strong as a yak. Her aluminium and stainless-steel pots lined the northern wall of the tent, with timber shelves from floor to ceiling. She must cater for very large numbers in the height of the caterpillar mushroom season. On this day, however, it was just myself, Dilip and Poona.

She squatted in front of the fire to prepare our tea, feeding the timbers under the pots to concentrate the heat. She has a gold crown on her left front tooth; I guess she must have gone to Kathmandu for such specialised dental treatment. She is prosperous in so many ways; her vitality being the key indicator, and she is very hospitable towards our small party. I admire her strength and wonder about the story of her life, what she has endured, how she came to be in this very remote part of the Himalayas; most likely many generations of Tibetan blood runs through her veins, but no other family seem to be present. I wished her well with all the kindness and respect I can muster. Namaste!

A hundred metres from her tent is a set of stone buildings that have been there a very long time. There were a number of men milling around the courtyard area and Dilip informs me this is the checkpoint into Dolpo; we were in fact crossing a border that would draw us ever so close to the Tibetan Plateau.

"...I enjoy the view of distant shadows that mark the

deep gorge of the Bheri River. Beyond the Bheri the steep mountains rise towards the snow peaks of the Kanjiroba Himal; on the far side of those distant peaks lies Crystal Mountain." (2) Peter Matthiessen, p.109**

We had been walking in tall pine forests since we left Tara Khet and with the formalities complete at the checkpoint, we crossed the river. I looked down at the foaming silver-blue river that flowed from the east and then turned to the north into dozens of mountains over five kilometres above the oceans. On the map it looks like a magical place that would eventually lead to Jomsom, but it would take many days to trek such a route. I longed for that wildness, the connection with Mother Earth that these people have enjoyed for thousands of years. They belonged here; they were a part of this landscape living in communities that supported each other every day in order to survive.

They are rooted in Tibetan Buddhism – which gives them a code to live by – and I marvelled at the strength I saw in the woman at the tea tent. She exuded an energy, a strength that is matched by this natural wild landscape where vibrancy is found at every bend of this wild river. It is a world that is becoming harder to find in 2020. We have populated these places, we have built cities to live in; there are so many of us but, at some deep level, I crave this natural beauty, this connection to the Earth that I know in deeper places of my soul. This is my birthright, my reason for existence. Somehow, I need to get that connection back and embrace this precious gift that is life. I saw this in the Tibetan woman's eyes as she cheerfully made our tea with a strength and beauty that belongs to the core of our being.

When I experience this, I ask myself: "Why do I stay in the West? What holds me there, when this life can be found here in nature?" There are, of course, many reasons my head tells me not to stay; my family back home, my Nepalese visa has an expiry date, the seasons will change to freezing in a month – these are just three reasons. But what if I really decided to go back and stay there – build a hut, fish, buy local supplies and breathe in this natural world every hour of every day I was there? I was feeling the call of the wild many of us feel living in our Western culture – that longing to be a part of a universal landscape that belongs to the heavens and the gods.

"My head has cleared in these past weeks free of intrusions – mail, telephones, people and their needs – and I respond to things spontaneously, without defensive or self-conscious screens. Still, all this *feeling* is astonishing: not so long ago I could say truthfully that I had not shed a tear in twenty years." (2) Peter Matthiessen, p.112

We cross the bridge and the trail winds its way up a ridge. I pass a Corn Flakes packet on the side of the trail faded by the seasons; it soon reminds me of my connection to the West. A little further along a massive tree with a metre diameter girth has been felled across the trail. There has been a portable mill at work, as a pile of 150x100mm posts are stacked for the mule teams to carry out when needed.

It's a very steep climb for several hours but the trail is in good condition, the trees become fewer, and the views down to the river are expansive, magical. That longing to be here, the call of the wild, comes up again; to live here, not just a traveller passing through. Is it a dream or something that could be real for six months, a year, or until a toothache developed or the Chinese border police booted me out? It's something to ponder on my death bed...what I did with my life rather than what I wished I had done for others? Remaining in the office doesn't come to mind...however, when raising three children this was necessary.

It is day twelve of the trek, the 28th of October 2019, and we begin following the Tarap Khola River northwest through steep country of barren hills and rock. Heavily laden bullock teams come towards us carrying grains and other goods I can only imagine; opium, cocaine, methamphetamine? I hope not. These are ancient trading routes linking China and Tibet in the north; Nepal and India in the south, and maybe these bullock teams are the real reason for the smartly dressed police carrying automatic weapons back in Dhorpatan – no intelligent government would allow such destructive drugs to infiltrate its people – just be sure we have a little alcohol...please!

The river carves deeply into the valley with campsites and tea tents along the route that cater for the caterpillar mushroom trade in April through to September and the odd western tourist, his guide and porter. The trail undulates but remains under 4,000m – it is very cold – the sun barely reaches this valley with mountains on both sides of us reaching 6,000 metres. Many fast-flowing streams crash down from these high places and into the Tarap Khola River on its journey to the southern lowlands of Nepal and India.

In some places the large pine trees are sheltered from avalanches and scree falls, and have flourished for fifty years or more. We stop for lunch at one of the tea tents very close to the river where a large rock – the size of a dinner table

– has Sanskrit carvings; **Om Mani Padme Hum**. The waters wash over these massive stone carvings and carry their Tibetan prayers down to the peoples in the southern lowlands of Nepal – precious prayers of wellness, strength and vitality, a universal connection. Namaste!

The tent has been through many seasons of trade, its canvas grimy from the weather. I photograph a mother and child in the tent; she wears a necklace of blue turquoise stones mixed with amber beads from Tibet. She is helping to prepare our lunch while holding her baby, and she beams with good health, as does her child. This mountain air and healthy produce that has travelled up and down the valley for thousands of years can be seen in this woman's eyes; she is alive and connected to her people, and her Bon religion.

We enjoy dal bhat with some dried goat meat washed down with tea. It is a delightful feeling to sit in these simple tents and hear the many stories that have been told here, of the caterpillar mushroom trade, fortunes won and lost. It sounds a little like the gold rush days of Australia. I just hope there are some laws attached to this lucrative trade now that it has become legal to 'prospect'. Better still, this 'soft gold' gets developed in a Chinese laboratory, which would help save this natural environment for future generations.

A large cluster of gold-coloured marigolds grows on the south side of the tent – how I do not know, as the area gets little sun. Inside the tent are carpets and low wooden planks that serve as tables. Around the internal perimeter of the tent are shelves with bags of goods and foods that will see them through the winter if they plan to stay, but the snow must lie in this cold valley and the river must freeze in many places.

IN THE FOOTSTEPS OF THE SNOW LEOPARD

It's not a hospitable valley to be in for the many months of winter.

An older Tibetan woman, perhaps in her fifties, wears turquoise stones around her neck mixed with the same amber-coloured stones I see many women wearing. She walks with us for some of the way; her husband has had too much rice wine as he stumbles along, muttering to himself. She seems to take it all in her stride, but it is not long before we separate from them. I ask to take a photo; her face is beautiful, weathered by climate and life, she's healthy and vibrant. She wears a black velvet blouse with small floral designs and has an orange/blue band, 150mm wide tied around her waist, Tibetan to the core of her being.

Along the steep trail we pass bushes of rosehip berries that I know so well from English hedgerows. I can only think they originate from the Himalayas, their fruits some thirty millimetres long and bursting with vitality. A nourishing drink can be made from rosehips, rich in vitamin C, but I don't see this being offered; black tea and Tibetan tea are the mainstays, along with coffee which grows in the lower regions of Nepal.

The mule man who shared tea with us at the tent offers to carry our packs for no charge; he is heading for his home in Nawarpani and would like us to stay in his tent house – I like this man's generous energy. It's almost nightfall when we get to Chyugur, a three-tent locality. I have no desire to push on into the night to stay with the mule man; I'm tired. He so wants for us to join him, and we promise to come for breakfast in the morning. He's a gentle man who treats his mule with great respect.

He looks to have done well in his trade of running mule teams, which would become very busy when the caterpillar mushroom business is in full production and the need for goods and services are at a premium. He wears a bright red leather jacket and black jeans. His rich black Tibetan hair and dark Tibetan skin make him a striking figure, and his hands work efficiently to adjust and tie the packs on his mule. He must be returning home from some smaller job to only have one mule with him; we are grateful for his generosity.

The small tent villages always have a flagpole with a string of Tibetan flags running the length and breadth of the area where the tents are pitched, designating protection by the prayers written on the white, red, blue, green and yellow-coloured prayer flags. They serve as a sign that this is Tibetan land; this is our culture and we are very proud to carry this forward to the next generation, and the next.

A grandmother is our host in Chyugur; she is minding a two-year-old boy whose parents are away on business. Dilip and Poona's kindness is heartfelt as they insist on setting my tent while I am left to rest and drink hot sweet tea with the grandmother and two-year-old boy. We three men are feeling the effect of the many passes we have crossed, but there is an urgency to keep moving through this cold valley to get to Dho Tarap in the next few days.

The resilience of these people is striking and I wonder where the Tibetan lady and her drunken husband ended up for the night – hopefully not in some cave with nothing but themselves to keep warm. The cold is a difficult thing to face in good health, quite possibly a death sentence when laced with too much rice wine or rum. I pray they are safe.

I see a rubber jumping deer in the storage boxes on the other side of the tent; I go over and pull it out for the little boy. He shows some interest as I am obviously someone new to entertain. Dilip and Poona return from their kind work and sit in front of the low timber tables and sip black tea and smoke. I love these two men...in a male kind of way – like packing down for a rugby scrum when I was a boy, directing play from my number "9" position. I'd have Dilip and Poona on my team any day. Dilip number "10", the trickster and playmaker; Poona number "3" to push hard with plenty of grunt.

I go to my tent and pull out my down sleeping bag and the many layers I will wear tonight; it will be another night with temperatures well below zero, there is little sun here during the day, but these people keep to their outpost. Perhaps it's about marking out territory for fear someone may take over their tent for the next season of caterpillar mushroom prospecting. I don't know, but I'm sure it's not to meet this Western traveller who likes to entertain a two-year-old with a rubber jumping deer.

The river is rushing just a few metres below my tent and I fall asleep listening to the sound of these waters that flow from the north of Dho Tarap. From there, Tibet is only thirty kilometres as the crow flies, but several mountain ranges must be crossed to reach the border and the trails weave and wind through deep valleys like the one we are currently in. They are very remote with small side trails heading to the Tibetan border. The thought is thrilling for some future trek, but I wonder what the Chinese Red Army reception might be like? Do they actually man these minor border crossings with soldiers, guns and mortars? It is interesting to contemplate, but not something a regular trekking company would be prepared to take on. The thrill of just getting to the border would be fascinating enough, as the country is remote and mountainous.

"From a biologist's point of view, in fact, most of the Himalayan region is still *terra incognita*. As George Schaller says almost nothing is known of the natural history of the snow leopard, and we are walking a long way indeed to find out some basic information about the relatively accessible Himalayan bharal." (2) Peter Matthiessen, p.120

Dilip and Poona sleep in the main tent along with the grandmother and child. The tent is large, nearly eight metres square, with two steel poles in the middle; by the looks of its wear and tear it has been here for many seasons. I wonder about the stories that have been told here and the many people who would have rested here over the years – and all the talk of trade and caterpillar mushroom 'gold' – all the while seeped in their ancient cultural heritage of Bon religion – something far deeper and more culturally inherent than the vibrant mushroom trade – far deeper than the whiskey bottles and rusting Ferris wheel I have seen scattered along this ancient trade route where few villages can exist.

CHAPTER XV

Let the beauty of what you love be what you do.
RUMI

We leave the hospitality of the grandmother and little boy and head further north-east to Nawarpani where the mule man is expecting us for breakfast; it is a two hour trek so I am grateful we stayed where we did. He is busy in his three-metre square kitchen, the ceiling so low I have to bow my head to find a place to sit. There is an older man – perhaps his father – helping, and three small children play near me. There is a little girl age about five in a maroon-coloured monk's gown; she is stunningly beautiful with her dark Tibetan skin, her glowing childlike eyes, and slender five-year-old frame. The river flows just ten metres from the tents; grey-blue coloured waters fed by glaciers and snow from the high mountains that will begin to thaw in March and April of next year.

Chapati and fried eggs are served with black sweet tea. The chapatis are delicious, made from local wheat flour, most likely grown at Dho Tarap. I am taken by the organisation of his camp; the large tent has an earthen floor with large colourful cushions on which to sit, and small timber stools. Outside there are 20 or more aluminium pots drying on a long timber plank, waiting for the snippet of sunlight later in the day. And a stone toilet – the first I have seen in a very long time – with water piped in to wash hands; it's almost unheard of in these parts.

I have gained the little girl's trust and I ask her father if I can photograph her with the gorge and mountains behind her. She is a natural and turns to look at me as I capture her delicate young beauty. Her skin has the dark lustre of Tibet, and her face has the cutest expression that was making me melt with love and affection, as only a father can. I feel so privileged to be here in this remote valley, and I am grateful for the generous hospitality this man is showing us.

I wonder if the maroon-coloured gown the girl wears is no coincidence; perhaps she is from a lineage of lamas and she is destined to follow in that direction. She carries herself well – with confidence; perhaps she is someone destined to great things. Dilip does not have the answers and really, it's none of my business; my job is simply to enjoy being here, soaking up the company of these Tibetan people. I am in the Himalayan Mountains, amongst the kindest of human souls.

Several hours upstream, the going has been steady, and we are gradually gaining elevation to our destination, Dho Tarap, 3,944 metres above the oceans. The river at one point disappears underground where fifty-metre cliffs rise rapidly; one of the many Himalayan secrets are these deep gorges – the deepest to be found anywhere in the world. We cross a timber bridge and eventually come to a single white calico tent where we decide to stop for tea.

The young man, about thirty, is very rude; he snorts and grunts and seems to have nothing but disdain for me as we take our place in the tent, such a contrast to the mule man's camp. There is a young woman barely sixteen, who I hope is his sister and not a child bride. She obeys his orders to get ingredients from the shelves but all does not seem well in this two-person camp and Dilip, Poona and I know it. Perhaps she is a child bride aching to be free.

The man seems not at all with it, as if he is on some type of drug. Dilip says to me later that perhaps he was on narcotics smuggled in from China. Either way it is obvious this young woman is trying to communicate to me; she is vibrant with life and obviously does not want to stay with this drugged man. As we are leaving, I ask Dilip what we should do, but he does not know so we begin to head for the trail. The man goes behind the tent, leaving the young girl alone for a few minutes; she smacks her hand on the palm of her other hand and shoots her hand to the sky like an arrow – it's obvious she wants to escape with us.

But this is not possible; this is not our problem, even though there is something plainly wrong here. A hundred metres up the trail I drop my pack and run back with a 500NPR (AU$8) note to give her, enough to buy food and shelter for a week. But the man is standing nearby, and he is suspicious that I have come back. I pretend to notice the large birds flying above us; they are vultures that seem to block the sun's light when they fly above us 'on creaking wings'. (2)

I pull out my camera and pretend to photograph the vultures; the man knows I'm up to something, and Dilip is watching on; **what do I do?** I begin to walk back up the trail and stop to tie my bootlace. There is a rock the size of my hand. I tuck the 500NPR note under the rock and keep moving. I pray the girl has seen what I have done. The man is now in front of her but I have to keep moving, we cannot do any more. I pray and hope the young girl gets free of the unhealthy prison she lives in.

Dilip has seen what's happened, and there is nothing more to do but hope she finds the NPR500. We continue on our way with heavy hearts. Within an hour we discover why there are so many vultures – in the next tent village, some fifty metres away, is a dead mule. The vultures take turns feasting on the mule's guts. They ruffle their feathers up to such a size they look huge, all in an effort to scare off the next wave of feeding vultures. There must be thirty of these giant birds on the hillside above the dead mule, all waiting their turn to feed. It's a hideous sight and somehow seems to connect with the tragedy in the last tent...we keep moving asking the gods: why?

There is a traditional timber bridge spanning twelve metres we cross to connect with a tent village of three. A woman is grinding legumes outside one of the tents, quite oblivious to the vultures and the drama down the trail. I want to ask her what she knows, but it's best to keep going, we have done all we can – I ask the gods to intervene, to bust up that unhealthy connection – it's obvious the will of the young lady held there will find a way.

About half an hour past this tent village there is an open cave that a large bus could be driven into; it will have served as a shelter for many generations of traders who passed this way before the caterpillar mushroom trade started. There is an open flat area between the cave and the river where mule teams could be tethered for the night. We keep moving, as Dho Tarap is our goal for tonight with several days' rest and acclimatisation before the leg up to Phoksundo Lake and the village of Ringmo. My skin feels grimy, my clothes need to be washed, and it will be good to stop and possibly connect with the outside world as there is an internet tower in Dho Tarap installed only a year ago by local authorities...or so I'm told through Dilip's interpretation.

We pass a herd of thirty bharal on the ridges above the river, and as we get higher the river opens out to fifty metres wide in places. There are Mani stone walls all along this route and I see an empty Red Bull can amongst some of the stones. I try not to notice as my mind collides with what these stones represent from several thousand years of culture... compared to this Red Bull can. The name "...Bull" seems appropriate.

We come to one last tent in the afternoon where we stop for tea before the final leg to Dho Tarap. There is a family inside; an older man watching a small television, and a husband and wife with a young baby. They welcome us. There is also another man who seems to be related. The tea is delicious, our tired bodies enjoying the sweetness and stimulant of the black tea. I ask if I can take a photo of them together and the father wants to look at my photos. Before I know it, he's taking photos of me, which causes riotous laughter from Poona and Dilip – the photo opportunity had turned to the Westerner! Huh! I get the joke....

The photo I have of this family is delightful, and I promise to post them a hard copy. They give me an address: White Tent near Dho Tarap, Northwest Himalayas, Nepal. When I get home to Australia, I dutifully write the address on the package and wonder if this will ever find its way to a tent somewhere near the Tibetan border near a village called Dho Tarap. I said I would send it...and so I do. The gods are in charge now...good luck little package from the land 'down under'...we love you!

I walked outside for some fresh air – there's only so much cigarette smoke I can breathe. I find a motorcycle strewn across the ground as if an attempt was made to fix it but ended with the extraction of the last nuts and bolts. When it came time to leave, Dilip asks one of the motorcycle riders how much it would be for a ride to Dho Tarap, a two-hour trek. The rider asks some ridiculous price; besides, the walk was much more open with plenty of sunshine as the river continues to snake its way to the northeast – such beautiful country. On your bike Mr Motorcycle Rider, we don't need you... the Earth is our quest!

A little way out of the tent village a young woman is carrying three-metre timber poles that lay suspended from her forehead in the same way Poona carries his basket. I was guessing these poles must have weighed thirty kilograms, and no doubt she was heading to Dho Tarap; strong as a yak.

The landscape is such a contrast to where we have come from. It's now an open valley with the river having a much wider, shallower flow. The hills that rise from here are still the same barren, rocky landscape. Our trail has many more walls of Mani stones less than a metre high, five metres long and a metre wide – they continue to fascinate me; their age, their wisdom, their design, their connection to Tibetan culture, an ancient culture, without any '...Bull'.

As we draw closer to Dho Tarap we come upon a herd of yak – real yak with large horns and a skirt of black fur that grows around their base and makes them appear to have short legs with heavyset hooves. They look almost cute in some ways but as we pass close to them the power of these animals, which weigh upward of eight-hundred kilograms, can be felt; their horns curl upward, which gives them an even greater appearance of power – Tibetan power!

A man and a woman are herding them back into the village; a herd of thirty mostly black animals, with a few grey and white in colour. They look part of this landscape; big and powerful animals, valuable to the local economy for meat and fur in this cold climate. Tibetan Buddhists include yak meat in their diet; the climate dictates this necessity.

Dho Tarap comes into view. The light-coloured stone buildings are well camouflaged with a darker shade of brown on their rooftops – animal fodder for winter – maize or buckwheat stalks from this year's harvest. At an elevation of just under 4,000 metres, the winter is long in this village with plenty of snow and ice. We pass a whitewashed chorten as we get closer, a small structure, some four metres high and three metres square made of stone and whitewashed; I earmark it as a place to explore tomorrow when I am refreshed with food and rest. It has been a long day, a steady climb up through the deep valley. We find a guesthouse and the middle-aged lady is not willing to bargain; it's NPR1,000 per room, and I make it clear that I want my own room. Dilip wants to keep me happy and reluctantly agrees to do business with this very cranky landlady.

I ask for hot water to bathe; it is late afternoon, and the sun has disappeared for the day. I ask where I can wash, expecting a room specially set aside for the job at these high rates, but no! I'm told to go to the front garden, where her horse is most interested in my activities. I try to explain that this is not in the 'tourist brochure' but she really has no sense of humour and it seems she couldn't care less whether we stay there or not. But the kitchen lounge room is lovely, as are the rooms.

I strip down to my undies in this refreshing open-air front garden of the Himalayas in full view of the village of Dho Tarap; it must be just a few degrees above freezing, but I am determined to wash my body with soap and remove all the sweat and grime of the past week. I am thankful the water is hot, and I use a lightweight towel to sponge my body clean. It's a refreshing experience to say the least, and I am sure half the village found great humour at this Westerner bathing so close to winter. I am most certainly sure that little to no bathing happens here for the long six-month winter – quite a ridiculous thing to do they most probably think, chuckling all the way back to their homes in Dho Tarap.

The horse gets the message after I shoo him with my towel; he moves to the other side of the grassy area. I am quick to put on fresh clothes and wash the dirty ones with what's left of the water. A quick rinse in some cold water and they are ready for the line which runs across the garden area. I trust the horse is trained to not chew the guests' clothes, but the horse and I seem to have reached an agreement, and he stays away. By morning the clothes will be frozen, so I set up a clothesline in my room and collect them before bed.

"Soon Mars appears over the dark split in the northern mountains where the Tarap River comes down from the Land of Dolpo, and in the snug warmth of my sleeping bag, I float under the round bowl of the heavens. Above is the glistening galaxy of childhood, now hidden in the Western world by air pollution and the glare of artificial light; for my children's children, the power, peace and healing of the night will be obliterated. (2) Peter Matthiessen, p.117

The landlady is no happier when we gather for dinner in her grand dining room. These people are prosperous and with a few questions over the next day or so, Dilip discovers the landlady's husband has recently been jailed for on-selling Buddhist artefacts stolen from this area. It's almost unimaginable that someone would be so stupid as to do such a thing in the warm embrace of their own village especially as they seem prosperous, and as Dilip discovers they also have a house in Kathmandu.

The full story we may never know but for her husband, he is jailed in Dunai, the centre of government affairs for this region and if found guilty, he will serve a very long sentence. The motivation for stealing just seems utterly ridiculous in a culture that is richly Buddhist. For myself as an outsider, I could not think of anything more stupid. These items are priceless and need to remain where they belong but obviously for some – my shell-owner from down the valley included – the temptation to quick riches is too strong; delusion!

In a village of only several hundred he would need to carry out these unforgiveable deeds in the middle of the night with a torch and headscarf. But then he still has to sell it, most likely to a Chinese market or possibly the odd Westerner who passes this way. The whole rotten scheme just doesn't make sense, and is the reason the landlady is so angry. Over dinner she barks at her son to help with our meals. He is a lovely young man, intelligent, and an assistant teacher at the large primary school an hours walk to the northeast – the trail we will take in a few days to Ringmo village on the shores of Phoksundo Lake.

Dinner is a sombre affair; the landlady's mood is affecting us all, but when we learn of these events, our sympathy is withdrawn. We talk of moving hotels the following day but as we are out and about most of the time, it really does not matter too much. I practice feeling compassionate towards her – we know only a little of the story.

CHAPTER XVI

*I love my friends neither with my heart nor with my mind.
Just in case my heart might stop. Mind can forget.
I love them with my soul. Soul never stops or forgets.*

RUMI

Before breakfast I walk back to the whitewashed chorten we passed on the way into town. It's large, eight metres square and almost as high, in three tiers covered in flat river stones. A flagpole at the top supports the many Buddhist flags that run across to a neighbouring building – reminders that we are just thirty kilometres from the Tibetan border as the 'creaking wings' of the vulture flies. *(2)*

There are relief patterns around the three tiers made from an earthen ochre and feature 900mm diameter artwork; horses galloping, Buddhist wheels, lotus, and intricate patterns in the corners of the building that look like the vines of a plant curling and growing from the building. Some of them have been damaged by the ravages of time, but I would guess this structure to be at least three hundred years old with many restorations along the way. It is so profoundly a trademark of this region, of the Bon religion of these Tibetan people, and their ancient past that stems from Tibet, the 'Roof of the World'.

Pigeons, in flocks of fifty or more, fly across the escarpment on the other side of the river. We have seen many of these birds on our journey; they are the ancestors of the pigeons that we have in our Western cities, introduced there several hundred years ago. It is also known as the rock dove and is found in its native form across the Middle East, Southern Europe, India and parts of Africa. And in our own home in Australia I have built birdfeeders using four 75mm timber poles rising two metres with plastic feeding trays; I place grains on two of them and fill the other two with water for bird bathing – the pigeons just love the grain while our Australian rainbow lorikeets muscle in for their share, along with magpies, butcher birds and pee wees. Our garden is nearly 100% Australian native plants that our native birds just love. *(25)*

I head back to our guesthouse, stopping occasionally to study the many Mani stones; they continue to fascinate me because of the love and devotion that has been applied to the carving of these texts, with many months – if not years – of work going into creating them for people like myself and the generations down the line to marvel at and be in awe of their creation.

They speak to me as though I have these ancient roots embedded in my ancestral genes – or is it simply that I admire their creation and the people who carved them almost twenty millimetres deep in places? The relief work when pitched to the sun is remarkable, a characteristic of these people, and I embrace them, love them as though they are my own ancestors, but then they represent the same human connection going back 100,000 years.

I meet Dilip and Poona for breakfast; I'll not mention the righteous anger of the guesthouse lady again. Her son serves us breakfast – fried eggs and black tea. He tells us the new mobile tower is not working so there is no internet – I'm getting very used to this and really couldn't care less, but he offers for us to come to his school later this afternoon and he will try to connect us. There is a silver lining in this household at last – the young son – although I can only wonder how this smiling young man really feels about his father being in prison for stealing and trafficking stolen Buddhist relics. What's more, how will the village judge this family? Hopefully they will take the Buddhist view and accept, understand and forgive. This young man most certainly deserves forgiveness as he is only connected by family – not deed!

Dilip and Poona decide to join me for the morning. I want to explore the village and head to the high Buddhist temple to the northeast, similar in design to the one I have just visited, although this one has a resident lama who, with some luck, will be interested in talking to me.

Dho Tarap is an extraordinary village and centre to several significant trails that eventually find their way to the Tibetan border to the northeast and Jomsom to the southeast. The thought of following these ancient routes one day fills me with great excitement; especially to make the crossing into Tibet – if at all possible – with enough US dollars in hand to pay off whoever needed to be paid off. That sounds very underhanded when in fact the Chinese Red Army may offer official channels for Westerners to visit; albeit with a personal military escort. I would find it challenging to hear their version of events and the current need for Tibetans to be re-educated this past seventy years – it just comes over as an oxymoron of words from a country driven by economic growth, power and domination – Tibet just happens to have the raw materials to help drive their economy, but then so does Australia – albeit at a higher price.

I cannot stomach this limited outdated version of the Earth – like the Earth is a commodity. Humanity, we are – *et mulieres sapientes* – and this is a time for great change and growth...of survival! Not just of this human species but the millions of species that connect us to fresh, clean air, water and food – the web of life. The life that traditional peoples the world over have known for thousands of years. This is a time for change – for planetary human change.

Our Earth screams for us to do this and, as I have said earlier, our Earth does not need us *homo sapiens* – she could shake us off within 30 years – and so life would go on. The planet would go on without us – this pesky *human species* that flatters itself to be the top of the food chain yet is struggling in 2020 to turn itself around to the traditional values of the peoples who truly did know: the North American Indians – killed and slaughtered by an invading white people; the Australian Aborigine – killed and slaughtered by an invading white people, taking just two hundred and fifty years – and still we blow up their heritage sites for raw materials, most of which is probably exported to China so we can have the 'good life'.

Now where we? Ah, yes breathing in that rich Tibetan air amongst the Himalayan Mountains. Dho Tarap is built of many thousands of river stones collected from the Tarap Khola, which flows steadily nearby, and is the source for the town's water needs. I see women washing clothes on the stony banks. There seems to be a system of thirty-millimetre black plastic piping to carry water up into the homes. Sewerage is dealt with by a large hole in the ground within the building – at least that's how it works in our guesthouse. There is a twenty-litre plastic drum of water next to the hole with a small pot to wash the sewerage away – but to where? The big hole in the ground, I assume. It seems to work; the village does not smell of sewerage – just the earthy smells of any agriculturally-based village with fifty head of yak parked in the adjoining paddock.

The buildings are no more than four metres high, and look as though a large stone saw has chopped them off, flat. The winter food for the animals is placed on these flat roofs along with firewood, all neatly cut and stacked. The forage is piled a metre high and is carried in from the neighbouring fields, which at this time of year look barren and spent. Stone walls a-metre-high link the homes, and timber doors blackened by generations of use guard each home from wolves and bandits. Tall flagpoles made from pine trees five metres high carry the Tibetan Buddhist flags, and they run across the village spelling out so clearly the culture of this beautiful, ancient place – across trails for trade from India, Tibet, China, and Mongolia.

The village is well camouflaged in its backdrop of rolling brown hills to the north, with a rocky escarpment nearing the summit. It's bathed in morning sunlight and it feels so very good to be here – to be alive on this planet. I can just make out the mobile tower halfway up the hillside and in many ways I wish it was not there, especially as it doesn't work. It is the only sign of the twenty-first century...and I wish it was gone!

In a large enclosure of stone walls not far from our guesthouse are the team of yaks we saw yesterday as we approached the village; some are being harnessed for work, others standing like sentinels, at home in their native land. I want to go over and hug them, thank them for being here, but their sheer size and power creates a presence I can only admire from a distance. Besides, the owners of these animals may not want my petty Western sentiments to spill over the stone wall. A small motorcycle putters past us, dispelling my theory that the tower is the only reminder of the twenty-first century.

We wind our way up through the stone walls and come to another guesthouse that looks equally swish...and hopefully happier. Dilip is keen to enquire but I am far more interested in this village, so I leave him and Poona to investigate. I'm ready for a little alone time after the past week of intense walking and the crossing of three high passes. I'm very sure they need some guide/porter-time to sip tea, smoke cigarettes and repeat and repeat – away from this Western man who has fallen in love with their country. I do enjoy their companionship, their attention to detail, always putting my welfare first over the past twelve days. I feel we could go on like this forever – or at least to Tibet – but that would most definitely change the end-goal of this journey with the Chinese Red Army to deal with.

I meet a young Nepalese man from the university in Kathmandu who is studying the elusive snow leopard. He has set up cameras in strategic locations in the surrounding mountains, but so far has not caught one on film – no surprise there – but there are signs, he says to me reassuringly. I wish him well and keep walking through the buildings. A woman is squatting – women don't sit in this land, they squat – on a small wooden stool to milk her cow who chews on fodder. She gives me a friendly smile and keeps going with her morning duties. She is distinctly Tibetan with her thick black hair, dark skin, and Mongolian eyes. She wears mostly black clothing with a large Tibetan waistband coloured blue and orange. On her wrists are large ivory-coloured bracelets that I hope are not from Africa – unlikely, as I see them on women everywhere.

A little further along there is a finely built home two stories high with a north-facing elevation of some ten metres. There are several windows on the second level with blue frames and lattice work. They must be breezy in winter as there is no glass, just heavy drapes. The facades to these windows are rendered with a grey finish and help to give the home a stately appeal. The owner must be someone of consequence, perhaps a trader in this region. I find several such homes in this prosperous village.

The stonework is professional, with a flat face and rigid corners that can only have been done by skilled stonemasons; the stones come from the river several hundred metres away. In the front garden area, penned in by a high stone fence, are six small horses that have much smaller ears than mules. They look to be resting after a long trek, their heads bowed with fatigue. Any direction from here is a long way through rugged mountainous country. There's a timber flagpole in the corner of the garden rising five metres with a vertical Buddhist flag of yellow, green, red, white and blue...what else?

Looking up to the monastery on the northern slopes, I see the Tibetan flags running to the north for fifty metres, supported by flagpoles in several places and then running south down the hillside another fifty metres. To the east and west where these buildings cluster the same prayer flags run, defining this place as a holy Buddhist monastery. The stupa with its whitewashed walls, earthen relief designs, three square tiers, and a gold painted crown is defining with the backdrop of the barren hills rising several hundred metres – adding further definition to this remarkable place. I am walking in the Land of Dolpo, very close to the Buddhist gods, and they call out: "Bonza little Aussie", and I reply, "G'day, from the land down under!" An enormous thumbs up appears from the heavens – the Buddhist gods rejoice. *(c)*

The stupa looks similar to the one I visited earlier this morning – Tibetan wisdom written all over its shape and earthen decorations; Buddhist flags run off for fifty meters in several directions - it is really just a larger version of a chorten being roughly eight metres square and nearly seven metres high. The trail leads me around to the left side of the buildings; a very old man sits in the sun and barely acknowledges me. He does not look well. I don't know what to do – should I give him money to buy food? I keep walking very respectfully past him, praying he is safe and in the right place. A long wall of Mani stones and prayer flags leads from the smaller chorten to the main stupa.

The stupa has the same deep earthen-coloured ochre relief work as the chorten at the southern entrance that I explored earlier. I find a small timber door that leads me inside to the temple; it is rich in Buddhist masks, and there is a statue to the gods sitting two metres high – which ones I do not know – but the colours are magnificent reds, blues, white, green and yellow – all defined with such purpose. The mask has a cranky face, and he's clearly not happy with the world; perhaps he knows of human activity that is in need of improvement on a global level. His skin is golden, his ears extend under the weight of gold-coloured earrings, and there's a heavy necklace sitting on his upper chest. There is a bowl in his left hand, and in his right hand I recognise the Tibetan vajra, a symbol of diamond being indestructible and the thunderbolt being an irresistible force. On a table below the deity are eight bowls of water with a tall metal chalice in the middle. He has a distinct message: "Don't piss me off anymore!" *(26)*

At Kopan Monastery one morning I rose before dawn to take part in the water bowl ceremony which had me emptying yesterday's water, wiping the bowls dry and then refilling them, all at a steady, loving pace that set me up for the day in terms of peace and tranquillity – well, as much as a Western person can have peace and tranquillity. One of the three monks supervising was from Australia; I heard her talk to another nun very quietly but when I tried to make some unnecessary conversation, she very quickly shut me down. How silly of me. I obeyed and got on with the task at hand – emptying, drying, refilling. The Tibetan Buddhists have been doing this practise for several thousand years. Ritual and Practice! Ritual and Practice!

On the walls there are six prominent pieces of art – three are a 'horror story' with very cranky deities, one of which has five skulls surrounding his head and flames all around. He holds a steel sword and sits on a tiger skin. He really has no sense of fun, with a belt of human skulls around his waist; he has long black Tibetan hair, his left foot pins a man down, and below is a burning figure of a man with wild animals watching on – yaks, horses and wolves howling –and more skulls. It is a very scary place that I have no interest staying in any longer. Where is the exit from this dark chamber, which is beginning to feel like some hellhole of evil spirits?

There is however one very beautiful painting of a Tibetan man in blue robes with white-capped mountains behind; in the foreground is a huge tiger and it appears the man is stroking the tiger, but the painting is quite damaged so it is hard to see if their togetherness is in kindness; but at least there are no burning flames, necklaces of skulls, and squashed men.

The remaining two art works are a juxtaposition of peace; a female figure in lotus position wearing a blue, red, and orange gown. White doves are below her; they perch on a lotus flower. I thank the gods that there is choice in this life, a choice of paths; however, in Buddhism we cannot have one without the other.

Finally, the mother of all fierce and angry Buddhas; six arms spread out fully and holding various items I cannot describe – but they aren't peace-loving. Behind his arms are five blue swords – at least that is what they appear to be. Above his fierce angry head his thick brown hair pulled back to expose many white skulls, and surrounding his deep blue garb are red enveloping flames. In each corner of this ferocious 'masterpiece' – it's certainly not something I would want hanging at home – are four circles of various entanglements, mostly human and serpents in vicious toil. There is much more I can add but it would only duplicate the viciousness of what I have just described. It could be the Bon religion's answer to two world wars or the Napoleonic Wars or the massacre of Australian Indigenous peoples during colonisation, but either way it was time to exit and look at the blue sky and the beauty of this day in such a peaceful place on Earth as Dho Tarap...in this very natural landscape. What the human mind is capable of – these destructive places deep in our psyche; these paintings speak of the Dachau concentration camp of World War Two, yet we are six and a half thousand kilometres away, with no internet. Why are these paintings here?

Further to the east there is another very old doorway – I'm guessing a hundred years old but it is hard to tell because of this harsh environment – the timber is so deeply worn, the pine grain has raised. There are three steel bands with large nails which pin the door together. On the right-hand side at the top is a chain that hangs to connect a lock to keep out the thieves who lurk in these parts. The hand-adzed beam above supports it; I can see the individual stroke-marks of the carpenter who shaped it. Inside is a brightly-coloured prayer wheel over a metre high and 500mm in diameter. It is supported by a steel reinforcing rod that is set on an earthen plinth some 200mm high all the way around the perimeter, which is over a metre in diameter.

I pay my respects walking around the left side, spinning the wheel as I go; it has an awkward lean to the left and is in need of some fine tuning to make it turn more freely. The ancient Sanskrit is painted in gold; the floral designs are green, blue and yellow, and the background is deep red – maroon. The surrounding walls are painted in green, red and yellow with floral designs that stand out in the darkness of this sacred Buddhist room into which I have let the sunlight flood. I close the doors when I leave. Thank you, Namaste!

There seems to be no one home in the lama's building, which is next to this grand stupa. I certainly do not want to disturb him. The views down to the village are spectacular with the earthen stone buildings lying flat on the landscape with the junction of the two rivers; the Thakchiu Khola running from the north, and Tarap Khola running from the east. The deep valley we emerged from yesterday runs up from the south. There is little wonder why this village developed into the important trading hub it has become over the centuries.

It is clear from this vantage point the fields have recently been harvested for winter storage; and come spring in April/May, this barren dry valley will be green to bursting with colour and new crops will be planted. The sky today is crystal clear – a rich cobalt blue made even deeper in colour by the foreground of a dry barren brown landscape that is remotely beautiful in this land of Dolpo.

I contour around to the east to check on the mobile tower that sits so 'proudly' on the landscape, but alas it does not work. I see myself tying three sticks of gelignite to each of the four supporting posts and lighting the fuse - blowing it sky high – the people in the village rejoice at this splendorous sight – the tower returns to earth and crumbles into a heap of twisted, broken metal. No more internet! The people rejoice even more and we can hear the gods in the mountains and the gods in the valleys cheering and clapping at this spectacle. "Go away Western technology", I hear from the villagers and the gods!

I feel rather self-conscious at this commotion – it was after all only twelve sticks of gelignite – I go over and mingle with a small group of Europeans, older than myself. They are on a tour of this region and thought my actions were a little excessive. They too are in awe of this village which lies before us. They too were hoping for some internet connection but somehow that's just not going to happen now with the twisted wreckage lying before us. The internet mostly serves as a distraction in this otherwise tranquil natural world we call the human psyche. The problem is in the West we have not discovered inner peace and tranquillity –more a type of chaos and destruction – hence the need for twelve sticks of gelignite.

I continue to contour around to the east as I have seen another monastery with a set of eight chortens, built in a row, whitewashed and standing five metres tall. There are around ten very fine houses in this area, built by master craftsmen.

The sun is low on the northern horizon heading towards the west casting light and shade on this desolate landscape. In front of me are several of the well-built homes, four metres high, with defined lines of skilled stone work rendered with earthen mud. Fires burn in several places and the smoke winds its way to the heavens. The walls of these homes are cast in shadow while the fields in the foreground are glowing in the low afternoon sunlight. The fields are fallow, their produce harvested for the on-coming winter; all that is left are the dry, dark brown stubbles of barely, maize and wheat.

Behind the homes, as the ground rises to the foothills, there is a mismatch of trails – mostly from livestock, goat and sheep – with boulders the size of 44-gallon drums strewn over the hillside, as if the gods got bored and started throwing stones one afternoon; the trails were running all around the boulders. A large trail runs through this mixture; it's made for human traffic and motorcycles, giving this landscape a most unusual texture with the predominant barrenness that belongs to the land of Dolpo.

I turn to the north to explore the monastery and chortens, all in a row. A central water tap is surrounded by ice; it appears to still flow with a drip, drip, drip into a ten-litre plastic water container; hopefully by sunset it will be full for the owner. Several friendly locals are enjoying the sunlight as I walk through this wealthy part of town. A timber plough stands against one of the homes; it is four metres long and skilfully crafted with local pine – skills passed down from one generation to the next. Internet access will not change the need for grain, and the soil's need for ploughing next spring.

The eight small chortens rising five metres run to the east, with a much larger stupa that looks more like a large house on the far west side. I try to enter but it is pitch black. I can just sense it's full of scary artwork so I am in no rush to head back up here with my torch. I far prefer the daylight beauty of this land to the violent paintings depicting figures burning and being crushed, similar to the horrors of two world wars. Not my cup of English tea, thank you. *(s)*

I'm not a learned enough student of Buddhism to fully understand them; they just begin to irk me after a while, like seeing too many men hanging from timber crosses in the southern areas of Europe, nails through hands and feet. I don't find inspiration in such depictions, especially so in 2019, where "Christ died for our sins". Can the assumption be more that we are human – we do make many mistakes – but we do in fact aim to make things right to the best of our ability? These 'man-made stories' make us wrong from birth – how can that possibly be? And I do not believe for a moment our future as a species has to endure such suffering – I believe life flows in a different direction from the dark ages from which we all have come.

Life has enough sadness, pitfalls, hardship and pain without being reminded of them by a good man nailed to and hanging from a timber cross, blood oozing from his rib cage. At least these Buddhist depictions are painted down inside the belly of these stupas – a reminder of life's struggles and represented in a more pictorial metaphor than a man hanging limply, only nails holding him from falling – "He died for our sins". He died from man's cruelty – nailed to a timber cross and stabbed in the heart – left to die – man's cruelty, nothing more.

So far, the heavens haven't opened with thunder bolts but

I'll promise to do my best and help this planet gain her true magnificence again; the heavens have opened – the gods are smiling. We may just be onto something here in the land of Dolpo – on Planet Earth in a small galaxy trillions of light years from anywhere. Perhaps that is why we humans feel so lost – it's because we are!

The chortens are a white and earthen colour, with relief work similar to the ones I visited this morning, steeped in the Bon religion. Bon is the term given to a Tibetan religion and is distinct from Tibetan Buddhism, although both come from the same origins and teachings. Dolpo is one of the remaining areas of Nepal in which Bon still flourishes. It is believed to have originated in the eleventh century. It has the characteristic reverse-facing swastika laid square which I see carved into many pieces of pine furniture on this journey, where carpenters are hired to build cabinets and tastefully decorate their work in the corners using the swastika, forty millimetres square. *(27)*

The chortens are smaller versions of the square three-tier design at the village's southern entrance; some have a rounded centre and four posts to support the layer above. There are several of these with intricate white and earthen-colour designs so tastefully spaced with a backdrop of the barren hills. Three of the chortens have slumped over from the course of time and weathering exposing their river rock construction, which I guess to be at least three hundred years old. Between the seventh and eight chorten are five-metre long Mani walls one metre high, with a flagpole of prayer flags at each end.

I photograph many of the Mani stones; they fascinate me –

IN THE FOOTSTEPS OF THE SNOW LEOPARD

their texture, their intricacy, their Sanskrit text of ancient times. I think of the people who carved them – most likely men, but I do not know – their patience, determination and pure religious devotion to their art. These people were skilled artisans – their work is too perfect for any other explanation. The main carving refers to the syllable mantra: *Om Mani Padme Hum* – the ancient Buddhist mantra that literally translates to *"Praise to the Jewel in the Lotus."* Some of the much larger and more detailed stones are entire Sanskrit scripts which would have taken enormous dedication to carve, for people like me generations on to appreciate and marvel at. *(22c)*

As I walk back into the village, following the Tahari Khola River, I see older people lugging twenty kilogram bags of grain – the younger people use small motorcycles to transport them up into the village. An interesting supply chain, I think to myself; a bit like a supermarket van delivering food around the streets of my suburban home. Some of the houses have 'glasshouses', 20 metres square and facing north, with a plastic sheet spread over the structure propped up by a matrix of timber beams, which acts as a roof and contains the heat from the day. They grow all manner of vegetables; tomatoes, green vegetables, climbing beans, potatoes, cabbages, marrow and aubergine. *(28)*

I watch a group of young men playing some sort of game in the warm afternoon sun; above them on the next level, a woman stripped to her waist sits cross-legged, meditating and enjoying the sunshine. Little do the young men below know of the lady's presence upstairs, her beautiful dark skin, rich black hair, and lovely firm breasts. I do my best not to stare and keep moving back to our guesthouse, trying not to be distracted by this very beautiful Tibetan woman amongst the buildings of Dho Tarap in the land of Dolpo.

Further downstream a group of five women labour with their weekly washing in the river; soap and much raw human energy goes into this process, which I have witnessed several times along this journey. Never do I see men washing clothes...except for myself. Now, I hope that horse hasn't eaten my washing...but then I remember I took them inside last night when Peter Matthiessen was admiring Mars and the heavens in the land of Dolpo. But he didn't see the lovely Tibetan maiden sunning herself in the privacy of the land of Dolpo – shut up! This is getting quite ridiculous....no more 'land of Dolpo'...Mr John Cleese.

At the guesthouse, I meet up with Dilip and Poona for a lunch of boiled potatoes, salt and chilli, washed down with black tea. The potatoes are delicious and no matter how careful I try to be with the chilli, I 'skilfully' manage to touch my eye and nose with my finger; the result is less than fun as this is potent, high-grade Himalayan red chilli. Washing the eye using a cool wet cloth helps as it cools the skin, a minor inconvenience that really burns. Hopefully, I will learn the lesson, but I think this is now the third time I have managed to burn my own face with this rich Himalayan grade of chilli. Ouch!

Dilip has organised a visit to the local school, as we have been invited to use their Wi-Fi. It's an hour's walk to the north on the trail we are to take tomorrow en route to Ringmo village. It's a pleasant walk in the afternoon sun, and gives another perspective on this extraordinary village built into the landscape that looks like it has been here as long as the mountains themselves. The only thing that gives the village away is the sharp construction lines created by the people who built these homes. They have far sharper lines than the traditional stupas, built hundreds of years before these modern homes; a healthy sign of their economy so long as the trade is not Chinese opium.

It is more of a road to the school which is used by tractors, motorcycles and groups of school children. The school services a large area and has over two hundred primary-age students. On the hillside to the north-west, a hundred metres from the school, is a ten-metre diameter coloured design in stone with its name – "Crystal Mountain School" – around the perimeter. It's a striking emblem of progress for all to see. The school was funded by a French not-for-profit, built in 1994; however, recent extensions have been completed. The new roofing iron is bright blue, and the walls are made of the familiar rendered local stone.

The Dolpo dialect of the Tibetan language is taught here, along with Buddhist philosophy, cultural performance art, and computer skills. It has an eco-focus with passive energy and waste management practices. The school operates for seven months of the year due to the winter but as heating options improve so will school attendance in the colder months. Once students complete grade seven they can go onto Kathmandu to complete school, university or other training. Most students return to Dolpo as teachers, nurses, health workers, project managers, or government employees. The principal aim of the school is to keep their Tibetan culture alive with an indigenous focus, good nutrition, sustainable energy and architecture. *(29)*

Dilip and I are given the Wi-Fi code and it was suggested we stand next to one of the buildings near the entrance to the school, as this is where the signal is strongest. Sure enough, in came the world magically on the little device that has been my camera and notepad for the past three weeks. While being absorbed into this outward world the gods obviously had a different idea as to what was important for us to do on this day.

There was a slight breeze from the valley below and then – all of a sudden – a massive wind gusts over us and rips off a third of the new blue roof. For some reason, minutes before this massive blow came, I walked inside the building to get out of the breeze and then all of a sudden, the tearing of roof timbers and iron lifts the roof some ten metres onto the other side. And so ended our meagre internet session, as though the gods were speaking to us; "Let it go, no internet today, Mr Tim!" "Yes ma'am," I quietly reply. "I will go back down to Dho Tarap and study the scary paintings." "Thank you," is her reply. I do not know what deity she was but her direction was clear and precise – hence the wind to remove the roof, just to make a point; now that's power, I humbly thought to myself.

And that was it – no more wind gusts, just a flurry of activity from the men in the school, including several Europeans who were working there. I was going to offer my services but the swarm of some ten men soon took control of what could have been a very damaging event for people and buildings – fifty square metres of roof ripped off and dumped on the nearby grass behind the building. Fortunately, all the students were inside so nobody was hurt.

The men soon got the metal back up onto the roof and I

can see the problem straight away. The builders had used seventy-five-millimetre bullet-head nails instead of roofing batten screws; an unpredictable gust such as this plays havoc with unscrewed roofs. I shudder to think as to what carnage could have ensued, but the gods were just out for a little fun it seems... "No internet for Mr. Tim today."

Dilip and I had lost all interest in the outside world; the men from the school didn't need our help, so we begin to head back down to Dho Tarap, impressed by the efficiency of the men who came from every direction and, as they put the sheets back up, they employed the old fashioned 'roofing screw' – five-kilogram rocks and lots of them – nothing blows them off.

In the school greenhouse – another plastic-roof structure with stone walls – it was past harvest time, with only remnant bean trestles remaining. A lady had set up her weaving loom in the greenhouse for warmth and is in the middle of making the most beautiful coloured mid-riff garment – deep reds, greens, blues, white and black. Many of the women wear these; they are a traditional Tibetan design and this wooden set of tools looked like it had been handed down through many generations as all the components were worn smooth. She looks up at me with great pride and contentment; here she was bathed in the warmth of the greenhouse, maintaining her Tibetan culture for possibly her mother or sister or great aunt, but one thing is for certain; the robust design and manufacture of this garment would last more than one generation.

So, with the roofing drama out of the way and many willing helpers to repair the roof, we head back to Dho Tarap, an easy hour-long walk down to our guesthouse. One of the horsemen from the French party is trying to bargain with the grumpy landlady for two cabbages. He tells us later he had to pay 500NPR (AU8$) for the cabbages, which is unheard of, but there is no choice if you are a tourist in town and the landlady has a husband in jail for stealing Buddhist artefacts. There are huge bags of grain stacked to the ceiling in several rooms of the hotel; no doubt they will be useful in covering costs over the winter months.

As the sun is setting, I go out to see where the French party is camped behind the hotel. The six mules are tethered within an area of the buildings; the hotel dog sits above them keeping watch. The dog is the 'informer' to the landlady – no one gets away with anything around here – not without paying for it at least. Tonight will be cold for these mules, at least minus ten; they seem unperturbed by the cold, and their handlers are generous with regular nose bags of grain tied around their necks.

The following morning, on departure, we are presented with a 10,450NPR ($144AUD) bill for our two nights stay with food. It's unbelievable and I feel like we are contributing to her sadness, as clearly money is not contributing to her happiness. Dilip was right to search for another hotel, but I didn't believe she would be this ruthless. In hindsight we could have refused to pay and simply left, but at the time we dutifully paid and hoped it would contribute to more happiness in her family...but that was probably unlikely.

In hindsight we needed to dig in our heels and tell her exactly what we thought of her 'daylight robbery.' Never mind the $8 cabbage 'theft' the horseman rightly protested about. If we stayed any longer there would have been a riot and boycott; clearly the landlady had lost her marbles to anger, resentment and fear. I wished her compassion, love and support through these difficult times; I hope her husband learns his lesson and finds inner peace and love – the gift of giving.

CHAPTER XVII

Love asks for nothing and risks everything.
RUMI

IN THE FOOTSTEPS OF THE SNOW LEOPARD

We are heading northwest to Tok-Khyu, passing a group of ten eager young students in blue uniforms heading for the Crystal Mountain School. The men who repaired the roof had used plenty of large rocks to hold the roof down; I was now concerned it would have the reverse effect and cave the roof in, but who was I to advise on such things? The rock method has been well proven in these parts for generations and this school just happened to be in a narrow part of the valley where winds could blast through at high speeds. I just hoped that was the only experience like this, as it could have been fraught with casualties if children had been outside for lunch.

We passed another series of eight chortens – all very neatly in a row; these were newer, smaller in size, and neatly painted white with a two-metre square base and a round second level with a gold painted top. The same earthen-coloured relief work decorated them and I wondered if they had been recently renovated as they were so neat. Behind them was the main stupa and monastery. For some reason I didn't badger Dilip to go in; he was probably still seething at the landlady's un-Buddhist practices but as I learnt in Kopan, detachment from such injustices is a good thing; besides, the next life will be balanced by the natural forces of Karma.

There was another flock of pigeons, fifty or more, on the northern slopes. They took off in a cloud and landed again some fifty metres up from where we were heading. I thought of Trafalgar Square, Times Square, St Mark's Square – just about every city and town the world over have flocks of pigeons that are descendants of these very beautiful medium-size grey birds who crane their green and purple necks in a characteristic gesture: "I'm a descendant of the Himalayan pigeon, please feed me rich healthy grains...and ignore the naughty Tom Lehrer song; *Poisoning Pigeons in the Park*". This was a favourite of my father, who would have guessed?

We pass a cow and goat-dung drying area; there is some twenty-square metres of poo laid out in the sun which will become a valuable fuel source over the winter. Tok-Khyu is another prosperous village with well-built stone homes, surrounded by fertile agricultural lands, but most of the people have gone, left for the winter to their homes in the south. There is a trail that leaves from Tok-Khyu to the northeast that connects to Tibet; how I want to follow this trail and go onto Lhasa....

At one point Dilip asks a goat herder if this is the way, as there is no one else in 'cooee!' I understand Dilip's concern, although the pass we are heading to is well known at 5,238 metres; Numa La Pass is the only trail to Ringmo village through this mountainous wilderness. *(29a)*

We stop for lunch by a five-metre Mani wall; I particularly like the shape and layout of the round ones, some 400mm in diameter. And the ones with hundreds of smaller characters; prayers repeating with Buddhist Sanskrit from another time...brought to this present day. I love finding these ancient stones – they speak to me and create continuity within *et mulieres sapientes*. The ones with the sacred prayer *Om Mani Padme Hum* carved deeply and with such conviction keep me fascinated; some of the Sanskrit is nearly 200mm high. I can picture the men carving them, resting them on a table or maybe just their thighs as they carefully shape the Sanskrit with steel chisels and hammers; such love and devotion repeated and repeated, showing us in the twenty-first century the wisdom of our ancestors.

Crossing the pass is done steadily – with confidence; my body has acclimatised well. On our rest day in Dho Tarap I was beginning to feel aches and pains in my feet, hips and knees. I was beginning to wonder how I would go on through these last two high passes, but I am very pleased to report my fifty-eight-year-old body is of good stock, well maintained and eager for more.

Such is the beauty this land holds for me; it's the blend of this Tibetan culture, the ancient trails that we follow, and the wild remote landscape that is described as the 'Roof of the World'. Or at least Tibet is so described, and with her borders now thirty kilometres away, I feel this plateau so close to the heavens and the gods that helps to make up this land of Dolpo.

We reach the summit with some jubilation; a cone-shaped mountain to the south is covered in snow. I drop my pack and head over to play in the snow. We have only seen snow in the distance and even these high passes are not always covered in snow; but then it's been nearly ten months since any snow has fallen, and there is another month before winter arrives – and arrive it will, with more clean white snow.

There are beautiful vistas as we climb the pass, especially to the north; the wild and dry escarpments seem to go on forever. It's not a landscape most would associate with the Himalayas due to the sparseness and absence of snow. At the pass, looking to the south, we can see Norbung Kang at 6,085 metres. It's an impressive mountain, covered in snow and a ridgeline that forms the boundary of Shey Phoksundo National Park on which we are now standing. We can also see the mountains and valleys that lead to our final pass, Bagala La, 5,169 metres above the oceans of Planet Earth, in a solar system within a universe, somewhere in space. Now that's a thought to be cherished by us Earthly types of *et mulieres sapientes!*

The landscape continues – barren and brown, a moonscape of ridges and valleys – with endless vistas that continue to the horizon; only the highest peaks having snow on them. The sky is a deep, cobalt blue. There are deep gorges with rivers that are still flowing. We see a lone yak three hundred metres below us, standing on gravel by the river; perhaps it has fallen from the trail as it doesn't appear well. Above us eagles are circling, six of them, waiting for this beast to weaken. It's an unpleasant death that awaits this poor animal with little way of protecting itself away from its herd. It's too deep in the valley for us to help; we keep moving in the Buddhist landscape of suffering, Samsara.

We see bharal, raptors and a several flocks of pigeons, but no snow leopard. Peter Matthiessen is correct when he says that the journey is far more important than actually seeing this elusive animal, but we know the snow leopard lives in this land – especially to the northwest of here where Shey Monastery and Crystal Mountain are, just thirty kilometres as a vulture flies, but many days' walk to accommodate the rugged landscape and elevation.

We camp the night at the base of Bagala La Pass, and it's the coldest night of the journey as literally no sun gets to this deep valley at this time of year; our elevation is 4,512 metres.

On our map the camp is known as Danigar. There are many frozen parts to the Panklanga Khola River just below us, which flows from the ridges leading to Norbung Kang. Before us to the west is the steep climb we will take in the morning. All around our camp are the remnants of rock dwellings, the outline of where stone abodes once stood, perhaps shepherd huts, but there are too many; more likely a remnant village abandoned due to the cold. Dilip cannot explain why they are here except to say there was once a village – a summer trading village in support of the caterpillar mushroom trade before the Chinese offered their calico tents.

I layer on every piece of clothing I have and Dilip lends me his spare sleeping bag. I don't sleep well as the extra sleeping bag keeps slipping off in the night and for some bizarre reason, I would rather suffer and stay cold for hours than turn my torch on for several minutes to remedy the problem. It's like the discomfort of moving for a few minutes is too much to bear for a night of possible sleep and more warmth. I have experienced this oddity before, where suffering seems to be the better option than actually resolving the problem. Perhaps it's the cold that has frozen my rational mind...or is it simply Samsara?

In the morning I find a quiet place some way off from our camp, and dig a hole in the cold rocky ground for my morning ablutions. I take in the beauty of the early morning and as cold as it is, this lunar landscape is beautiful; I hear the 'quietness' that comes from being in such remote places – a wilderness with no human sounds – just the mountains and the river not far off. The silent heartbeat that belongs to our planet; she wants for us to find, and to understand, her existence where economic indicators are not part of her needs – they are a human construct for human needs. But to come here and to listen to the Earth's silent heartbeat is something that cannot be bottled and taken home, as it lives inside each one of us – a journey we can and must take if we are to survive as just another species who shares this precious ecosystem of Planet Earth.

While climbing to the summit – a slow and deliberate effort at this altitude, my lungs drawing heavily for oxygen – I ask Dilip if there will be a tea stall at the top. My little joke runs flat as a pancake as he too is struggling with the ascent. It's seven hundred metres of elevation from our camp but it takes over three hours as it's straight up to the pass at 5,169 metres. There are many Tibetan flags strewn across the rock cairns and flagpoles. Poona, of course, takes it all in his confident stride, his thirty kilogram basket on his back.

The landscape is rugged and barren, sculpted by millions of years of weathering. A stubble brown grass grows in places, but closer to the pass there is only rock. My breathing felt suffocating at times and I would stop every so often, lean on my walking poles – take several short breaths – then keep moving. It's important to keep moving so your body doesn't 'fall asleep', collapsing from the exertion at altitude. At the summit Poona tells me it is a good idea to leave 10NPR to the Buddhist deities, and I follow his lead. The two-metre-high rock cairn represents a Buddhist stupa with Tibetan flags running away for thirty metres in several directions.

I sit and feel the Earth's quietness; its stillness and peace here on the pass summit. The Tibetan flags wave their prayers out into the world. It is so beautiful; the rich brown valleys, the snow-capped peaks, the remoteness and a landscape that seems to go on forever. It's like there is nothing more important in the world than this feeling – this isolation, this wilderness – and it is something the indigenous tribes the world over knew well and lived with every day. So, what happened? We became industrialised, mechanised, digitised – bigger, faster, more 'intelligent' – to the point where we are now a species out of control, lost and distant from ourselves and the natural boundaries the Earth provides.

CHAPTER XVIII

On this path, let your heart be the guide.
RUMI

As I write this – 6 April, 2020 – the world is in coronavirus lockdown, three weeks into what will be at least another six months. Governments will prop up our economies if they can and still the virus is spreading – but the curve is looking to plateau. At least here in Australia and New Zealand, it is beginning to be contained, but only time will tell.

What's extraordinary, however, is hearing stories of the hole in the ozone layer starting to get smaller; the planes have stopped and so have the motor cars; the pollution over our cities has gone; and people are communicating far more meaningfully. Perhaps it is the virus we need to help bring us back in touch with the Earth, and with ourselves. She certainly will not always be this patient with us, and her power could shake us off like some pesky flea, eradicated from existence – no more. But there is always the opportunity to learn the lessons, hear the Earth's call for us to follow – and follow we must if we are to survive.

We keep moving over this lunar landscape heading west to Ringmo village, just two days' trek away. A mineral leaches from the ground and forms a dry creek-bed for a hundred metres, its ferrous red colour spilling out over the landscape.

A mule man stops to talk with Dilip and Poona; he has news from Dunai. The husband of the Dho Tarap guesthouse couple has been found guilty of stealing and trafficking Buddhist artefacts. He will remain in prison for ten years. No amount of excessive guesthouse charging can help this family now. It is so very sad, but they knew the rules before they went down that path – and maybe there is more that we don't know. I have only love and compassion for the family, particularly the young man who was so cheerful and helpful to us in Dho Tarap. I wish him a new life.

Dilip finds us a lunch place and Poona cooks tuna and noodles, which we wash down with sweet milky coffee. I'm aware of my tiredness and aching joints. The smallest of things begin to irritate me like adjusting the straps on my pack; it is, after all, day eighteen and I dream of getting to Ringmo, a place to rest, explore and relax in this important spiritual and trading village of several thousand years.

Further down the trail we come to a group of men riding on ponies; they have travelled from Ringmo. They ride in procession with the lead rider wearing a traditional Tibetan hat, grey in colour with red decorations. He holds his right hand up in a type of salute as he passes. And then comes a man wearing a fox skin hat which sits high on his head; he too salutes us as we pass. And behind them are two other men riding with pack saddles, dressed very ordinarily – most likely they assist the two men leading.

Do they salute me because I'm a white western man or does everyone get this honoured treatment of respect? Dilip thinks they have performed a marriage ceremony in Ringmo and now head home to Dho Tarap. These two men look like they are half asleep, recovering from a wild party with gallons of rice wine – fortunately their ponies know the way home. Dilip however assures me these are respectful men doing spiritual, ceremonial work. They are most likely tired from days of festivities, Dilip assures me – no hangover, no party – just traditional village work. OK Dilip, I believe you....

The trail continues to descend following the north side of

the Ghuchun Khola River, which plunges over a fifty-metre cascading waterfall and is joined by another river from the southeast. The land levels out here and a well-constructed hut is built of stone with a grass roof. It has its very own rubbish hole, over a metre deep. We decide that it is a good place for lunch. Unfortunately, the inside of the hut has been used as an animal shelter so we are forced outside to sit in the sunshine, something we have had in abundance on this trip.

Large rocks the size of dinner tables have fallen in many places from the surrounding mountains – as if the gods had been really pissed off: "Damn these humans, they just don't get it; we give them all the cues to a good life, a sacred life that nurtures the Earth and its perfect ecosystem designed by us – the gods – and they just got to screw it up, like they're some dumb species that never seem to learn!" As I sit there quietly eating my lunch, I actually can see the gods in a rage above me throwing these massive rocks down, crashing into the ground and breaking into smaller pieces the size of dinner tables – they are really pissed off with us!

Dilip and Poona just watch on as if it's all part of the human condition and the gods behave this way in the Himalayas – it's where the gods come when they need therapy to rejuvenate their souls – away from the pesky human species. But Dilip assures me we are quite safe – the gods love us to visit and experience their world – that is, in fact, why they created the Himalayas – to re-connect our human souls, our spirits, our value for this Earth; that she is not a commodity and that we are human beings – god-like in our own way, with potential beyond anything we have ever known before – a healing potential for ourselves and for this Earth.

IN THE FOOTSTEPS OF THE SNOW LEOPARD

The valley running to the west from here will take us to Ringmo – our aim tonight is a small deserted village called Dajok Tang at an elevation of 4,080 metres. It takes us several hours to reach and another very cold night awaits us. There is little sun in this valley – the reason the village has been deserted until next spring – but the Tibetan flag poles rising five metres remain, showing the people where their homes are when they return. The homes are well constructed using stone, with pine poles as roof beams, and they have flat grass roofs. Behind us to the east is Norbung Kang, but it's not clearly visible through the grey wispy cloud that now forms around us.

It's another freezing night, perhaps minus fifteen-degrees. It is day nineteen of our journey and I feel the exhaustion; I'm a little teary this morning, missing home, family, friends, a hot shower, a shave, and the pleasantries of a civilized, privileged life. I strip off my clothing layers from sleeping and change into my walking clothes. Dilip brings me a hot milky coffee with his usual good humour and gentle nature. I thank him and Poona for their kindness and the way they have looked after me on this epic journey through the mountains of Dolpo; through some of the most extraordinary Tibetan culture. They are a resilient people who I have tried my best to describe in this story, and who I will never forget for all they have taught me. They are a people I deeply respect and love because of their gentleness, their inner strength, and their cultural knowledge, several thousand years old.

In these constant cold temperatures, small things become irritating – like brushing teeth; the water is so cold; trying to dig a hole in frozen ground to crap, my hands do not work so well. It is no surprise my moods are often frayed during these experiences when I am at my most tired, exhausted, vulnerable; but this is why I come here – to test myself and to go beyond the normality of daily living in our comfortable Western homes, in comfortable cities, with comfortable jobs an eight-hour plane flight away, the carbon un-neutral aspect of my journey.

May our scientists soon develop a silent, carbon-neutral air vehicle. It's got to be at least on the drawing board somewhere. If we are capable of inventing enough 'military might' – *nuclear missiles, F118s, Iron Curtain, extreme weaponry, Predator Drones, Project Thor, The Ghost, Sea Dragon, Poseidon Missiles* – to name a few of our human creations currently developed in 2020, all of which could destroy life as we know it – we could invent a silent plane that is carbon neutral or better, one that cleans the atmosphere as it travels. Get to it chaps – no time to waste! *(29b)*

There is a light snow this morning and as we prepare to leave the ravens are calling; one of their feathers floats down to my boots; I pick it up instinctively and place it in a small hole in my hat, something my father would have done. According to one interpretation, a black raven feather is: "A message from angels, a message of protection, you're not alone; there is magic, balance, cunning, skill, boldness and release from past belief". I'm grateful for this feather and its meaning; it suits my circumstances very well, especially as I awoke feeling so fragile, exhausted from the cold after nearly twenty days of trekking to heights over 5,000 metres on several passes. I feel I'm in very good hands with Dilip and Poona – reminded by this feather floating down from the ravens and landing at my boot – extraordinary. *(29c)*

Dilip believes we have a half-day walk, and I'm very happy with that. We walked through the stone buildings of the village – four in total – with dried brown grass still growing on the roof. In many places along the river and creeks we pass bushes a metre high with bright red leaves, and now they are here again as the trail follows the Maduwa Khola River that takes us all the way to the Phoksundo Khola, which flows from the massive lake of the same name. The trail edges high along the mountainside, and in some places there are magnificent views to the snow-capped mountains to the west that form the boundary of the Shey Phoksundo National Park; Mukuteshwar Himal, Mutuchula Himal and Paile Himal – all over five thousand metres. To the south of these mountains, just ten kilometres as the raven flies, is Juphal where we will be heading for our flight back to Kathmandu within a week.

Below us in the farming valley there are remnant fields from harvesting this year's crops, barley and maize, but there were few people or livestock to be seen; they must have already begun their descent to warmer climes where they will take their grain and livestock to bargain and trade.

I stop on the trail to admire a huge Mani stone, some three metres long and two metres high, it looks to be work in progress and may have only been started in the last few years as the stone cuts still look fresh; there is more depth to be given to the Sanskrit. It will be a work of art and perhaps intended as a welcome into the village of Ringmo, which is now only an hour walk away.

At one point on this section of the trail the red leafed bush is mixed with clumps of light brown grass, forming a carpet-effect that disappears over the hillside to the river below; it's utterly beautiful. The months of May and June, when the rains come, must totally change this landscape into a valley of green where wildflowers abound.

The valley is narrowing and there are pine trees growing on the northern slopes where it gets more sun throughout the year. It is such a dramatic landscape and the southern slopes remain the barren lunar terrain we have been traversing for several days. As we turn to the north, we are walking in a pine forest with trees rising thirty metres; their bases a metre in diameter. The highest waterfall in Nepal comes into view to the west and it doesn't disappoint, with its massive water flow that cascades down two hundred metres. In May and June, it will roar with the monsoon rains and melting snow adding to the thunder and power of this dramatic landscape.

We are just thirty minutes walk from Ringmo village and soon we get views of the famous lake that stretches for seven kilometres north through the mountains towards Shey Monastery; it's over a kilometre wide and in 2004 its maximum depth was officially recorded at a hundred and forty-five metres. It's a strikingly turquoise blue colour that can change in intensity depending on the position of the sun and clouds. The local spelling of the lake has the syllable 'sum' – meaning three – and reflects the correct number of arms to this grand lake that sits 3,612 metres above the oceans. *(30)*

CHAPTER XIX

If light is in your heart, you will find your way home.
RUMI

Shey Phoksundo National Park came into existence in 1984, largely due to recommendations to the Nepalese government from zoologist George Schaller from the time he spent here in 1973 with Peter Matthiessen studying the bharal and the elusive snow leopard. They never actually saw the snow leopard; however, they did discover its scat not far from the northern end of Phoksundo Tal.

We cross the final bridge to Ringmo village, and Dilip seems to know exactly where he is going in terms of guesthouse selection. I'm lost again – in my mind – taken over by the chortens and Mani walls that greet us in several directions. I am to revisit these ancient treasures in the two days of restful wanderings I will have here. I can't thank these men enough – Dilip and Poona – for bringing me safely through this extraordinarily and unique landscape of Dolpo.

Somewhere below this bridge is the huge rock that Peter Matthiessen describes, which has the Buddhist prayer carved mid-stream – which meant whoever did the work must have swum out every day to chisel and carve and somehow lashed themselves to the rock as they carved. Alas, I didn't find this rock amidst all the other interesting things in this village, but its somewhere between the large waterfall and the village from Peter's description. It rings of Buddhist devotion:

"...and just above this bridge, in the roaring waters, is a boulder that was somehow reached by a believer, OM MANI PADME HUM has been carved there in mid-torrent, as if to hurl this mantra down out of the Himalayas to the benighted millions on the Ganges Plain." (2) Peter Matthiessen, p.135

Ringmo village blends into the landscape like Dho Tarap. The houses are made of river stones, flat roofs of timber and earth and – characteristically – on the roofs is the winter fodder, a red/orange colour, buckwheat cut, waiting to be fed to their domestic livestock throughout the winter. Buddhist flag poles abound on nearly every house rising five or more metres; the flags nearly always look new so the gods know these people are devout. It's their place in the world, so close to Tibet and the rich tapestry of the Bon religion that springs from there and reaches out across this world despite the Red Army's best attempts to crush the Tibetan people's spirit since 1959.

Ringmo has around two-hundred residents, mostly of Tibetan origin. Their ancient Tibetan religion, which uses the left-facing square swastika, is carved into cabinets and in earthen relief on the stupas and chortens that abound in this village.

Dilip leads us to a guesthouse on the north side of town just ten minutes' walk to the lake, and the landlady is a delightfully friendly woman; obviously her husband earns an honest living. One can only feel compassion, be caught stealing artefacts in this strongly etched Tibetan Buddhist land of Dolpo.

Very near the guesthouse are two large green tents where a wedding ceremony has been going for days, most likely the place our hung-over horseman with the fox fur hat had come from. We spot our friendly mule man in the red jacket from the valley before Dho Tarap. He is lining up to pay his respects and he gives us a big wave – so delightful to see him again. He is at least three days' ride from home and I wonder who is looking after his precious little daughter in the maroon gown; hopefully mum is not far away.

Two carpenters are working outside the guesthouse. They have almost finished two cabinets in a local pine timber, and they have carved the distinctive left-hand square swastika and continuous design that belongs to the Bon religion. I admire their work and they show appreciation that I'm so interested. Their tools include a large timber plane, a smaller steel plane, fret saw, chisels and clamps – all of which I have used when I too once made my living from working in timber, a trade and skill I loved as a young man. One of the men has a pencil stuck behind his ear. He has a friendly smile and the gentle poise of a man accomplished in his trade, and before him is an example of his skills that must be sought up and down these wealthy Himalayan valleys.

We are shown our rooms upstairs; mine has two beds on which I spread my gear and air my bedding. There is one small window which I won't need to open and a set of double doors that have been handcrafted. We are asked by the landlady to lunch in a large cosy lounge room opposite my room. It is decorated in timber cabinet work, most likely made by the carpenters outside. The cabinet timber has been stained a dark brown and around the walls are photographs, a Tibetan tea-making tool, and a dranyen. The atmosphere of this guesthouse is so much brighter than Dho Tarap where a dark black cloud hangs over the 'Caravan Guesthouse' and, sadly, will for many years.

Lunch is a rich blend of boiled potatoes, chillies and salt washed down by sweet black tea. I have come to love this dish that seems to ward off the cold weather and provide much needed carbohydrates – and the fact that I have learnt to keep my fingers away from my nose and eyes is simply a bonus. Dilip and Poona found great humour in my misfortune, but nothing has beaten the reversible camera 'show' just south of Dho Tarap – the gods too were laughing at this one – silly Westerner. The valley was resounding with laughter, and I was pleased the joke was on me!

I pack a water bottle and map into my day pack and head off to explore; it's a relief to be free of my seventeen-kilogram pack, made heavy with books I don't need on this trip. For some reason I wanted to carry *The Snow Leopard* to be reminded of the wonder of this trip – but I learned early on I had my own wonder on this trip, different to Peter Matthiessen's, but just as remarkable. And as a footnote, I don't do electronic screens when I read; I love the texture and feel of a paper book...but I understand this could be an over 50-year-old issue. I do however find reading unnecessary on these journeys as I'm so absorbed by what I'm seeing, immersed by my note taking; sleep takes precedence, breathing in and soaking up in awe of where I am, connected to the Himalayas. Why escape elsewhere into a book when it's all here for the taking and absorption, so to speak. I also carry the Dalai Lama's book, *The Power of Compassion* – now that I did read in small, nurturing amounts.

I have the greatest respect for the Fourteenth Dalai Lama, even more so since reading his autobiography and discovering his human qualities through his deeply rooted Buddhist eyes – such an extraordinary man, alive in 2020. A man driven from his cultural homeland of Tibet on 17 March 1959 to Northern India, when the Chinese Red Army invaded. The Chinese

Army were to be exposed for committing unspeakable crimes no different to the traumas and chaos of two world wars; the Tibetan people were killed, tortured, thrown into re-education camps, their ancient temples destroyed, and yet all through this time the Dalai Lama maintained a calm composure and has great hope for the strength and deep wisdom of his people to survive and retain their culture in lands other than Tibet. *(30a)*

"Tibet is also rich in other resources including lead, zinc, molybdenum, asbestos, uranium, chromium, lithium and much more. Tibet is China's only source of chromium and most of its accessible lithium is in Tibet. These raw materials are used in the manufacturing of household goods, computers and smart phones, among much else." This is the reason why the Chinese invaded Tibet in the first place – they wanted these raw materials for economic advancement globally. *(30b)*

The Dalai Lama's biggest concern to this day is the environmental damage caused by Chinese mining activities operating on the Tibetan Plateau; especially the extraction of raw materials such as uranium. It is the by products produced when mining these minerals that are His Holiness' major concern, as it could well affect future generations of humans, as well as native flora and fauna. However, he holds strongly to the fact that Buddhism is on the rise within China especially amongst the younger generations, and that is a positive point forward for the Earth...as is the fact that the majority of young people in China are now opposed to the illegal trade of ivory from Africa. *(30a)*

The Dalai Lama also holds great hope in his belief that his successor may well turn up in Europe, Australia or the United

IN THE FOOTSTEPS OF THE SNOW LEOPARD

States. Since the dispersal of his people to many countries across the planet due to the Chinese Red Army's invasion, the Buddhist gods may choose a Western country in which to birth him or her. In Buddhism we are a universal being and with the Dalai Lama still with us, the world is in good hands despite the seemingly insurmountable mountains of human made b/s. *(30a)*

Around from the alley where the carpenters work are five horses feeding on salt that the landlady has scattered onto a small tarpaulin. It's a helpful supplement for these animals with winter approaching; in Australia salt is offered to cattle when our blistering summer drains them of goodness and market value. An elder cow cocky from Galway Downs – a 1.5-million- acre property in far Western Queensland – once told me that when there's a drought these animals would survive by licking the gibber stones that stretch for miles. In the crevices and cracks of these stones are seeds and other vital nutrition for when the rains don't fall.

I'm heading to the lake which is taking on a deeper turquoise-blue colour as there is much cloud cover coming down to the lake from the north. A large black raven flies to the west and I see a way down to the lake edge where Buddhist flags abound. Two large green tents are pitched near this entrance; they appear to serve as a kitchen and dining room. I see Western men airing their sleeping bags, drying their tents and climbing equipment. They must be army, I think to myself, as the tents are all in a row and their hair is short, to military standard.

At the lake edge there is a small chorten supporting a flagpole three metres high and Tibetan prayer flags run off in multiple directions. I strip to my shorts and do my best to bath in the very cool waters. There is something magical about this lake as I look up the four kilometres to where it turns northwest for another three kilometres and then to the northeast for another kilometre; in total it is 494 hectares of lake. It's a deep turquoise colour today with the heavy white clouds almost touching the lake to the north.

There's a grey/white silt on the stones under the water for about ten metres and then the lake descends into a deep turquoise-blue that extends out across the water. I feel like I have it to myself – if I was in Europe there would be thousands of people and signs telling me what I can and can't do, power boats and water skis, but here it is just me, the lake, and these mountains – not forgetting the constant reminder of the Bon religion going back a thousand years or more. This world is so very beautiful as I fill my lungs with fresh Himalayan air, untouched by 'human noise'.

I can see the trail carved into the steep rock walls on the west side of the lake that heads to Shey Monastery, where I plan to go on my next visit – Part II of this journey. I have to be willing to pay US$500 for the privilege of going there; a Nepalese government fee which I trust will come back to this national park for the sole purpose of environmental research and trail maintenance.

I photograph a wispy grey/brown flower that so delicately hangs onto its metre-high stem waiting for the winds to blow it to the far corners of this land of Dolpo in preparation for the next growing season in March/April. The bushy red-leafed plants that frequented the trail on the last section heading into Ringmo are also growing, hanging onto life before the full affront of winter and the snow descends – the land will be bare, hibernating till spring in a boundless cycle on an Earth we humans are so fortunate to share – where life teems with natural splendour, too vast for words.

I follow the lake around to the start of this northern trail – it's tempting to just keep going as my body is tired but my spirit wants to spur me on. Shey Monastery, Crystal Mountain... the snow leopard! For now, though, this is where I will stop. I will finish this journey into Upper Dolpo and this story of what I discover here – *In the Footsteps of the Snow Leopard* – nearly fifty years on from Peter Matthiessen's journey.

It is humbling to be writing this story but even more so to be walking in the footsteps of Peter Matthiessen as he writes so commandingly; his knowledge is from a deep well of understanding particularly of Tibetan Buddhism, in which he is aided by Lama Anagarika Govinda, Dr David Snellgrove, John Blofeld, and Dr Evans-Wentz. I do not pretend to compare my knowledge and story with Peter's; my intention is more to build on his inspirational journey... this is my journey.

I am deeply inspired by Peter Matthiessen and George Schaller, and what they achieved back in 1973 with limited equipment and funds. My trip is made so much easier with the development of trails and particularly the suspension bridges, and food supplies – but not the plastic wrappings I find too often.

This is why my trip is in Peter's footsteps. I love the way he writes, the way he sees the landscape, the fauna and flora they find, his understanding of Tibetan Buddhist culture and, of course, the elusive snow leopard that places his wild spirit in these mountains for us and who, most certainly, watched Peter and George as they went about their zoologist work around Shey Monastery. A snow leopard who may well have spotted our small party of three, particularly around those wild, remote passes of Bagala and Numa La where we saw many tasty bharal but no spots of the snow leopard with its large heavy tail designed for balance and warmth and large paws designed to cross the snow at speed and assist with stealth for the kill. An intelligent animal we can but admire and respect as part of this vast universe – on this precious planet – barely a speck of dust to the gods.

"High above the lake George Schaller turns to wait; he points to something on the trail. Coming up, I stare at the droppings and mute prints for a long time. All around are rocky ledges, a thin cover of stunted juniper and rose. "It might be close by, watching us" murmurs George, "and we'd never see it." He collects the leopard scat, and we go on." (2) Peter Matthiessen, p.142

The mountains rising from the east are over 5,000 metres and have recent dustings of snow. I can make out a cluster of several stone buildings on the east side of the lake which is Thasung Choling Monastery. I will visit the monastery in the morning when I am fresh. For today, I am happy to sit next to the lake edge and ponder what we have achieved; making it here to Phoksundo Lake, one of the planet's most remarkable destinations... but please don't tell anyone. I don't want to come back and find 'human noise' – condos, water-skiing, jet skis or any other unnecessary noise from Western human beings who are lost in needing to find such amusements – lost in finding themselves and the traditional connections written into the Mani stones that mark this landscape in the land of Dolpo on Planet Earth, in a solar system, in a universe of unlimited wisdom and knowledge. Humanity is a blessed species to be part of this – it's our responsibility to treasure this privilege.

I walk to the small timber bridge that links the trail to Shey Monastery and Crystal Mountain from Ringmo village. It is time to stop; this is the end of my journey, for now. I know I will return to complete the second stage when the weather is not so close to winter; and with good fortune when COVID-19 allows us to travel again. I will look forward to connecting to Mother Earth and in turn connect to myself, this adventurous part of myself that yearns to explore lands of ancient cultures.

To write about these adventures, these Earth connections, far from my own Western culture is the true gift for me; being able to share and to inspire others. Somehow the development of a book cements a resource for future generations just like the hundreds if not thousands of Mani stones I have seen, that I have marvelled at and run my hands and fingers over – these ancient peoples telling me something of an ancient culture – and there is much to be learnt by their work, from hundreds and thousands of years ago. I believe we need this connection more than ever – we need to draw from this deep well of ancient wisdom, here in COVID-19 2020.

Being surrounded by the Bon culture is also helpful in this process of understanding; an Earth bound by a living breathing nature. We need these places like we need oxygen in our lungs; they sustain us, nurture us, and truly supply us with life, which comes with connecting to the heartbeat of our precious Earth. I need to go home and tell the world that economies need to speak of heart connection, human connection, and most importantly Earth connection. In Australia, this means moving on from coal as a means of bolstering our economy with the mantra of jobs, jobs, jobs – hollow as a black hole!

But let's stay in the peace and tranquillity of Bon religion and breathe deeply the air that is Dolpo, in the Himalayas, the Roof of The World. Breathe in fresh clean air, breathe out generations of Western afflictions; breathe in fresh Himalayan air, breathe out generations of Western afflictions and repeat and repeat...breathe in fresh clean air of the land of Dolpo, Bon religion...breathe out generations of Western afflictions.

I turn – rather reluctantly – back towards Ringmo, passing what has to be a small army camp; I will investigate that further tomorrow. As I walk back into the village, I see a small boy, about eight, with a basket on his back picking up goat and sheep dung – earning his pocket money by providing fuel for his family. Ask a Western boy to do that – I'd guess he'd be far more interested in an electronic Game Boy made in China where he learns to kill aliens or zombies – about as much Earth connection as a plastic wrapped lolly.

May we become the Earth-focussed species we are meant to be – for every day of our lives – in Earth-focussed cities run by Earth-focussed governments for the future of humanity – for the future of this life-sustaining planet. We cannot escape this duty, this call for Earth-focussed responsibility.

CHAPTER XX

*The light that shines in the eye
is really the light in the heart.*
RUMI

The wedding celebrations in Ringmo village are still ongoing. There are over twenty older women who enter the tent with elaborate headdresses and brass-plated garments; these are traditional Tibetan costumes. Traditionally the brother and other relatives give a dowry that they can afford, to help the couple on their journey together.

I meet up with Dilip and Poona at the guesthouse; they are feasting on hot potato chips, deep fried in oil. I ask for a bucket of hot water with which to bathe; I'm told the toilet downstairs, outside and round the corner from the main entrance, is where 'silly bloody tourists' go to bathe. There is no room to strip off, never mind bathe, and the smell of this toilet is well developed from many years of no maintenance, so I exit and forget all modesty, choosing the small garden to strip to my undies – not caring that a wedding is happening less than fifty metres away. It takes me only a few minutes to bathe and re-dress into fresh clothes. I take my time washing my dirty trekking clothes, and hang them in my room. They will freeze outside overnight and besides, a horse may come in search of Western fodder – or possibly a thief seeking Buddhist relics.

The late afternoon light is upon us and I now have five layers of clothing on. The bath stirs my bloodstream – it was worth it, every refreshing droplet – this silly Western activity so close to winter. I get the feeling the locals don't often partake in such rituals between September and April, if at all, from birth to death. But I did hear the complaints from a boisterous three-year-old in Dhorpatan, nothing a lolly wrapped in plastic didn't fix. Huh!

Upstairs in the handsome lounge I ask for rice wine, and sit with Dilip and Poona who are still chewing on hot potato chips. They are tasty, mixed with salt and chilli. An elderly man comes in to join us by the fire. The landlady barks at him, then serves him tea. I wonder what he has done wrong – they are obviously related; perhaps he is the father-in-law, has little money, and therefore has to accept his daughter-in-law's tongue...or maybe it is her father whom she doesn't like. She barks at him several times, scolding him like a child. I feel for the elderly man but I know nothing of the details and don't want to interfere. I ask Dilip to translate but he shrugs his shoulders as if to say, "Enjoy the rice wine and warmth of the fire, Mr Tim," so I do.

The night is full of celebration for the wedding party and in the lounge room of our guesthouse sleep four musicians who stumbled in at 5.00am, their half-full rum glasses sitting next to them. I enjoy the singing and celebrations from my bedroom; Dilip tells me we could have gone to the wedding, but I am happy to have slept even if the night air was one of jubilance and celebration for the union of this Tibetan couple. I pray they have a long and prosperous life together. They certainly seem to have the support of the whole Dolpo community, including the kind mule man who cooked our breakfast in the deep valley before Dho Tarap.

Three attractive young Tibetan women join us for breakfast in their traditional dresses and help the landlady, who works hard to keep her guesthouse going – there are horses, goats and chickens to feed, and a constant flow of visitors. The Tibetan tea runs out and I offer my glass to one of the women, who finds this very funny; I can only guess as to what gender gap I just breached in my Western ignorance.

The night was as cold as expected but I was warm, with my many layers and a comfortable bed. After a delicious Tibetan breakfast of fried eggs on chapati I leave Dilip and Poona to enjoy the local hospitality while I head off to visit the monastery on the eastern side of Phoksundo Lake, a forty-minute walk contouring around the edge of this majestic lake of deep turquoise; it is no surprise there are precious Tibetan stones of this colour worn by the women, mostly around their necks.

It turns out the army camp is in fact British. I talk to one of the men; he is a Nepalese Gurkha and speaks very good English. He tells me of their aborted climb just two days ago; a peak near Shey Monastery. It's less than six thousand metres in elevation but the weather closed in on them and one of their men had to be rescued by helicopter due to altitude sickness; even the military are not immune to such illness.

He tells me their party consists of eight English personnel and eight Gurkha/Nepalese personnel; he is the Gurkha captain while the English captain is the only woman on this expedition. I make a mental note to try and talk with this young woman, and learn more of her skills and bravery to command this contingent of sixteen British Army personnel; something unheard of in the days of my father, a British Army lieutenant in the Royal Horse Artillery. How impressive are these times, where women are seen as leaders in what were traditionally only male gender roles.

I leave him to continue airing his gear along with the other men, but the female captain is not to be seen; none of them are wearing army clothing or badges of rank. Their gear could be that of any civilian expedition – but there is a definite air of the military about them.

There is a herd of twenty black yaks on the far eastern bank heading to the lake edge – it's obviously time for morning ablutions as they charge in like nine-hundred-kilogram bulls, which of course they are. They drink and stand up to their stomachs in the icy waters. I just pray they don't crap in the beautiful, pristine turquoise water and send their 'blessing' down to the plains of Nepal. But that is highly unlikely; their turds probably weigh ten kilograms...urrgh...hence the reason I treat my drinking water. Surely there are more godly things we could be talking about? Like the monastery on the eastern side of the lake.

The trail to the monastery is well formed and passes through large pine trees that filter the morning sunshine and the deep turquoise lake to the west. There is an elderly man heading towards me who I assume is from the monastery. He carries an axe and looks none too friendly. He seems to be objecting to me passing this way, but I insist my presence at the monastery is honourable and peaceful; please take your 'madness' up into the trees to chop and collect fire wood for the resident lama. I'm impressed by my non-verbal communication as the 'clouds' part and I can continue on my way with a brisk pace in case he follows me. Fortunately, firewood collecting is his goal rather than rousting a tourist who means no harm.

I'm guessing the stone structures to be three hundred years old as they are crumbling to gravity and limited footings. Before me are a row of eight chortens, three metres high in two square-ish layers, with the characteristic earthen relief decoration that now seems synonymous with this region.

They are in various stages of repair, and I am pleased to discover that rebuilding funds have clearly made it to this cultural epicentre – the Bon religion is alive and well. Mani stones feature in nearly every direction I walk, beautifully carved deeply into the rock with impressive lines that spell out their Tibetan heritage.

The Tibetan flags rise from the chortens and run across to other flagpoles near the lake, forming a criss-crossed message of love and compassion. The legend goes that this place was once shelter to hunters who killed many animals in the area – a Buddhist lama made claim to the land and, in so doing, protected the animals that lived there. Several of the buildings had the Bon swastika embossed on the walls and a decorated small timber window – weathered dark brown – was high up on one wall, as if to provide a vantage point to spy on those approaching. It certainly had an impressive decorative appearance about it, and I had seen these windows in other Buddhist monasteries. *(31)*

In the process of exploring the buildings and discovering the main doors to the temple locked – we know of thieves in these parts – I was greeted by three British Army officers, not that I realised at the time, as they were wearing civilian North Face clothing. One was the Gurkha captain who I'd met earlier, and another Gurkha who spoke beautiful English, and then one, all 167cm of her, was a woman! The really odd thing was I didn't connect the dots until much later in the day; she was the captain of this British Army expedition – "stone the crows!" as we say in the land 'down under'. How wonderful for this Western woman knocking over traditional barriers – the Buddhist gods were cheering too. *(o)*

IN THE FOOTSTEPS OF THE SNOW LEOPARD

The British Army contingent of three had the resident lama in tow and he was more than happy to open the temple doors. Inside was revealed the most beautiful of Buddhist shrines with a deep red-coloured mask that looked as fierce as the devil himself. He had a large third eye and glowing white eyes and teeth. The artist had used a gloss paint to emphasise contrast. On the other side of the room was a deep blue mask with more white skulls and a third eye painted directly onto the forehead – fearsome.

Paintings decorated the walls in all range of colour, some showing ferocity while others showed love and kindness. On one side, painted directly onto timber slats, are the burning deep blue deities with three faces, wide white eyes, and sharp fangs. Around the tops of the heads are seven smaller white skulls. They ride on a red horse with gaping white teeth, and the head of a man hangs from the horse as though his body is squashed by the raging blue deity. Behind all of this are raging orange flames that come out in all directions; one of the six arms of the blue deity holds a large steel sword in a threatening pose – there is no 'loving kindness' in this painting whatsoever – the devils within have come out to play! On either side of this painting are two more of equal ferocity. *(33)*

On the opposite wall are the same blue deities but in a peaceful lotus pose; they look out into the room with passionate embraces in two parts of the painting. There are no aspects of life left out of these Buddhist works. The colours are deep blue, yellow, orange, red, green and white. In all there are fifteen deities in various stages of telling a story about life through this ancient Bon religion. The 'bird-man' I have seen before at Kopan; he stands with blue feet and fluffy feathered white legs and a beak that holds a snake stretched out between his arms; behind are the blue wings symbolising the bird with blue tail feathers. I conclude these are teachings as represented by the Dharma; the cosmic law and order as applied to the teachings of the Buddha and as a way to avoid these fiery beasts coming into your life as portrayed here. Lesson 1: don't steal Buddhist artefacts or ignore these wild deities; they represent great purpose. *(31a) (33)*

The shrine itself is no more than thirty years old. The gold-coloured Buddha sits nearly a metre high with a crown of embedded coloured stones. The Buddha is draped in green and yellow cloth with a special white material on which the Eight Auspicious Symbols of Buddhism have been embossed. There was a large brass drum, trumpet and cymbals on the left side of the room, ready for the next puja to celebrate the Buddhist deities. They do enjoy their puja, these fun loving, sincerely happy Buddhists. I had met them in Kopan – the monks exuded vitality and a deeply felt happiness; a life free of Western burdens. *(32)*

The beams above the shrine are decorated with intricate designs and paintings of a mythical dragon, complete with leopard spots and I wonder, was this meant to represent the snow leopard? On the left side there is a sculpture of a ten-armed deity with three heads decorated vertically with gold crowns; the main head has ears stretched from wearing heavy stone earrings. She is made of plaster and wears a red cloth with the same auspicious symbols draped around her, covering eight of her ten arms. *(33)*

On the opposite wall was another sculpture of an eighteen-arm deity with serious anger issues; white ferocious teeth and skulls hung down his sides. His five heads are displayed horizontally, looking equally ferocious. Draped up his body is a woman surrendering herself to him in an exciting, erotic manner – lucky bugger I think to myself, as I make my way to the door.

It was indeed a great experience to have been able to see such an interesting shrine so alive with the Bon religion in 2020. This traditional Buddhist religion was flourishing in one of the remotest parts of the Himalayas. I left a donation with the Lama to thank him for a very special tour and to honour him for being here, nurturing the love of Bon on the banks of Phoksundo Lake. May the water-skiers, condos, gambling dens and every other conceivable Western menace FOREVER stay away...and of course they will; the gods will be very clear about that.

"When B'on was the great religion of the Land of B'od, of which this religion was once part, there was a village where this lake now lies. In the eighth century, the great Buddhist saint Padme Sambhava, the "Lotus-Born", came to Phoksundo with the intent of vanquishing the mountain demons. To this end, he persecuted the B'on demoness who, fleeing his wrath, gave these villages a priceless turquoise, making them promise not to reveal that she had passed this way. But Padme Sambhava caused the turquoise to be turned to dung, upon which the villagers, concluding that the demoness had tricked them, betrayed her whereabouts. In revenge, she wreaked upon them a disastrous flood that drowned

IN THE FOOTSTEPS OF THE SNOW LEOPARD

the village beneath turquoise waters." (2) Peter Matthiessen, p.134

In the afternoon I go to inspect the hydro scheme under the suspension bridge that was built in 2014 with funding by the World Wildlife Fund and several American not-for-profits. It's an impressive structure built of concrete, but the hydro blades have been knocked out of action by the monsoonal rains. There does not appear to be any protection for the hydro blades from floating tree trunks or perhaps the sheer power of the water, which quite possibly washed the hydro blades down to India or at least the southern lowlands of Nepal. The blades are nowhere to be seen; the concrete structure sits and waits for repair by someone who holds the blueprints and can make the necessary adjustments for them to work in these powerful waters of the Himalayas. That may take some time – the gods will consult and tell us when they are ready. But the problem remains – Western blue prints, the power of the Himalayas, Bon religion – a formidable mix.

Back up near the village, I find a man busily shaping a wooden plough out of timber. I'm excited to witness this very important job, and obviously he feels it necessary to be prepared for next year's harvest. He is nearly finished and must have put several days' labour into building the plough as all around him are piles of timber shavings that only a carpenter can make. He has used a local pine timber and I ask if I can take a photo of him with his craft, so essential to these villages' wellbeing. He is not very interested in a Westerner taking a photo of his handmade wooden plough; "Can't you get a diesel tractor air-lifted into here?", he says. My answer is as Buddhist as I can get, "But your work is important for your village, thank you for sharing your skills and love for your people – you don't need a bloody diesel tractor dripping oil and other pollutants in this otherwise pristine land. Next, you'll want chemical fertilizers air dropped. Why don't you people listen to your Gods? What's more, you are teaching me!"

I enter the chorten near the suspension bridge to study more closely the paintings of deities that appear on all four walls high up near the ceiling. They are painted with nine mandalas – all are different, but they share the bright colours of Bon. The deities are much calmer than those in the gompa by the lake, with a pattern of three main deities surrounded by many smaller ones in rows, perhaps one hundred to each wall. One wall has the flaming deity of the protector, Guru Dragpo, complete with white skulls above his head and a leopard skin draped around his body. *(33)*

What strikes me most about these paintings is the use of colour – bright reds, greens, blues, yellows, oranges and white; the overall effect is bright and life-enriching when one stands below them in a building purpose-built to show that this is Dolpo and here is their Bon religion. In this relatively small village, there are five of these structures, mostly at the entrances; a welcome to visitors and an acknowledgement of what they stand for as a people – a culture that is ancient, at least 2,000 years old.

"...we question everyone about Kang-La and Shey Gompa, as the crowd gives off that heartening smell of uncultivated peoples the world over, an earthy but not sour smell of sweat and fire smoke and the oil of human leather. Goats, a few sheep, come and go. Both men and women roll sheep wool on hand

spindles, saying that blizzards have closed Kang La for the winter. On the roofs, culled buckwheat stacked for winter fodder has a bronze shine in the dying sun, and against a sunset wall, out of the wind, an old woman with clean hair turns her old prayer wheel, humming, humming." (2) Peter Matthiessen, p.136**

I cross the bridge to the east side where we first entered the town. The late afternoon light is shining and I sit and watch the many women who have been gathering winter fodder into their large cane baskets. They stop briefly, and sit next to me to catch their breath – I so wish I could talk with them, but we seem to manage communicating silently with acknowledgment and respect for our human connection of some 100,000 years. Namaste!

They then head across the bridge with the one last output of energy required to get them home for the day. Some have baskets full of goat and cow dung that they will dry and use for fuel over the winter months. Not all in the town leave for warmer climes; some must remain to keep an eye out for thieves and bandits. The suspension bridge was built by the British Gurkhas in 2015/16; how much easier and safer village life has become thanks to these foreign investments.

I walk back into the village and see an elderly lady collecting cow dung in the apron of her dress. I walk past, a little ashamed to be wearing AU$120 sandals, AU$80 trousers, AU$150 thermals, AU$40 Merino gloves, AU$40 thermal beanie, AU$400 down jacket and AU$280 outer jacket. I am humbled by my privilege, yet I have such admiration for what these people have – a strong, tightly knit community, a dependency on one another to survive, a connection far closer to the Earth than any of us in the West know, unless we are driven to find it.

I realise this is what drives me, and has done since I was nineteen when I rode my motorcycle to the tip of Cape York to spend many nights under the heavens, connecting to the natural cycles of the Earth; marvelling at a full moon over the waters of the Kennedy River and hunting with the Indigenous peoples from Lockhart River Mission who accepted me into their tribe. Now, some thirty-nine years on, my adult children flown from the roost, and I seek this solace again, this need to understand indigenous culture and to hear the silent heartbeat of Planet Earth.

I recognise this as my underlying journey in this world; it's what I seek to be part of and, most of all, to share with those who may not wish to make this journey yet want to understand the calling of Planet Earth, to understand the deeper knowledge of connection and wisdom that indigenous peoples the world over have known for tens of thousands of years.

I believe the time has come – particularly in the West – to incorporate this knowledge into our lives; *et mulieres sapientes* have always known, but for the past two hundred or more years we have stepped away from Mother Earth through industrialisation, mechanisation and now digitisation. It's time for a quiet, peace-loving reformation to claim back what is our birthright as human beings, and may the Buddhist deities cheer from the balconies of Boudhanath, Mecca, St Paul's, St Peter's Basilica, Blue Mosque, Imam Mosque, Batu Caves, Duomo Di Milano, Koutoubia Mosque, Notre Dame, Meenakshi Amman, La Sagrada Familia, Saint Basil's

Cathedral, Muhammad Ali Mosque, the Great Mosque of Mecca, Glastonbury Tor, Swayambhunath and the central deserts of Australia. Namaste!

I pass a woman working on a loom in the forecourt of her home. These machines of timber, fibre, and an extraordinary amount of love have been passed down through generations; this woman sits with the timber spools in her hands, and before her the white base strings with which she will build a traditional woollen fabric. I love to see her face with the knowing satisfaction that comes from generations of knowledge woven into a well-supported community. I just need to bottle ten thousand litres of this knowledge to take back to the West – *et mulieres sapientes*!

She feels a part of her village as does the ploughman, the women who collect firewood and fodder for their livestock, the carpenters who build the cabinets for our landlady, and the lama who showed us through his Tibetan gompa. I'm but a traveller here, but I have been shown so much, and I have learnt so much from these wonderfully intelligent people. I feel such gratitude for this window, this opening into their lives that has existed as far back as my own family from Mercia, as it was known from 527AD. *(33a)*

I like the story from Poona, translated by Dilip in the late afternoon at our guesthouse while sipping tea and smoking cigarettes. Poona's ancestors are from Mongolia, which is evident in his darker skin, more rounded face, and thinner eyes. They were a nomadic people and most of their violent warlike activity was to the north into Russia, west into the Middle East, and south into China and Tibet. Genghis Khan, who lived in the thirteenth century, was the most formidable of these Mongolian warlords, a man of extraordinary ability and drive. *(34)*

Poona believes his family crossed into Nepal in the eighteenth century from Tibet, and possibly passed on this very route we had travelled from Beni. He is certainly a man I want on my side with his incredible strength, calm, and respectful manners – his ancestors' warrior blood running through his veins. I can picture Poona in Mongolian military armour, ready to push forward with the next conquest. However, in 1990 a peaceful revolution was conducted that saw the Mongolian People's Republic overthrown, and cease to exist in 1992. In 2002 Mongolia was recognised as a democracy by Taiwan, paving the way forward to her own autonomy. *(34)*

And having got to know Poona, even without the gift of language over this twenty-four-day journey, I see him as a gentleman with a strong heart who loves to smoke, sip tea and get the job done when it came to crossing the high passes with thirty kilograms on his back supported by that ingenious head-strap that propels him forward. At the conclusion of this trek, in Giri's office, I have an envelope that I had carried in my money belt the whole journey next to my passport and visa; US$100, which is a considerable sum of money to him, but worth every dollar to me. I am delighted to offer this to him in gratitude.

I give Dilip the same amount – US$100. He is more used to such gifts, but to Poona this was a gift from the gods, and he came to me as I sat in Giri's office with his hands outstretched, the white envelope in his hands, head bowed – he was so very grateful – as I was for his abilities on this journey. It was my pleasure to offer this gift with gratitude and love.

That evening I show the elderly man my photos of the gompa while his daughter-in-law yells at him and pours him more Tibetan tea – maybe he is just deaf? The elderly man is thrilled to see my photos, and appreciation for his culture; this precious Bon religion he has known all his life. He has brown timber Tibetan beads around his neck that he threads through his fingers. There is much I want to ask him but for now we enjoy each other's company while his daughter-in-law continues to yell at him. For all I know she could be just asking what he would like for dinner, but somehow the tone is more like; "Why did you gamble the family's money away?" I do so hope it is the first response for this family's sake.

A woman enters the room wearing a deep blue headscarf, black clothing, a wide colourful woollen mid-rift, Tibetan beads around her neck, colourful bangles on her wrists, silver and turquoise blue earrings the size of my thumbnail. She is a striking figure and good friends with the landlady. Two younger women enter dressed in a similar way; one looks to be pregnant, and I smile as only a man can in the presence of such beautiful feminine energy. These women work hard, as does the landlady; I can see their strong hands have calluses from working to support their village and people. They do their share in this unforgiving cold landscape where tonight the temperature will drop well below zero.

A young man comes in and sits behind me. It seems he is the butt of some joke amongst the younger women; he carries a small stringed instrument, a dranyen, and begins to play. I find it lovely, no matter what he has done wrong. I take a guess that he has an interest in one of the younger women but she's clearly not interested – that could be his crime, being too persistent when the answer is NO!

The younger women eat oatmeal porridge by the teaspoon like it's a treat in these parts; maybe it is laced with wild honey or sugar, but they are having an enjoyable feast of it despite the advances from the young man who is playing his dranyen – an instrument that has belonged to these mountains for as long as the paintings I found in the gompa today that tell the story of Bon religion.

Poona and Dilip are busy behind me eating potatoes, salt and chilli; I join them with my rice wine. They offer no explanation as to the proceedings before us so I too focus on the potatoes, which are freshly cooked and delicious. This is the third time I forget about the chilli on my fingers and go to scratch my eye, and then my nose, which by this time has erupted into a flaming fire equivalent to the paintings I was walking amongst earlier today. The landlady is the first to jump to my aid – it's a common problem in these parts, even for the locals. She offers a cool, wet cloth to place on my eye. Dilip and Poona chuckle to themselves; "It must be time he learns the lesson, silly Westerner. So good he doesn't speak Nepalese, chuckle, chuckle, chuckle."

It is the twenty-first day of our journey, and only three days until we are to fly back to Kathmandu from Juphal; a three-day trek with an elevation loss of over 1,200 metres. Our journey is drawing to a close and my body is grateful for this, and for the two friends I have made on this journey; Dilip and Poona. We have shared some remarkable experiences, from the bizarre when the young women wanted us to help her gain freedom in that cold vulture-ridden deep valley – I wished I could have done more, but as a traveller I only knew some of the story – to the funny, when the landlady in Dhorpatan compares her potatoes with Dilip and Poona's testicles and probably mine for that matter – I just wished I'd stayed up for that one , and then to exhaustion when we climbed the two high passes, Bagala and Numa La, at over 5,000 metres.

In all we crossed seven passes together – the sheer beauty, remoteness and connection I felt with the Earth was incredible. These are special experiences I shared with Dilip and Poona; they are precious memories I will have until it's my turn to accept the Buddhist wisdom; that life is impermanent and detachment is an important learning on this journey through an often precarious life from which no human, no sentient being, escapes alive, Samsara.

CHAPTER XXI

Whatever happens, just keep smiling and lose yourself in love.
RUMI

As we depart from the village of Ringmo heading south-way west, we pass through the winding village lanes in the early morning light, smoke spiralling up through the sunshine from these quaint buildings that form part of the landscape with their stone frames and flat timber roofs with animal fodder and firewood stored above. Many buildings rise four metres, and some use horizontal timbers every two metres to support the stone structure. It's simple yet marvellously effective way to cope with the ground movement caused by the Himalayan tectonic plates.

We come to the final chorten on the southwest gate to the village and we say our farewells to Ringmo. I know I will be back – there must be a Tibetan word for this – as they are such a travelling, exploring people – Namaste! The white and earthen-coloured chorten was built at least three hundred years ago, and has a Mani stone wall running off to the south. It is a gateway, both welcoming and, in our case, farewelling. Hopefully with the blessings of the gods we will be back to this chorten; the gateway to Ringmo, Phoksundo Lake, Shey Monastery, Crystal Mountain and Saldang…and to finding the snow leopard.

I would like to come back to sit in this place and listen to the Earth, silently, deeply – and I may even sight a snow leopard; but as Peter Matthiessen and George Schaller both discovered in the 1970s, this is an unlikely outcome – it's just the allure and the reason to visit. A snow leopard is too wild, too instinctive, too clever – tapped into the Earth's vibrations – to be spotted by humans. The real reason for me to come here I have learnt; my purpose for this trip is for the connection to Mother Earth amongst a Tibetan culture easily as old as my own from Mercia, over 7,000 kilometres to the north-west.

The trail takes us over the top side of the massive waterfall we could see on our way into Ringmo. There are many scree slopes and areas needing repair work from the washouts which can only get worse in the monsoonal rains of April and May. No trail can withstand this sort of movement for more than a few months, and I wonder who is responsible for its upkeep and maintenance. It's a specialised job by people who have assisted journeys like mine and those who carry food, equipment, village goods and caterpillar mushroom 'gold'. These trails must stay open no matter what the climate throws at these resilient people.

As the trail turns south into the main valley there are several villages with significant building projects in the final stages of completion. One village has a new medical centre two storeys high, and another has a new school three storeys high, with a brilliant bright-blue roof the colour of the sky. I continue down into the valley hoping they have used cyclone grade batten screws...another roof uplifting would be too much to bear.

The trail stays close to the roaring Phoksundo Khola River as it hurtles down the valley through pine forests and large rock outcrops. In places there are small clusters of farm buildings abandoned for the winter. We pass a team of bullocks well laden with produce for Ringmo; three men walk with them. Below the trail the turquoise waters thunder through the boulders as they have done for millennia. The sun barely makes it into these parts, and steep ridges rise from the river with pine trees growing precariously, waiting for their turn to fall victim to gravity and the ground's inability to hold any permanence. Nothing in this life holds permanence – we humans from the West just like to think so.

"Disputing the path is a great copper-coloured grasshopper, gleaming like amber in the sun; so large is it, and so magical its shimmer, that I wonder if this grasshopper is not some old *naljorpa*, advanced in the art of taking other forms. But before such a "perfected one" can reveal himself, the grasshopper springs carelessly over the precipice, to start a new life hundreds of feet below. I choose to take this as a sign that I must entrust myself to life, and thanking the grasshopper, I step out smartly on my way." (2) Peter Matthiessen, p.125

Some of the trees we pass are nearly a metre in diameter, tall and straight – a logger's dream in the West – but here they will remain until they die of old age or are pulled into the currents below by gravity and become part of the river's tangled web, a wilderness which is part of this valley that has been travelled for at least several thousand years.

By mid-afternoon we reach the small village of Chepka, elevation 2,678 metres, where we will stop for the night. It too clings to the banks of the river with agricultural land rising up into the hillsides. I decide another 'bath' is in order as a bucket of hot water can be purchased for 200NPR (AU$3). There is a campsite on the north side of the village which the British Army contingent has taken over along with their eight-strong party of porters and guides, not forgetting the six mules. They are very polite and some of the Englishmen address me by my first name which I find extraordinary, as I haven't really talked with them as much as I would have liked. The captain is happy and greets me with "Hello" but nothing more; she must know I'm writing a book. Obviously, this is a 'top-secret mission' for Her Majesty's government. I was waiting for 007 to appear from the skies by parachute to deliver their secret documents, but thankfully it didn't happen. I found a spot for my 'bath' right next to the bog hole that one of the Gurkhas helps me to flush clean with a gallon bucket of water.

It was a productive, fertile village with several cows tethered beneath the buildings, and red chillies drying in the sun on tarpaulins three metres square. A man weaves a basket just like Poona's; his strong hands work skilfully with the slats of bamboo. Rows and rows of corncobs dried in every possible location that caught the winds or sunlight. Some of the rows of corn had dead crows tied above them to remind the living crows this will be their fate if they eat the corn. God knows what they killed the unlucky crows with; a shotgun I guessed, or maybe a lure trap using grain.

We spend the evening talking with the friendly British Army Gurkhas and a group of school children travelling with their teachers. In all, about twenty of us sat in this travellers' den. One of the Gurkha soldiers who spoke very good English was helping a little girl about seven years of age with her homework, and I was also very happy to help these eager, smiling children that made my heart melt. My good friend Steve Bellamy, who wrote the foreword to this book, set up an Australian charity, *The Pencil Tree,* to help Tibetan children just like these little gems with so much potential, sitting with me in this travellers' den.

None of these men looked like soldiers in their civilian

clothing; they had the gentlest of manners and were very well educated, representing the elite of Nepal's military force, connected to the British Army for over two hundred years. And here they were sitting around a fire in some of the world's most beautiful wilderness helping a seven-year-old Tibetan girl with her English lesson. It was enough to make a grown man choke on tears at the thoughtfulness, and deep love this man – this soldier – had for his people and culture.

My bedroom is on the second level and it requires skill to negotiate its access; first I must make my way through the flurry of cooks and porters busily preparing dinner for the British Army. Then there is a set of stairs steep and narrow enough to be more of a ladder, the only distinguishing factor is the hand-width step treads. Then I must negotiate two low doorways, and walk along a narrow corridor with timber windows that open onto the street – one last low doorway, and there is my little room packed with bags of grain for the winter. Fortunately, I don't suffer from hay fever or the night would be sniffingly long.

At breakfast I am offered a rare treat – mountain oats as Dilip describes them. Essentially these are oats ground almost to powder after which Tibetan tea is poured over the top. It has an earthy flavour that comes from these mountains. I am appreciative – certainly it must be nutritious. I tell them about the 'soccer game' that was going on in the ceiling of my room – rats they say! Yes, that did come to mind. I tried to explain that at home we have a 'rat poison' for such jobs, but it seemed to land on deaf ears. These animals are sacred and I certainly wasn't going to 'rock the rat boat' of Buddhist belief.

On the trail heading south soon after leaving Chepka we

come across a small hydro plant operating from a river flowing in from the east. There is a two-hundred-millimetre steel pipe feeding a turbine that is locked inside a small box-shaped building. From the east, in goes the steel pipe at a forty-five-degree angle, and on the west side of the building out come electrical wires that feed a transformer; from there the wires run up and down the valley delivering power to several smaller villages. It is almost magical in its creation and delivery, just a shame about all the suspended wires that ruin my wilderness photographs, huh!

I was thinking of home and wondered how long I would greet people with the Earth connecting phrase:

Namaste* – *"I honour the place in you in which the entire universe dwells. I honour the place in you which is of love, of truth, of light and of peace. When you are in that place in you and I am in that place in me, we are one!"

I will be contacting our Prime Minister and religious leaders to tell them we have it all wrong and the Australian 're-education' camps must be established not just in the deserts of Australia where our indigenous people lived but also up here in the mountains close to Tibet – this way we can connect with *"Namaste"* daily. Forget about our obsession with the economy and especially our preoccupation with that nineteenth century fuel called coal. Up here in the north-west Himalayas can be found the true meaning of life; clean air, water, food, shelter – an Earth focus with daily meditation eight hours per day. I'm very sure the Fourteenth Dalai Lama would agree with me; so, let's get cracking chaps, a new world order awaits us.

On a high section of the trail on the western side we meet a mule team of six with two men leading the way. The mules are well-loaded with what looks like grain, but it is the head mule I find most entertaining. He's wearing a grandiose headdress that stands nearly one metre above his head, with flowing white mule hair hanging down, decorated with gold Buddhist scarfs. The mule has a large metal bell around his neck, with a chain of bells and more gold Buddhist scarfs tied on for effect. The animal seems quite unperturbed, simply happy to be doing his job, eyes and ears looking forward with the alert attention of any lead horse. To me this animal was a walking embodiment of this colourful culture, going about his day. I keep wanting more of these people, their culture, and connection to the universe.

After several hours of walking in the fresh mountain air following the pounding, fast-flowing river, we come to a small open area with a tea tent, several walnut trees, and lots of places to 'park' mules. Dilip orders our tea, and then we set about trying to break and extract some of the walnuts. This is no mean feat, as these are wild trees so the nut is not so developed as the ones we can buy in our supermarkets. The flesh of the nut is so entwined in the kernel it becomes a numbing experience rather than enjoying a fleshy reward, so we go into the tent and sip our tea. Dilip and Poona chat with the tent man who has a five-year-old boy – but where is mum? – I think to myself. The dad is an attentive parent, so I relax and sip my tea. *(28)*

In Peter Matthiessen's time there were none of these modern steel suspension bridges and I think of all the crossings we have made so easily this morning. In Peter Matthiessen's time, it would have been achingly cold and dangerous in the fast-flowing waters hanging onto ropes tied to rocks or trees; their leather boots heavy with water and their packs weighing them down. Their porters may not have been happy to be there; their payment was meagre and the conditions were tough for sixty-four days.

With warm tea in our bellies we continue southward, losing elevation with every step. We make it to a small village high above the river for lunch, and the British Army contingent catches up to us. I don't envy the size of their party and the scurry of effort the porters must go through every day to make breakfast, lunch and dinner for their party of twenty-five. I can only think of all the things that can go wrong... and sure enough one of the kerosene cookers from the 'last century' is leaking, and no pressure can be maintained. I see if I can assist as I have some surgical tape that might just hold under the pressure. I get a 'gold star look' from the cook; I just hope it holds for the duration of their trip.

I so prefer the simplicity of our team; a caring guide and porter who are willing to do whatever it takes to get this Western man through this high-altitude landscape. I continue to feel gratitude for Dilip and Poona's kindness on this twenty-four-day journey, prompted by Peter Matthiessen some fifty years ago – may I help pave the way for another generation of hikers who seek answers for themselves, and for our world. This Himalayan landscape is mind-expanding to say the least, along with the Tibetan culture that just fits with these mountains that form the *Roof of the World!*

While waiting for lunch I peek into the local store to see what delights are there. I am quickly repelled as I see the "C" drink, lollies by the jar full, bubble gum, chips, dry noodles in plastic packets and a further assortment of Western inspired 'stuff'. I go out into the sunshine to regain my composure and see a pomegranate tree with hardened fruit from last season. These fruits remind me of my father – he was forever impressed by their composition. When they are cut open their delicate red fleshy seed is wrapped so tightly that one can barely extract enough to eat. And there are layers of rough skin that hold the fleshy seeds. It is a fruit to admire but not really worth the effort, in my humble opinion – best left to European painters of the eighteenth century.

I try one last time to 'crack the British Army vault' and talk with the Army captain. She sees me at fifty paces and buries her head into the game of poker she plays with four other men; her back firmly turned towards me. OK, I understand, you don't want to talk about how you became a captain in the British Army – nothing was going to allow that to happen – so I left them to their poker game and cigarettes.

At this point on the trail the British Army and their entourage of porters, cooks and guides were turning southeast to Dunai where we knew of a man in prison for stealing Buddhist artefacts; we were heading west to Juphal and our flight home to Kathmandu in just two days. The trail continues to descend and we pass another small village selling enormous cabbages and chokos – which I thought only belonged to Colonial Australia – chillies by the basket full, and other green fleshy vegetables of great vitality. We pass several flat roof spaces with two-metre diameter circles of red chillies drying in the few hours of sun that penetrates this steep valley; the winter sun is now low on the northern landscape where most of the mountains rise to six kilometres above the oceans; sunshine is short-lived in these parts especially this time of year.

We eventually reach the junction of rivers where the thundering Thuli Bheri River flows from valleys as far north as Dho Tarap some sixty kilometres northeast and the Suli Gad, which we have been following most of today; they meet to form a seriously large river with an enormous steel suspension bridge to cross. I think again of Peter Matthiessen and their huge team crossing here. It would have been very cold and wet to say the least, with the very real danger of losing one's footing and being washed downstream to India. Maybe a porter volunteered to swim across with a rope – something to hang onto at least – icy cold, wet, dangerous work.

Dilip thinks we need to camp the night somewhere at this junction as Juphal is another four hours' walk and there is little to be gained by pushing forward; my tiring body agrees. In the late afternoon light, I am interested to wander in this deep valley as all around us are mountains rising over 3,000 and 5,000 metres; the river charges through with the power of a hundred snow leopards. We are 2,080 metres above sea level, the lowest we have been in weeks.

"The typical Snow Leopard has pale frosty eyes and a coat of pale misty grey, with black rosettes that are clouded by the depth of the rich fur. An adult rarely weighs more than a hundred pounds or exceeds six feet in length, including the remarkable long tail, thick to the tip, used presumably for balance and for warmth, but it kills creatures three times its own size without much difficulty. It has enormous paws and

a short-faced heraldic head, like a leopard of myth; it is bold and agile in the hunt and capable of terrific leaps; and although its usual prey is the blue sheep (Bharal), it occasionally takes livestock, including young yak of several hundred pounds. This means that man would be fair game as well, although no attack on a human being has ever been reported.

The Snow Leopard is the most mysterious of the great cats; of its social system, there is nothing known. Almost always it is seen alone; it may meet over a kill, as tigers do, or it may be unsociable and solitary, like the true leopard." (2) Peter Matthiessen, p.145

We set our tents in the garden of the family who offer to cook us dinner; my tent is less than twenty metres from the raging river that I will listen to throughout the night, to wash away the tiredness I feel in my precious body that has performed so graciously. I am grateful again for this human vessel in which I travel these mountains, these Himalayan Mountains. But why does this Tibetan culture speak to me more than my own? Is it the eastern rim of Western civilisation that I grew up in – Australia, with our history, our lack of understanding and recognition for the Indigenous peoples that are arguably the oldest culture on the planet?

And still in 2020, "WHITE AUSTRALIA HAS A BLACK HISTORY"; the wealthier and whiter we are, the less we want to understand this factual statement that needs more understanding. There's never been reconciliation, at least not on black terms. No wonder 'Namaste' falls flat on our shores; that concept died two hundred and fifty years ago in this land called Australia when Western culture invaded a rich black cultural diversity with over three hundred languages and over five hundred individual territories. *(33b) (33c)*

As a nation, thinking individuals are still trying to come to terms with what happened, our destruction of an indigenous culture that has been part of the Australian landscape for 60,000 to 100,000 years – what were we thinking? Colonisation was the only thought of that time and now we must find reconciliation on Indigenous terms if we are to truly evolve and grow as a nation.

There are mandarin trees in the garden – I pick two of the ripened fruit and head upriver – I find the family's vegetable patch and can't resist the healthy fresh carrots growing in the rich alluvial soil. I pull three big plump ones, break their stalk and wash the sandy loam away. They are crisp, full of flavour, and I binge on them; I have missed fresh produce like this. I will tell the owners of my 'theft' and offer to pay for their fresh produce. I keep wandering upstream, chewing on the deep orange flesh as I go. I come to a small shed with two solid timber spokes, longer than my arm and three hundred millimetres in diameter, that grind grain into flour using large round stones shaped specifically for the job.

We share dinner with the family and their five children in a small room on the western side of their home. We sit on the earthen floor while the father cooks dinner on a timber stove with a chimney cut through the roof. There is a gas cooker – perhaps they use it only in the summer months – and a single table in this small room, some three by two metres. We are between Juphal and Dunai so transport with supplies is good. The mother has gone to get us rice wine; she nurses her baby and the other children mill around or play just outside.

The family enjoy our company. I'm content to sit, the silent guest, soaking up what is before me with these gentle people, and outside I can hear the roaring Thuli Bheri River. The nine-year-old plays with her phone; it's so warm and snug in here with this friendly Tibetan family. A corrugated iron ceiling, black from the fire, tools jammed between the timber battens and the roofing iron, ever ready for the next job; pliers, cutters, screwdrivers, small hammer; nothing hi-tech here, just human hearts and souls.

The mother cuts the vegetables into her hand. The father has been stripping boxing today from a water channel that will supply their home. They work hard, and it's ground into the palms of their hands; hands that don't type or use a computer eight hours per day – they have no need for a gym.

Fresh eggs sit on the table, fresh radishes, greens, fresh carrots – I tell them of my garden 'plunder' this afternoon; please add them to our bill. My body feels excited to receive such nourishing fresh vegetables from the Himalayan soil. The eight-year-old has damaged his toe and looks at his father awkwardly. I show the father a photo of an Aboriginal sculpture made of chicken wire, painted black with a blood red scarf – it resounds of eldership – Indigenous Australian eldership and another rich traditional culture.

The meal of rice, vegetables, goat meat and various sauces is delicious. I just want to climb into my little tent as I'm exhausted by this grand adventure, this journey... *In the Footsteps of the Snow Leopard,* inspired by Peter Matthiessen, made possible by Giri and his men, Dilip and Poona, who steered me through this portal of knowledge and wisdom. I hope this story brings inspiration and fascination to others; these are my intentions, my hope.

I brush my teeth and face the roaring river; the heavens above me, there is no moon tonight that I can see. I'm surrounded by these enormous foothills that belong to the Himalayas in remote northwest Nepal, so close to the Tibetan border. I sleep with these words a friend has given to me earlier in the year; their meaning is more deafening to me than the river; ancient tribal words:

"WE ARE EARTH PEOPLE ON A JOURNEY TO THE STARS. OUR QUEST, OUR EARTH WALK, IS TO LOOK WITHIN, TO KNOW WHO WE ARE, TO SEE THAT WE ARE CONNECTED TO ALL THINGS, THAT THERE IS NO SEPARATION."

(Lakota proverb)

The Lakota are a Native American tribe from the Great Plains of North America; an indigenous culture that understood the Earth before our noisy Western 'machine' arrived and marred our senses and soul connection with a living, breathing planet that doesn't need our human noise. She wants our love and intimate connection just as the indigenous peoples the world over have known for thousands of years. We need to alter course, become 'Earth people'; we have a living planet to nurture. *(35)*

CHAPTER XXII

You will learn by reading, you will understand with love.
RUMI

Our final walk to Juphal took less than a day; we followed the Thuli Bheri River for several hours then turned up into the hills, a four-hundred-metre elevation gain on a good trail that passes through fertile cropland with metre-high terraces to accommodate the steep slopes. My body is feeling the pinch of this twenty-four-day journey and the altitudes we have reached, not forgetting the freezing conditions for so much of the way.

At the river this morning I notice a red-tailed black bird as long as my hand, with a white head. I have seen many of these along the rivers. A flock of fifty pigeons soar as one to the south, then turn east and then south again – such commanding aviators. I am thinking this is their morning exercise routine and preparation to fly south before the winter envelopes them. They remind me of the massive flocks of Australian budgerigars in our desert regions; so wild and alive – attuned to the Earth's vibrations. They fly like a black cloud that moves over the red sand dunes, turning as these pigeons do.

As we draw closer we can see Juphal village, which clings to the hillside; a huge rock below the village has a homeless man living under it. I could see the things that made it his home; a mattress, clothing, blankets. This homeless scene reminds me of a man who out of choice lives under a pile of plastic bags in an affluent suburb that is my home town, and no amount of coaxing will get him to re-locate. He has been there for years.

We walked up through the buildings with steep stairs that seemed to go on forever. It was obvious we were on the outer suburbs of this significant trading hub, with its own rather special airport. Dilip finds us a guesthouse thirty minutes' walk from the airstrip, which runs at twenty degrees down to a cliff-hanger of a drop off. The pilot has six-hundred-and-sixty metres to get his twin-engine Otter airborne and thirty metres width to land. The runway received a tar seal in 2017, another engineering feat. I can but guess as to how it was done with tonnes of asphalt required and heavy machinery to manoeuvre and roll it into place. *(36)*

The guesthouse is large but there are few guests; a French couple with their five-year-old daughter camp in the spacious garden. A Hindu ceremony with ten participants is taking place in the garden when we arrive; it is still going after nightfall, a quiet and persistent process. I take great pleasure in washing some of my gear, including my boots, in preparation for the plane journey to Kathmandu. Dilip finds me a barber, so off I go to have this wildness cut and shaved from me. I cannot stay like this forever, the 'Wildman' from Robert Bly's *Iron John*. *(36a)*

The barber shop is located among narrow streets that seem to hold every type of small business imaginable. The steepness of this small town requires the shops to be contoured; the barber's shop is no exception. It has two levels, yet is only several metres long. The barber looks at me with some astonishment: perhaps he has never cut and shaved a Western man before; perhaps he can't see the need; perhaps he is impressed by my bushy grey-dusted beard.

He asks me what I would like through a young interpreter. I try to explain – short, neat and clean shaven – but this seems to get little understanding, so I point to a photo pinned to the wall of a young man looking very chic. He sets to work with an electric razor. A small gathering of younger men appears; they are fascinated by this Westerner in the hands of their local barber – they are genuinely interested, and they watch in fascination. I try to keep a brave face, not wanting to disappoint the small crowd that has gathered; eventually, the barber and I relax into the flow of this sixty-minute process.

The shave was the most interesting experience for me; he uses a cut-throat razor after he has removed the bulk of my beard with the electric razor, and then he takes his time using several hot flannels to soften and open the pores of my skin in preparation for the razor. I am by this stage humming somewhere in the mountains over Tibet; and thinking of home, my children, family and friends after what can only be described as one of the most extraordinary journeys I have ever done; the Himalayan landscape, the rich Tibetan culture, and the two men who made it possible for me, Dilip and Poona.

I floated from the barber's chair to the Tibetan plateau of my mind and also had some understanding of why women love to go to the hairdresser, but I will steer clear of this very lovely female domain – which one of my daughters has followed as her profession. "Two hours is standard, Dad, and so is $300." I can understand this now as I float back to the guesthouse; Dilip and Poona are sipping tea, chatting to some Nepalese guests and, of course, enjoying a cigarette or two.

They too are celebrating in their own quiet way; they have nearly got this Western man home safely. No mean feat considering the number of times I fantasized about running off into the mountains to set up a permanent camp and visit the Tibetan border to bribe Chinese guards for an entry permit. But I was a 'good boy' – and we are bathing in the glow of accomplishment, a team effort.

I watch a local man declaring his love to a woman in the garden below – they were both past their prime; I watch as the guesthouse owner walks over and 'biffs' the man. I thought this rather an odd way to treat someone in full view of his guests, although I was the only guest witnessing it seemed – then he 'biffed' him again and again! I wonder if I should intervene; Dilip and Poona had gone to their room for a nap – what was I to do?

Fortunately the guesthouse owner walks away – he had made his point; it seems he didn't think the man virtuous enough, as the couple were at least in their forties. Maybe this was requited love but I thought the guesthouse owner was being rather brutal and I found myself rather suspicious of him – his behaviour was not at all Buddhist. Thankfully, we were only here one night. The guesthouse itself, however, was lovely, positioned high on a ridge overlooking the valley we had come from and the Himalayas unfolding beyond, all visible from the dining room.

The ninth of November arrives and we depart early for the airport, a thirty minute walk up through the steep contoured streets to the western side of town. Dilip performs his magic – the number ten playmaker; he gets us through the large crowd of locals. Security is sharp; the passengers are counted before being allowed onto the airstrip. A young Australian woman who we met briefly last night at the guesthouse pushes her way through to Dilip. She wants to change Australian dollars, but Dilip refuses. What was she thinking? Why didn't she change them in Kathmandu? Why is she even travelling with Australian dollars? And here she is in Juphal planning to head up to Phoksundo Lake with winter nearly upon us...madness! We keep heading for the gates; "Goodbye and good luck," I call to her. I truly meant it. I wished I had spoken more to her last night, to find out her plan – if, in fact, she had one.

I see an official-looking woman standing about mid-way down the airstrip. The plane is due to land very shortly. I can only guess her job is to ensure no goats, cows, mules, buffalo, yak or people wander onto the airstrip, which has a fence of sorts around it. We can hear the Twin Otter – that beautiful little Canadian plane that can land almost anywhere, is as reliable as a Himalayan winter, and can carry twenty passengers and crew. It is perfect for this mountainous region, so near the 'Roof of the World'.

I watch as the plane straightens and levels to land on the black tarmac which runs uphill at twenty degrees; the brakes are barely needed with the pull of gravity. It's shiny white paintwork glistens in the sun, and oil lines run from the two props – nothing to be concerned about here in Nepal. The pilots give us a wave as they pass – that's always a good sign – happy pilots entrusted with our lives.

They taxi into a level loading bay and I watch as five kayaks are unloaded along with other Western expedition gear; again it seems odd so close to winter to be doing such a trip – the rivers will soon be low on running water or frozen, but I really couldn't care less; we had done the journey that we set out to do. It had gone very well and I had much material to write; connecting to the Earth, this Tibetan culture and following in Peter Matthiessen's footsteps was my purpose

– my quest. My special thanks to Peter Matthiessen for inspiring me with his most remarkable book, *The Snow Leopard;* we had followed the same trail from nearly fifty years ago...ancient trails.

We have another half hour to wait while our baggage is loaded and the plane is refuelled – how do they get the fuel in here, or the tarmac for that matter? Don't care, want to go home now. My seat is near the rear and I can see the pilot and co-pilot; they are possibly Indian or Nepalese – they have that jocular courage and confidence that pilots certainly must need to carry out their 'quests', landing at these high altitudes in all manner of weather.

The plane is full of passengers – I am surprised no goats or chickens are travelling with us – the pilots taxi the Twin Otter up to the top of the runway; the brakes are applied and the throttle opened. I can feel the power of this little plane as the pilot releases the brakes and opens the throttle wide. We have six hundred metres to gain enough speed and altitude to lift us into the air. We do it easily – the passengers are elated and so is the pilot. We enter the valley then bank south sitting just above the foothills of the Himalayas.

The passengers and crew are jubilant as we cruise in this 'little tin can' with more technology than I can begin to imagine. I'm just thankful to be heading home, to write this story and tell the world that Peter Matthiessen was right; Buddhist philosophy is very useful, the Earth depends on us to change; *et mulieres sapientes!* That we as a species could be made redundant, not needed for the Earth's purpose. This knowledge gives us no choice but to adapt, and be part of the natural, ancient workings of Planet Earth.

We need a return to Mother Earth and tribal knowledge combined with the technology and intelligence that salutes our planet. Other life forms from the outer reaches of the universe may choose to 'like us' and make contact, realising in fact that we are not totally stupid, and there is hope for this human species. "Much potential we have seen – but then they stuff it up with their wars, pollution and unwillingness to change – but maybe, just maybe, this time they have got it right, so let's join their social media – give these humans some universal 'airtime', once they've fixed all their 'dumb arse' self-defeating problems; climate change being top of the agenda – leaving coal firmly in the ground for two – and three, let's go for plastic stuff stuffing the oceans and the millions of organisms they aren't even aware of – maybe this time we can invite them into the universal community; the driving life-force they want to be a part of...let's pray and consult the gods!"

Our flight included a three-hour stopover in Narayangarh where we wandered around in the airport, waiting, eating less than wholesome food, until finally we were boarding a much bigger plane to Kathmandu. It took less than an hour to reach Kathmandu and the 'cattle yards' of people, queues, and what felt like such chaos after our twenty-four days in the wilderness of the Himalayas. All I wanted to do was get to my hotel, wash all my gear, drink some beer, and stare at the heavens from the rooftop of my guesthouse.

It had taken us over seven hours to arrive in Kathmandu from Juphal, but Giri wanted us to call in to his office for the final 'Welcome Home Oh Great Western Man'. Thank you Giri, can I go now, I'm exhausted! I said my heartfelt farewells to Dilip and Poona; they were so grateful for their US dollar bonuses; they had been exceptional in their efforts in looking out for me. We would meet again, we knew this.

Giri's driver took me to the Hotel Shechem, where this journey had begun – the hotel with the beautiful garden, large clean rooms, and delightful rooftop garden – only to find there was a mix up with my booking. The manager very kindly took it on herself to walk me up to another hotel – the Tokiyo – a twenty-minute walk uphill and through some very large steel security gates. This very new hotel was painted a pristine white and was on two levels, with views to the city. On the high ridge to the west was Kopan Monastery, where I had spent ten days sitting, learning to meditate and being silent. It was as if the gods had orchestrated this rather wonderful set of circumstances. I humbly thanked the manageress with a bow and 'Namaste'. I was getting very good at this beautiful Eastern greeting and the genuine heartfelt connection I had for these kind, loving Nepalese people.

As tired as I was, I wanted to wash – everything. My room had an adjoining bathroom that was spotlessly clean in which everything worked, even the hot water. I stripped my gear down and washed it; first my pack, which had served me well and nurtured my back the entire time, then my boots, which had nurtured my feet the entire time, my sandals, sleeping bag, liner, socks, undies, shirts, thermals – even the dry bags that carried my clothes. There was something cathartic in this process that said I was homeward bound, and the journey was over...for now.

I found a place on the rooftop to hang and dry everything. The large steel gates that I entered and the surrounding three-metre-high wire fence with coils of razor wire on top made me feel I could leave trekking gear out overnight; these treasured items were my lifeline when visiting such places.

I dined in the hotel dining room and was soon talking with Rita, an Irish woman who was working for a not-for-profit education organisation. It was good to talk to another English-speaking person, and talk we did. She was fascinated by my trip, and knew of Peter Matthiessen's book, *The Snow Leopard*. I was nearly falling asleep in my dal baht but we pigeonholed a time to meet after her work to visit Boudhanath; she had been coming here for ten years and knew the best millet beer houses. I was definitely up for that.

I had four days in Kathmandu before my flight home to Australia. Giri wanted to have one last dinner with me, and I spent many hours watching my gear dry on the rooftop – the winter sun was delightful – to stretch my body, to read, to stare lovingly at Kopan Monastery and remember all I had learned there. It was like a re-education camp for Western minds, and the Fourteenth Dalai Lama was the headmaster. I came away feeling humbled by the life-long lessons I had been shown there.

Karen, a seventy-year-old woman from Sweden who came to Kathmandu in the 'sex, drugs and rock'n'roll' days of the 1970's, discovered Buddhism and Kopan Monastery and never left; she was our teaching nun. She knew a lot of what was behind the masks we Westerners wear and I could not help but feel she knew more about my life than I did – but it was for me to discover. I did not feel she was open to counsel with me – perhaps it was her European heritage – a little too cultured for the humble likes of me – perhaps my life was too devilish to share. However, the Australian 'de-robed' monk in his early sixties – now, he was a different story; I found him as open and friendly as any other Australian. He provided much counsel and I loved his quiet and efficient delivery at Buddhist school every afternoon at 2.00pm.

Rita and I walked to the Boudhanath, a thirty-minute paced walk through bustling noisy streets. Our plan was millet beer and dinner at a place she knew down one of the alleys off from the Boudhanath which was glowing in Tibetan Buddhism. It was disappointing that the yak butter lights were not a nightly occurrence at this time of year – winter was not quite officially upon us in the Buddhist world and I had to suffice with the splendour and grandeur of this magnificent structure, which has been a continuous place of spiritual worship for over two thousand years, and the receiver of travellers for the same period. There is a Dolpo art gallery that Rita took me to upstairs, with views out to the brilliant white dome of Boudhanath where the light was fading quickly into night and the thirteen-tier golden capping was beginning to glow with the Buddha-eyes looking out to the North, South, East and West – to Dolpo.

It was a challenging process to drink the beer as there is thirty millimetres of millet seed to wade through using a metal straw. We asked to have it topped up with hot water for as long as the flavour remained. I can safely say the extra weight of the liquid in my stomach was dinner enough but we did have something to eat; however, you'll need to ask Rita what it was. I was floating off with the Buddhist gods back over Dolpo, through the mountains, valleys and rivers; the birds calling me back and somewhere in that mix, the snow leopard, sitting with its large tail wrapped around its haunches, blending into the Himalayan landscape like a bharal sheep.

How I loved where I had been – the adventure – but more the 'education' classes I attended for twenty-four days and nights; not forgetting the ten days in Kopan Monastery. I was a new Western man, ready to face our Western world but also, to connect with my family, the hearts of my three children who had now all returned from London, having done the Australian adventure of touching their Anglo-Saxon roots in the land of Mercia. And to see my ninety-one-year-old Yorkshire mother who still carries her spirit of a good life, a respectful life, an accepting life.

Giri's driver collected me for my last night out in Kathmandu; he wanted to take me to a fine restaurant in Thamel. The food was excellent, but I do not remember what it was; he was filling me up with beer and thanking me for extending his business to the remote northwest. It had been a learning experience for him too. And we discussed the use of my photos of which I had given him a copy; I was insisting he had to give recognition for these photos if he was using them in his business, which of course he was – Giri is always the businessman, and a very clever one at that.

In one breath he refers to me as his 'father' and then he wants to take me to some Kathmandu bar with pretty girls. Somehow those two things – father and bars with pretty girls, possibly wanting a ticket to Australia – just don't go together. As tempting as it all sounded, I was still fatigued and would be for many weeks, especially when I return home to Australia and a scorching summer with bush fires raging out of control for months – Mother Earth was telling us something, indeed! Climate change!

I said my heartfelt goodbyes to Giri before he bundled me into a taxi, floating in beer for a second night. It was a forty-minute drive back to my hotel. I think back to Giri 'torpedoing' me at Kathmandu airport two years earlier; his very good English, his impeccable manners, grey suit, polished black shoes, and incredible business tenacity. It was as though the Buddhist gods had organised our meeting – he was now a very good friend. His business had been of enormous help to me and we would do more trips together, we both knew that.

Your work is to discover your world and then with all your heart give yourself to it.
BUDDHA

Thank you, and may the gods shine down on your dear human soul!

GLOSSARY

(a) **Anzac Day:** Australia and New Zealand Army Corps, that was established early in WWI, a day of commemoration to the veterans who served, a part of our national story but far from complete if you read Stan Grants', Australia Day or Henry Reynolds', Frontier Wars. https://en.wikipedia.org/wiki/Anzac_Day

(b) **Billy:** a metal container often made from a tin of peaches to boil water on an open fire to make tea; very much part of early Australian life. https://en.wikipedia.org/wiki/Billycan

(c) **Bonza Bottler:** Australian slang meaning that all is good, if not in fact excellent. https://www.bonzabottlerday.com/how-did-bbd

(d) **Chapati:** originally from India, a flat bread made from wheat or maize flour, a welcome alternate meal with deep fried egg. https://en.wikipedia.org/wiki/Chapati

(e) **Chorten:** a stone monument built for a distinguished Buddhist, such as a lama; it is generally smaller than a stupa. https://tibetpedia.com/lifestyle/chorten-stupa/

(f) **Deity:** a god or goddess with divine status. https://www.google.com/search?q=deity+meaning

(g) **Dharma:** cosmic law and order as applied to the teachings of Buddha. https://en.wikipedia.org/wiki/Dharma

(h) **Drongo:** Australian slang for 'not very bright', a mild insult. https://en.wikipedia.org/wiki/Drongo

(i) **Gibber stones:** stones that form part of a boulder plain in Australia, usually small in size 70 x 50 x 40mm and stretch to the horizon. https://www.google.com/search?q=gibber+stone+meaning

(j) **Gompa:** a Buddhist monastery, a place of learning. https://en.wikipedia.org/wiki/Gompa

(k) **Hard yakka:** Australian slang for hard physical manual work. The name is believed to be Aboriginal in origin from the 1880's. https://www.macquariedictionary.com.au/blog/article/604/

(l) **Puja:** in Hinduism and Buddhism, a daily ritual with reverence, honour and worship. It can be performed individually or as an event to celebrate spirituality. https://simple.wikipedia.org/wiki/Puja

(m) **Samsara:** the beginningless cycle of repeated birth, a life of suffering and of death. https://en.wikipedia.org/wiki/Samsara

(n) **Sanskrit:** Buddhist text as found on Mani stones on this journey; originally from the Indian sub-continent, the text is believed to be 3,500 years old. https://en.wikipedia.org/wiki/Sanskrit_Buddhist_literature

(o) **Stone the crows:** an Australian saying when something remarkable happens; a surprise, amazing or simply emphasis. https://en.wiktionary.org/wiki/stone_the_crows

(p) **Stupa:** a stone and earth structure that serves as a monument to Buddha, marking a sacred area, generally larger than a chorten. https://www.britannica.com/topic/stupa

(q) **Tallie:** Australian slang for a large bottle of beer; also known as a 'longneck', they contain up to 750ml of beer. https://www.google.com/search?q=tallie+beer

(r) **Wuss:** Australian slang meaning ineffectual person, weak, cowardly, timid https://en.wiktionary.org/wiki/wuss

(s) **WWI, WWII:** World War One and World War Two, mostly played out in Europe but also Japan, United States, Russia and Australia. https://en.wikipedia.org/wiki/World_War_Ihttps://en.wikipedia.org/wiki/World_War_II

LIST OF REFERENCES

(1) https://en.wikipedia.org/wiki/Foundation_for_the_Preservation of_the_Mahayana_Tradition

(1a) https://en.wikipedia.org/wiki/Bharal

(1b) https://www.himalayancompanion.com/shey-gompa-and-crystal-mountain-upper-dolpo **Note:** At the time of printing, this website disappeared and I was unable to find another source. My only thought is it has been unable to be maintained through COVID-19 but this legend must be available from other sources.

(2) Peter Matthiessen, *The Snow Leopard*, 1978 Vintage Random House 2010, London SW1V 2SA, ISBN 978-0-099-77111-1

(3) https://www.thoughtco.com/snow-leopard-facts-4584448

(4) https://local-moda.blogspot.com/2012/10/how-women-adorn-their-noses-in-nepal.html

(5) https://en.wikipedia.org/wiki/Bindi_(decoration)

(6) https://en.wikipedia.org/wiki/Animal_sacrifice_in_Hinduism

(7) https://en.wikipedia.org/wiki/Cannabis_indica

(8) https://en.wikipedia.org/wiki/Eleusine_coracana

(9) https://en.wikipedia.org/wiki/Magars

(9a) The Lonely Planet, *Trekking in the Nepal Himalaya*, Bradley Mayhew, Lindsay Brown, Stuart Butler, 10th edition, p. 272

(10) https://www.imnepal.com/dhorpatan-hunting-reserve-nepal

(11) https://www.britannica.com/topic/Homo-sapiens

(12) https://www.britannica.com/science/Cenozoic-Era#ref586067

(13) https://www.climbmountkilimanjaro.com/practical-information/what-to-take/medical-kit/diamox-what-is-it-and-is-it-worth-taking

(14) https://en.wikipedia.org/wiki/Women_in_Nepal

(14a) https://en.wikipedia.org/wiki/List_of_people_with_bipolar_disorder

(15) https://www.webmd.com/depression/ss/slideshow-depression-overview

(15a) https://www.geolsoc.org.uk/Plate-Tectonics

(16) https://www.livehistoryindia.com/history-in-a-dish/2017/05/28/chhang-the-beer-of-the-himalayas

(17) http://www.hinduismfacts.org/hindu-symbols

(17a) https://noriohayakawa.wordpress.com/2016/02/10/the-difference-between-the-buddhist-swastika-symbol-and-the-nazi-swastika-symbol/

(17b) https://en.wikipedia.org/wiki/Swastika

(18) The Lonely Planet, *Trekking in the Nepal Himalaya*, Bradley Mayhew, Lindsay Brown, Stuart Butler, 10th edition, p. 274

(19) https://en.wikipedia.org/wiki/Bon

(20) https://en.wikipedia.org/wiki/Ophiocordyceps_sinensis

(21) https://www.bioceuticals.com.au/education/article/caterpillar-mushroom-and-its-uses-in-traditional-medicine

(22) https://ngs.org.np/2018/09/27/origin-of-arsenic-and-other-heavy-metals-in-the-rivers-of-nepal/

(22a) https://www.environment.gov.au/biodiversity/invasive/weeds

(22b) Fisher, James F; *Trans-Himalayan Traders*, 2017 second edition, Orchid Press, Bangkok, pp 19 to 28, p.54

(22c)   https://en.wikipedia.org/wiki/Mani_stone

(23)   https://mastermindcontent.co.uk/the-symbolic-meaning-of-the-conch-shell-in-buddhism

(24)   http://www.religionfacts.com/conch-shell

(25)   https://en.wikipedia.org/wiki/Rock_dove

(26)   https://en.wikipedia.org/wiki/Vajra

(27)   https://en.wikipedia.org/wiki/Dolpo

(29)   https://visiondolpo.org/crystal-mountain-school

(29a)   'Cooee', an Australian bush call when one needs to attract attention; our bush is vast, as you can imagine.

(29b)   https://www.youtube.com/watch?v=fZvTuNKTW8M

(29c)   https://otherworldlyoracle.com/feather-symbolism-feather-magic-omens/

(30)   https://en.wikipedia.org/wiki/Phoksundo_Lake

(30a)   Fourteenth Dalai Lama of Tibet; *Freedom in Exile*, Hodder and Stoughton Ltd, 1990, Great Britain

(30b)   https://www.freetibet.org/about/environment

(31)   https://www.youtube.com/watch?v=kOLON_-7d5Y

(31a)   https://en.wikipedia.org/wiki/Dharma

(32)   https://www.exoticindiaart.com/article/symbols

(33)   https://www.andyweberstudios.com

(33a)   https://en.wikipedia.org/wiki/Mercia

(33b) https://en.wikipedia.org/wiki/Australian_Aboriginal_languages

(33c) https://info.australia.gov.au/about-australia/our-country/our-people

(34) https://en.wikipedia.org/wiki/History_of_Mongolia

(35) https://en.wikipedia.org/wiki/Lakota_language

(36) https://en.wikipedia.org/wiki/Dolpa_Airport

(36a) Robert Bly, *Iron John*; 1990 Addison-Wesley Publishing Company Inc. A book about mythical men written by a famous American poet, Robert Bly; the 'Wild Man' lives in the wilderness away from the town and holds the key to men's souls if they dare to leave the comfort of the town. An extraordinary story of mans' psyche, and a story that can be read again and again; a beautiful work by Robert Bly.

POSTSCRIPT

It's October 2020 and my original plans to return to Kathmandu and the northwest region of the Himalayas have been thwarted by COVID-19. Realistically, the opportunity to return will be when a vaccine has been developed, most likely September/October 2021.

In many ways this story is not complete without Shey Monastery, Crystal Mountain and Saldang in the Upper Dolpo region; a very cold and remote place on the edge of the Tibetan Plateau.

To visit there will complete this journey – *In the Footsteps of the Snow Leopard* – as those areas hold great interest to me in terms of the Tibetan culture, the remoteness and of course where Peter Matthiessen and George Schaller did most of their fieldwork in regards to the beloved snow leopard.

In regards to this story of my twenty-four days and the profound experiences I had there in terms of feeling the ancient rhythms of Planet Earth and our need as a species to nurture this Earth, I believe we have no choice but to dramatically alter our current course. I hope this is what you have gleaned from this story and I hope it spurs you on to be part of that crusade in whatever way you can.

And may future generations of people thank us for having the foresight and strength to move beyond the current limited structures that make up our lives, but which don't necessarily honour the planet that keeps us alive. I believe anything is possible for our future and we do have the intelligence to change course to that which nurtures our Earth.

With love and compassion,
Tim Easton

Instagram link to over 800 images:
goingbeyondexpeditions
Tim Easton, Brisbane, Australia

www.timeaston.com.au

PROLOGUE

It's important for me to thank the many hundreds of Nepalese and Tibetan people I came into contact with on my journey. They are a people like no other. They not only thrive in their own high-altitude landscape but they have a radiance and thirst for life that flows out into the world. In many ways this book is a portal for their very special energy that can never be crushed despite the efforts of the Chinese Red Army.

For myself, as a 58 year-old man from the West, this journey was a gift in so many ways.

Firstly, that my body not only could undertake the twenty-four-day trek; it in fact thrived in this cold mountain landscape far away from the 'madding crowd'. I am thankful to my forebears and their strong genetic code that enabled me to undertake this journey through so many valleys and passes at high altitude.

Secondly, I find the Nepalese and Tibetan people very inspiring. They are for me a gift from the gods in terms of understanding our place in the universe. Their rich colourful culture, hundreds of generations old, never ceases to amaze and thrill me. Of course, they live among the highest mountains in the world which adds a certain magic: easily found at such high altitudes.

On this journey, just a days walk from Ringmo villag, near to Phoksundo Lake I come across large boulders the size of car bodies. It's as though the gods got really pissed off with us humans and threw these boulders to the ground as part of their anger management therapy on the 'Roof of the World' where they go when they need therapy or to heal their wounds from this self-destructive human species on the brink of climate change.

I hope dear reader that you find inspiration in these pages and may it propel you to find answers that will appeal to the gods as we are forced into this funnel of change which, with some luck, will see us come through as et mulieres sapientes (or wise men and women).

I can only hope future generations will praise us for the timely changes we simply must make, all 7.8 billion of us.

ABOUT THE AUTHOR

Tim Easton at Kopan Monastery © Francoise Resler

I was born in Stanthorpe, southeast Queensland on 9 October 1961 to British migrants John and Diana Easton.

Stanthorpe is a very beautiful part of the world, an imposing granite landscape rich in vineyards and fruit orchards. But for my mother, an Englishwoman arriving there in 1960, Stanthorpe was a hot and dry place with thousands of black flies that managed to fossick for moisture in nearly every orifice of the human body given the chance. Stanthorpe can be an unforgiving place to live especially as my father was away most of the week selling Caltex fuel and oil to prosperous farming communities.

I had two older sisters, Helen Coromel and Heather Easton. At the tender age of thirteen a terrible tragedy struck our family when I witnessed my sister Heather fall to her death from Lost World on Lamington National Park's western plateau.

In trying to understand this tragedy I've searched for answers. In my late thirties I sought professional help to understand the depth of my depression. It's no surprise that it was directly related to Heather's death but it was also living for the better part of twenty years with my parents' grief.

So why did I do this trip – alone? I can quickly say for the deep love and respect I have for my very British parents and their sense of adventure. The family motto is Esto Quod Audes (be what you dare) my ancestors chose this, I see only benefit in living up to their request. I even had this Latin inscription tattooed onto my left shoulder when I was aged 46, along with the Australian Indigenous flag out of respect.

By 2009 my world came crashing down with mental illness that in 2012 was diagnosed as bipolar disorder. With the help of a very good doctor I have got my life back on track but it's been a long, almost ten-year journey that one can never really 'get over' – one simply learns to manage the illness - and with the correct professional help it can be managed. There is hope!

In 2000 while renovating two homes, I graduated with a Communication degree from Griffith University, Brisbane. I somehow always knew I would study journalism but I didn't think I would wait until I was thirty-six years old to take it up. But I flourished at university and discovered that my gift was more for radio than writing.

I ran *Men's and Women's Stories* on Radio 4EB in Brisbane from January 2014 for almost five years during which time I was the carer for my now ninety-two-year-old mother. A mutually beneficial arrangement during a time I was building my strength.

Today I'm a proud father of three young adult children. May they always know their mother and father love them dearly and may they travel to the Himalayan mountains one day to discover the richness and beauty of the Tibetan/Nepalese culture.

Thank you, and Namaste!

With love and kindness,
Tim